RETAIL SALES TAX

RETAIL SALES TAX

An Appraisal of New Issues

Daniel C. Morgan, Jr.

Madison and Milwaukee, 1964

THE UNIVERSITY OF WISCONSIN PRESS

Published by
THE UNIVERSITY OF WISCONSIN PRESS
Mailing address: P.O. Box 1379, Madison, Wisconsin 53701
Editorial offices: 430 Sterling Court, Madison

Copyright © 1964 by the
Regents of the University of Wisconsin

Printed in the United States of America by
George Banta Company, Inc., Menasha, Wisconsin
Library of Congress Catalog Card No. 64-12723

ACKNOWLEDGEMENTS

The people to whom I owe most are Professors Harold Groves and Robert Lampman, and my wife Mary. I should also like to thank Lee Van Zant, who compiled most of the information on the sales taxation of services; John Gronouski, John Wilke, and Alden Hayes for their gracious assistance and for permission to use data from their work sheets at the Wisconsin Department of Taxation; Carey Thompson and Richard Heaps, who took an interest in the work throughout its process; and Gerry Hinkel at Wisconsin and Bonnie Whittier at Texas for their secretarial help.

Daniel C. Morgan, Jr.

Austin, Texas
July 1963

CONTENTS

TABLES

ix

APPENDIX TABLES

RETAIL SALES TAX

I

THE NEW SALES TAX ISSUES
AND THEIR IMPORTANCE

The state retail sales tax in America can be likened to an illegitimate child that was not wanted but that came anyway. Being unwanted is not really unusual and it is certainly no bar to normal growth. It is even possible for the illegitimate to gain respectability.

The retail sales tax has grown not just normally but abnormally. And apparently it has gained respectability. Three decades ago the retail sales tax was almost unknown in the United States. Only West Virginia (since 1921) and Georgia (since 1929) had had any experience with it. Today, thirty-seven states levy retail sales and use taxes. In almost all of these states the sales tax is the most important source of finance. And if we combine the yields from taxes of all kinds for all fifty states, we find the retail sales tax to be first in importance. Apparently the trend to sales taxation is world-wide.[1] Even such welfare states as Norway, Sweden, and Iceland are adopting retail sales taxes to finance their expanding programs.

An economist or a political scientist who advocated sales taxation thirty years ago would hardly have been considered respectable in his profession. But today we see scholars of all political persuasions, including welfare staters, socialists, and modern liberals, who tolerate or even actively endorse this form of taxation.

It is not my purpose to try to establish the reasons for the favorable shift of opinion toward the sales tax. But my purpose is closely related to this: I wish to analyze in detail the recent issues of economic literature which bear on the appraisal of retail sales taxation.

New Hypotheses in Relation to Sales-Tax Appraisal

As one reads and listens to scholarly discussion of the sales tax, he is struck by the fact that a new set of issues is emerging.

Until recently, debate followed a predictable pattern. The opponent of the retail sales tax deplored its regressiveness and its burden on large families. The advocate emphasized that the tax is easy to administer, that it raises a great deal of money (including some from nonresidents); he argued that the sales tax is relatively favorable to saving and investment and to industrial location in one's state. These traditional arguments survive, surely, and may have some merit. But investigation has brought the validity and the significance of some of them into question. Whatever the reasons, many of the old arguments no longer persuade.

Public finance scholars are now engaged in fresh controversy. They debate the merit of the retail sales tax as "an instrument of social balance"; they analyze whether it is *really* a consumer-burden tax; they measure its progressiveness and its neutrality according to "permanent income"; they question its rationality as a form of business taxation.

Many of the new issues derive from only four propositions. One of the four is the "social-imbalance–affluent-society" thesis of John Kenneth Galbraith. Another is the "factor-burden" theory of sales-tax incidence with which Earl Rolph challenges the conventional consumer-burden doctrine. New hypotheses of consumer behavior are responsible for a third set of issues: of the new consumption theories Milton Friedman's version of the permanent-income hypothesis has had the most dramatic impact on sales-tax analysis. A fourth group of arguments has emerged with the mushrooming realization that retail sales taxes apply to sales in production as well as to transactions between retailers and household consumers.

As these new hypotheses have been applied, they constitute a revolutionary challenge to conventional views about the effects and the merit of retail sales taxation.

Implications for Sales-Tax Analysis

Earl Rolph tries to puncture the popular illusion that sales taxes are a burden on consumers in general. Sales taxes work to restrict the output of taxed goods and to raise their prices. But they increase the output of exempt goods and lower their prices. Consumers in general may be no worse off because of the sales tax—they lose on the one hand but gain on the other.

The implications of Rolph's hypothesis are intriguing. Sales taxes are really like taxes on factors of production. Who can say on whom they fall? The groups with the loss may be owners of resources employed in the taxed industries, owners of resources on which consumers economize as a result of spending more for the sales-taxed goods, or owners of resources that compete with either of these groups. If the economy is competitive enough, Rolph's hypothesis leads to a modern diffusion theory: though the sales tax is placed on selected goods, its burden is distributed like that of a general factor income tax with a proportional rate. So if we are studying the progressiveness of a typical retail sales according to a size bracket distribution of income, the best first approximation may be that it is proportional. The sales tax is thus relieved of its stigma as a regressive levy. And if Rolph is right, there is no special merit in a food exemption as a device for alleviating sales-tax regressiveness. Nor is there any reason to exempt from taxation sales to charitable, religious, scientific, or governmental organizations. The burden simply is not borne by buyers of products. It is borne by sellers of resources.

Most economists voice at least a qualified rejection to Rolph's hypothesis. Suppose that we accept this consensus and conceive of the sales tax in the conventional way, as a tax on family consumption expenditure. New hypotheses of consumer behavior force us to revise our ideas about its effects. Most startling of the new hypotheses in its implication is Milton Friedman's version of the permanent-income hypothesis. Friedman posits that families consume not on the basis of their current incomes but on the basis of their expectations of their long-term resource positions. In other words, their consumption is based on their normal or "permanent" income, which, roughly, is expected average income over a period of several years, discounted. Friedman contends that if we could take a sufficiently long period of receipt and consumption—defining consumption to include only the use value of durables—the consumption-income ratio would be the same for all levels of income.

Consider the implications for retail sales-tax analysis if Friedman's hypothesis were acceptable:

1. If families at all levels of permanent income spend the same fraction of that income, regressivity is apt to be apparent, not real, for most retail sales-tax schemes.

2. Current consumption may be superior to current income as a measure of the relative economic positions of persons, and therefore of their relative abilities to bear taxes. That is, current consumption might equate better than current income the relative capacities of receivers of fluctuating versus permanent income or wealth, and of persons of different age.

3. Several "established" conclusions about the neutrality of retail sales taxes are brought into question. The conventional view is that sales taxes discriminate: against large families as compared with small; against families headed by both young and old persons as compared with families headed by middle-aged individuals; against white as compared with Negro families; against urban as compared with rural families; and against manual, clerical, and service occupations as compared with professional, managerial, and self-employed groups. The conclusions are arrived at by running regressions of current taxable consumption on current ("measured") income and finding that the former group in each case above has higher taxable consumption than the latter. But under the permanent-income hypothesis equal measured income can correspond to different levels of permanent income for the groups being compared. So we must reformulate the neutrality tests according to the new hypothesis to see if any of our conventional conclusions are affected.

Other theories of the consumption function explain the observed data about as well as Friedman's theory and compete with it for acceptance. The patterns of consumer behavior on which these theories are founded differ from Friedman's behavior assumptions. The differences can lead to different conclusions, normative as well as positive, concerning the consequences of retail sales taxation.

A more direct rationale for the retail sales tax has been presented by J. K. Galbraith. Galbraith argues that our society is characterized by a social imbalance. We produce too much in the private sector of our economy relative to the public sector. We need to transfer resources from the private to the public sector. At the state and local levels of government, taxes must accompany the resource transfer. For several reasons income taxes of the requisite yield are unacceptable or impracticable for state and local governmental bodies. And property-tax yields are too inflexible, too unresponsive to growth in income and wealth. The sales tax is an ideal instrument. The degree of progressivity of the tax employed is not so important as it once was, according to the Galbraithian view. Our society is affluent, so affluent that it takes Madison Avenue to convince us that we need the consumer goods our industrial complex is able to produce. Today's poverty is either insular or it is caused by a peculiar quality of the personality of the individual experiencing it. Proponents of Galbraith's theory are persuaded that the kind of tax adopted is no longer so important. The critical factor is to get it adopted or to get it increased in order to effect social balance. A good tax is a high-yield one which is income elastic.

We have been assuming that retail sales taxes burden only household consumers. But any realistic appraisal of the effects of retail sales taxes must consider the sales tax on transactions between business enterprises. Most people do not think of sales taxes in this way. They think that if a man buys an item from a retailer for his personal use it is a taxable retail sale, and that otherwise it is exempt. Actually, most sales-tax statutes consider a retail sale to be any sale in which the buyer does not intend to make a further sale of the item purchased. The sale of a typewriter to a department store is a retail sale. The sale of capital machinery to a manufacturer is usually a taxable retail sale. Even so, most of our studies of the progressiveness of sales taxes proceed as if they are simply taxes on household consumers. The studies either allocate the entire tax yield to the income classes in accordance with their sales taxable consumption, or else they simply ignore the existence of what we call "the business portion" of the tax.

Most public finance treatises continue to teach that the retail sales tax is a single-stage tax. Being single stage it does not discriminate against nonintegrated firms, as do multiple-stage sales taxes. The truth, of course, is that the sales tax is not necessarily a single-stage tax. It can apply at several points in the production and distribution process. And it can fail to apply at points at which consistency might call for its application. In short, it is a capricious hybrid between a single-stage sales tax and a turnover tax.

Increasing numbers of people recognize the existence and the importance of the business portion of the typical retail sales tax. With this recognition several critical questions suggest themselves. Which of the sales made by one business to another are taxed? Which enterprises are hardest hit by the tax and which are least affected? Does the business portion in most states account for a negligible or for a substantial part of sales-tax yield? What is the incidence of sales taxes whose impact is on firms engaged in production and distribution? How does the business portion affect the rationale of the sales tax? Finally, what sense does the sales tax make as a business activity tax?

These are the new issues that will form the subject matter of this book. Consider what they can do to our conventional ideas about the sales tax. Sales taxes may not be taxes on consumers after all; they may be taxes on factors of production. Presumably they are proportional or neutral in equalization effect. Or at any rate they are probably not very regressive. This follows from Rolph's hypothesis. But even if they are consumer-burden taxes, they are far more progressive than we have thought. And they may not discriminate in the ways we have assumed. These conclusions follow from Friedman's theory of the consumption function. But even if sales taxes are regressive and if they fall relatively hard on low-income families and on large families, it may not be very important in this affluent society, which has to contrive desires for what it produces. What really matters is getting the necessary revenue for stepping up public spending. And this the sales tax does admirably. This is Galbraith's proposition. Finally, a good portion of the typical sales tax falls, at least initially, on nonretail business. And this "business portion" makes the sales tax all the more uncertain and all the more likely to be capricious. Even if Rolph has not succeeded in destroying the image of the sales tax as a consumer-burden tax, recognition of the business portion of the tax may destroy the simple consumer-burden image.

It is my opinion that because of their novelty the new issues are being oversold, and I shall try to put these issues in perspective.

What We Mean by "Retail Sales Taxes"

I am interested in the broad impact of these hypotheses on public finance thought. But my immediate concern is with their meaning for the appraisal of state retail sales taxes. If asked to say precisely what we mean by retail sales taxes, there is only one honest answer: we mean what everybody else means, whatever that is. In other words, we are forced to take refuge in the classification systems of our leading tax guides and in the other books on retail sales taxation.

There is really no alternative to this approach. It is impossible to say precisely what it is that distinguishes what we refer to as retail sales taxes. Legislators give these taxes many names and many forms: retail sales taxes, general sales taxes, gross receipts taxes, consumers' sales taxes, retailers' occupation taxes, and gross income taxes. We cannot distinguish them as taxes on either "consumers" or "sellers": the statutory obligation of what most people mean by sales taxes rests about equally between sellers and buyers in the sales-tax states. A classical distinction considers the retail sales tax to be one form of "indirect" tax, as opposed to a "direct" tax. This dichotomy presents two difficulties for our purposes. First, it relies on a particular theory of incidence which is under attack. An evaluation of this attack constitutes one of the subjects of our book. Second, even if we accept the classical dichotomy we must realize that there are dozens of forms of "indirect" sales taxes besides those taxes we call retail sales taxes.

One classification of sales taxes turns on the frequency with which the goods are taxed as they turn over in the production and distribution process. Many years ago the National Industrial Conference Board suggested such a classification system. It suggested that there are multiple-stage sales taxes and single-stage sales taxes. The multiple-stage taxes apply at several points in production and distribution. Multi-stage levies include turnover, transactions, and transfer forms. Single-stage levies are supposed to apply at only one stage. They include such forms as the manufacturers' sales tax, the wholesalers' sales tax, and the retailers' sales tax. This classification scheme has much to recommend it. But it is not strictly accurate for what is commonly meant by "the retail sales tax." One of the aims of this book will be to demonstrate that retail sales taxes are often applied at more than one point in the production-distribution process. They are by no means single stage in the sense of applying only to transactions between retailers and household consumers.

Another useful way to distinguish a general retail sales tax is that it is usually characterized by rate uniformity. Unlike selective sales taxes (excises) and turnover taxes, the retail sales tax is said to apply the same ad valorem rate to a wide range of goods. But the exceptions are numerous and they are increasing rapidly. Several categories of items sold to nonretail businesses are granted preferential rates by many states, especially Southern ones.

Because of the difficulties, it seems wise to follow convention. Thus, we list thirty-seven states in our tables (see the Appendix) as states that employ retail sales and use taxes.

Problems of State Finance in the Coming Decade: What Role for Sales Taxes?

Why do issues about the effects of sales taxes matter? For a period during the 1950's it was fashionable to think that the source of finance for state government was not very important. What was important was the level of taxation, not the form. But the vogue seems to have passed. Most of us have returned to the view that it is indeed important how a state finances a given level of expenditure. Many will say that, as both the absolute level of taxation and the portion of income going to state government rise, the source of finance is increasingly important.

Indeed, it appears that state government's share of income or output will continue to rise in the coming decade. Such a prediction is consistent with the historical trend. And it is confirmed by our leading projections of state and local governmental expenditure. The projection of the National Planning Association[2] concludes that between now and 1970 outlay by both state and local government will rise at a rate of 6.5 per cent a year. This rate of increase is somewhat more rapid than that which occurred in the 1950's—and we have not forgotten the tax crises of that decade. A rate of increase of 6.5 per cent per annum is also faster than we anticipate for national income. We should expect, therefore, an increasing share of income to be taken by state government.

The projections of the Committee for Economic Development[3] are lower than those of the NPA. Even so, the CED estimates that state and local spending will rise faster than income. Dick Netzer presents another group of well-reasoned projections[4] for three standards of performance: (1) no change in standards, (2) moderate improvement, and (3) substantial improvement. Netzer concludes that if the economy continues to grow at a real rate comparable to that of recent years the likelihood is that state and local tax yields combined will double between 1957 and 1970. He believes that if his projections prove correct only modest increases in tax rates should provide substantial improvement in the quality of public services. However, at the Conference on Public Finance in 1959 the critics of Netzer's work were not nearly so optimistic.[5]

Nor is Robert Lampman so sanguine as Netzer. Lampman demonstrates[6] that there are three very important reasons why in the next decade we may expect a larger part of our dollar to be spent on education, welfare, health, and research and development. The reasons are (1) the price disadvantage problem faced by government; (2) the population increase and its changing configuration; and (3) rising standards for the public sector.

The price disadvantage problem refers to the fact that the prices of what governments buy have been increasing much more rapidly of late than the prices of things that household consumers buy. The GNP deflator index in the 1950's indicated an increase in prices of all goods and services of about 2 per cent a year. But the deflator for state and local government purchases rose by about $3\frac{1}{4}$ per cent a year. Government's demand is directed predominantly at services and construction materials. These are, of course, the very items that have been rising fastest in price. The deflator for services shows a rise for the 1950's of $4\frac{1}{4}$ per cent annually. So government, like Alice's Red Queen, must run faster to stay in the same place. If government were to hold the scope and the quality of its services stable, it would not be possible to hold money costs stable. Employee compensation would still have to rise about as much as it does in the private sector—say 50 per cent in a decade. While there might be some offset from productivity gains, most observers feel that rising employee costs in state governments are at best only partially offset by demonstrable increases in productivity. The implication is that it probably takes an increase in money costs of 2 per cent a year simply to maintain a prescribed standard of performance. Such an increase is to be anticipated even if there is no growth of population and no improvement in the quality of services.

But these other factors do not remain constant, population least of all:

Our age group [World War II and postwar parents] has displayed what is, in historical terms, a remarkable rise in reproduction. . . . The major problems of the next twenty years will be paying the full price for the established pattern of high fertility.[7]

For our enthusiasm for reproduction we must pay not just one price but two. One price is the loss of potential per capita product, which is the consequence of the fall in the proportion of our population which is of working age. The second price is a loss of consumer goods and services. This second loss we incur in redirecting a portion of our product toward schools, roads, public works, and housing. As Lampman observes, this second price we need not pay, but we neglect paying it only at great risk to the quality of our civilization.

Many of the expenses of state government are best related to the size of the population or to its growth. So as a first approximation we might expect state governmental outlay to increase at the same rate as population grows. Let us put this at 1.7 per cent per year for the coming decade. More important, however, is the age distribution of the population. In the next ten to fifteen years the number of very old people and the number of young people will increase very rapidly while the working age population will remain practically stable.[8] It is the old and the young—especially the school-age population—who are expensive in terms of provision of governmental service. Yet these age groups are very low in output per head.

Taking all factors into account, we may expect an increase in state expenditure of more than 2 per cent a year just to meet population growth and its changing age configuration. Any quality improvement will be in addition to this.

It seems reasonable to conclude that the pressure on state treasuries is likely to continue throughout the current decade. There will be more tax crises. We are not yet out of the woods.

The retail sales tax is the number one state tax source, and it is expanding rapidly along with other sources. Should this situation continue? Should the form of the tax be modified? New hypotheses challenge conventional ideas about the effects of this tax, and to answer such questions we should know more about its true nature and effects.

II

TAXATION OF BUSINESS UNDER
THE RETAIL SALES TAX

It is fashionable to talk about the "image" of personalities, places, and things. Let us so consider the retail sales tax. Its image is of a tax on family expenditure for certain items and also of a single-stage tax. We think of the typical sales tax as applying to sales to families for their personal use, but not as applying to sales to businesses of items used in production. Even public-finance economists sometimes tell us that the retail sales tax avoids pyramiding and does not discriminate against nonintegrated concerns. The reason: it applies at only one point in the production process.

Actually, retail sales taxes are more than taxes on transactions between a man behind a counter and a customer who lives down the street. These taxes apply to a wide range of transactions between business units at various stages in the production and distribution process. If we think of sales-tax impact as falling on the purchaser rather than on the seller, business through its purchases pays a healthy portion of total sales-tax yield.

This business portion of the retail sales tax has been given surprisingly little attention by economists, although lawyers and tax administrators have explored its legal and administrative aspects rather more thoroughly. Neglect by economists is puzzling because the implications are sufficient to put a new face on appraisal of sales taxation. Once we recognize the importance of the business portion of the retail sales tax, several questions need answers. For example,

1. Which transactions between business units are taxed, which are excluded, and which are exempt?

2. What part of total sales-tax yield is paid by business as purchaser?

3. How are different types of businesses affected?

13

4. Does the impact burden follow some rationale, or is it capricious?

5. What is the incidence of the business portion?

6. How is the rationale of the retail sales tax affected by the recognition of the tax on business?

The body of this chapter will be heavy with detail and methodology, but I shall present my tentative conclusions at the outset. In brief, I posit the following.

Taxes on transactions between business units are not a negligible aspect of the yield from retail sales taxes in most states. Research indicates that the business portion should account for a tenth to a third of total sales-tax yield, depending on the nature of the sales-tax statute. If a state employs a strict component-part convention and provides no reduction in rates for business items taxed under the convention, the business portion can yield up to a third of total yield from the sales tax. Under a very liberal direct-use convention, 10 per cent of total yield might be a representative figure. The percentage for most states will probably range between 15 and 25 per cent.

The selection of items used in production and distribution which are to be taxed has little economic rationale. The items selected and the rates applied differ widely among sales-tax states. There are two principal conventions employed—the component-part convention and the direct-use convention. But there are many hybrids, and there is diversity within each convention. Thus, generalization is hazardous. But in most states, and especially in states that follow the component convention, the sales tax is as much a tax on investment goods as it is a tax on consumer goods.

The impact burden of the business portion is discriminatory. Hit with relative severity are the contractor or builder, the farmer, the capital-intensive firm, and the firm which uses large quantities of fuel. Lightly hit are service enterprises, labor-intensive industry, and distributional activities.

The incidence of the business portion of the sales tax is very uncertain. Who ultimately bears the burden of a sales tax on the furniture bought by the purchasing department of a company producing industrial chemicals? Is it borne by owners? Is it shifted forward to consumers—and if so, which consumers? Is it shifted backward to labor or to other factors of production? What part is borne within the original state and what part is shifted to residents of other states? About all that is certain is that the incidence of the business portion differs from the incidence of the household portion. Yet most studies of sales-tax incidence implicitly assume that the pattern is the same for the two portions. Tax studies assign the entire yield of the sales tax to income classes in accordance with their consumer expenditures on taxed items.

The business portion is slightly regressive, according to our methodology. Many people would expect it to be progressive. Critics of retail sales taxation do not stress the regressivity of the business portion, however; it is the uncertainty of its incidence to which they object. As it works in most states, the sales tax cannot be a precise instrument of policy. It is likely to be capricious in its effects.

Conventional arguments for the retail sales tax are tarnished by the existence of the business portion. Consider a few of the traditional arguments. Many scholars incorrectly think of the retail sales tax as a tax on consumer expenditure exclusively. They think that as a consumption tax it will fall with neutrality on families with equal capacities to bear taxes. Others find the effects of the sales tax on "growth" appealing, relative to the effects of income taxes. Because the sales tax does not tax saving and investment, they say, it is relatively favorable to industrial location in one's state, to work effort, and to domestic investment. Still other scholars find the retail sales tax appealing because they believe that it is a single-stage tax applying only to sales to households and therefore that it does not discriminate against nonintegrated concerns as do most multiple-stage sales taxes. Each of these arguments is somewhat discounted when one appreciates what the sales tax actually does. It taxes a part of the final value of consumer goods and services, but not all, a part of the final value of investment goods and services, but not all; and it taxes a part of the final value of product more than once.

Concept of Retail Sale Under Existing Sales-Tax Statutes[1]

"Retail sale" has been defined by the statutes of most sales-tax states along these lines: a sale of tangible property,[2] and sometimes services, to a consumer for any purpose other than for resale.[3] The criterion is the disposition made by the purchaser: we must determine whether the purchase is for use or for resale. If the item is for resale, no tax attaches. If for use, it is not certain that the tax will apply. It depends on the statutes of the state. For making the determination in the latter case, two general tests are prevalent. One is called the component-part or physical-ingredient rule. The other is called the direct-use rule.

Table 1 suggests the following arbitrary classification of states with a sales tax, according to whether the state adheres most nearly to the component-part rule, the direct-use rule, or a hybrid of the two.

States with Component-part (Physical-ingredient) Rule (23): Arizona, Arkansas, California, Colorado, Florida, Hawaii, Illinois, Indiana, Iowa, Kansas, Louisiana, Maine, Maryland, Missouri, Nevada, New Mexico, North Dakota, Rhode Island, South Dakota, Texas, Utah, Washington, and Wyoming.

States with Direct-use Rule (8): Connecticut, Michigan, North Carolina, Ohio, Oklahoma, Pennyslvania, South Carolina, and West Virginia.

States with Hybrid Rule (5): Alabama, Georgia, Kentucky, Mississippi, and Tennessee.

COMPONENT-PART (PHYSICAL-INGREDIENT) RULE

Most sales-tax states employ the component or ingredient rule in deciding whether an item bought for use is a sale for resale or a statutory retail sale. Only the statutory retail sale is taxed. An item is considered to be resold if it becomes a physical ingredient or component part of another good which is sold. But if goods do not become a physical part of the unit's product, the sales are statutory retail sales and are taxed.

It is not essential that the property retain its identity in the article in which it is incorporated—for example, buttons on clothing or tires on an automobile. If the materials of which an item is composed become a physical part of some other article through physical or chemical processes, the sale is said to be a sale for resale and therefore is excluded from tax.

Fuel is not considered by most states to become an ingredient or component. Nevertheless, half the states with component-part rules, and most other states, exempt fuel used for industrial processing. But they tax fuel used for heating. (Here and in following material, see Table 1 for an enumeration by states.)

Sales of tools, machinery, equipment, lubricants (generally), building materials, office equipment and furnishings, cash registers, and show cases have all been ruled to be retail sales under the component or ingredient test. It is immaterial that they enter into the sales price of the ultimate consumer good.[4] Refrigerants, including ice, are in about the same position as fuel in the states with strictest ingredient rules; since they do not become part of the further article, they are usually not considered sales for resale.[5]

Sales of fruit trees to orchardists are final sales and taxable under the logic of the ingredient test. They are probably exempt under the logic of the direct-use test. Similarly, under the logic of the ingredient test, sales of livestock for breeding and dairying would be taxable.[6] So would feed sold for fattening swine, cattle, etc.,[7] be taxable. Nevertheless, each of these items—trees, livestock, and feed—is usually granted statutory exemption.

Sales of cartons, containers, and wrapping materials in past years were usually considered to be taxable retail sales. But many states have of late followed the lead of Ohio (a direct-use state) and have exempted wrapping and crating materials and cartons. There is precedent and logic for holding that nonreturnable or expendable containers are purchased for resale and hence are not subject to retail sales taxes when sold empty to a processor.[8] Almost all states give immunity to such containers in practice today (see Table II of the Appendix). But sales of bottles to bottlers and of milk bottles to retail distributors have most often been considered to be taxable retail sales.[9]

The general rule regarding construction materials and contractors' items is clear. Iowa's law is typical:

Sales of building materials, supplies and equipment to owners, contractors, subcontractors or builders for the erection of buildings or the alteration, repair or improvement of real property, are retail sales in whatever quantity sold.[10]

Illinois, perhaps, stood as the lone exception to the rule until recently.[11] There is often a question of whether the service as well as

TABLE 1. Taxable Status of Items Employed by Business Enterprises in the Production-distribution Process, by States, April 1963

	Raw materials, components, etc.	Industrial machines, tools, equipment	Fuel for industrial processing	Office equipment and supplies, display equipment, etc.	Construction materials, supplies, etc.	Feed, seed, fertilizer	Livestock, trees, etc.	Agricultural machines, tools, etc.
Component-parts states								
Arizona	E	T	T	T	T	E	E	T
Arkansas	E	T[a]	T	T	T	E	E	T
California	E	T	T	T	T	E	E	T
Colorado	E	T	E[b]	T	T	E	E	T
Florida	E	T	E	T	T	E	E	T
Hawaii	E	T	E	T	T	E	E	T
Illinois	E	T	T	T	T[c]	E	E	T
Indiana retail sales	T	E	E	T	T	E	?	E
Iowa	E	T[d]	E[b]	T	T	E	E	T
Kansas	E	T	E	T	T	E	E	T
Louisiana	E	T	E	T	T	E	E	T
Maine	E	T[e]	T	T	T	E	E	T
Maryland	E	T	E[b]	T	T	E	E	T
Missouri	E	T	T	T	T	E	E	T
Nevada	E	T	T	T	T	E	E	T
New Mexico	T[f]	T[g]	T[f]	T	T	E	E	T
North Dakota	E	T[d]	T	T	T	E	E	T
Rhode Island	E	T	E[b]	T	T	E	E	T
South Dakota	E	T	T[h]	T	T	E[i]	E	T
Texas	E	T	E	T	T	E	E	E
Utah	E	T	E	T	T	E[j]	E	T
Washington	E	T	T	T	T	E	E	T
Wyoming	E	T[d]	E[b]	T	T	E	E	T
Direct-use states								
Connecticut	E	E[b]	E[b]	T	T	E	E	T
Michigan	E	E[b]	E[b]	T[k]	T[l]	E	E	E
North Carolina	T[f]	T[m]	T[f]	T	T	E	E	T[n]
Ohio	E	E[b]	E[b]	E[o]	T	E	E	E
Oklahoma	E	E[b]	E[b]	T	T	T[p]	E	T[q]
Pennsylvania	E	E[b]	E[b]	T	T	E	T	E
South Carolina	E	E	E[b]	T	T	E	E	E
West Virginia	E	E[b]	T	T	T	E	E	E
Hybrid states								
Alabama	E	T[r]	E	T	T	E	E	T
Georgia	E	E[s]	T	T	T	E	E	T
Kentucky	E	E[t]	T[u]	T	T	E	E	T
Mississippi	T[f]	E[v]	T[w]	T	T	E	E	T[x]
Tennessee	E	T[y]	E[b]	T	T	E	E	T
Often included as sales-tax states								
Indiana: gross income	T[f]	T[f]	T[f]	T[f]	T[f]	T[f]	T[f]	T[f]
Wisconsin	E	T	E	T[z]	E	E	E	E

Key: T = Taxable; E = Exempt.

[TABLE 1, continued]

Sources

Commerce Clearing House, *Sales and Use Tax Statutes*, Rules and Regulations of the Various States; and *All-State Tax Reporter*; and Commerce Clearing House, *State Tax Review*; Clinton Oster, *State Retail Sales Taxation*, p. 85; Ohio Department of Taxation, *Retail Sales Tax Comparative Tables*; Tax Foundation, Inc., *Retail Sales and Individual Income Taxes in State Tax Structures*, Project Note No. 48, p. 25; Federation of Tax Administration, *Administration News*, January through June, 1963.

Notes

[a] Exempt from use tax if used for replacement or expansion of existing facilities.

[b] If used "directly" in manufacturing, processing, etc.

[c] Act of Illinois legislature, 1961, should end long doubt about exemption of construction, building, etc., supplies, equipment, fixtures, and the like. These items were most often not taxed before this action.

[d] Exempt when "not readily available" in taxing state.

[e] Except expendable items expected life of which is less than a year.

[f] Taxed at wholesale or reduced rate.

[g] Some agricultural machinery and equipment is exempt, however.

[h] Exempt from use tax.

[i] Seed for commercial agriculture is taxable in South Dakota.

[j] Seed is taxed if used to grow feedstuffs in Utah.

[k] Offices, etc., related to production and processing are exceptional.

[l] Construction materials for real-estate improvement are taxed at a 1 per cent lower rate, effective May 10, 1961.

[m] The following items are exempt: mill machinery, parts, and accessories sold to manufacturers; agricultural machines, parts, and accessories; sales of machinery to laundries, dry cleaners, and freezer locker plants; switchboard equipment; boats and supplies sold to commercial fishermen; medical and dental supplies and instruments; manufactured products sold to other manufacturers, producers, wholesalers or retailers for resale. Other items may be taxed.

[n] Taxed at only 1 per cent.

[o] Exemption applies only to property "used directly" in making retail sales (display merchandise, show cases, refrigeration merchandise, shelves, store furniture, fixtures, etc.).

[p] Only feed is exempt in Oklahoma.

[q] Trade-in allowance on machinery excluded from sale price.

[r] Rate of 1.5 per cent for most items.

[s] Machinery used directly for "new and expanded industry" (only) is exempt effective April 1, 1963.

[t] Machinery used directly for "new and expanded industry" (only) is exempt.

[u] All fuel used in manufacturing, processing, mining, or refining is exempt to the extent that it exceeds 3 per cent of cost of production.

[v] Gas, petroleum, electricity, and fuels for industrial, commercial, and agricultural purposes are taxed at 1 per cent. Sales in excess of $500 of industrial machinery to be used in the state are exempt.

[w] Gas, petroleum, electricity, and fuels for industrial, commercial and agricultural purposes are taxed at 1 per cent.

[x] Farm tractors taxed at 1 per cent in Mississippi.

[y] Machinery for "new and expanded industry" taxed at 1 per cent only.

[z] Office supplies such as forms, paper, other expendables, are not taxed.

the value of materials is taxable, however. And there is sometimes a question as to who will remit the tax.[12]

We see that a large portion of the tangible goods which enter costs of production are taxed in component-part states. Many materials are taxed, fuel is usually taxed, and so are construction materials taxed; purchases of machines, tools, and equipment are taxed; and the purchases of items used by the administrative, sales, and distributive branches of business are invariably taxed.

Since sales by one business to another are in fact so often taxed, the same value can conceivably be taxed several times. The value of a taxed item may enter into the sales price of a commodity which one business sells a second, the second in turn incorporating the commodity into its product and selling it to a third business, etc. Clearly, under the component convention the retail sales tax bears a family resemblance to other kinds of multiple-stage sales taxes— turnover, transactions, gross receipts, and gross sales taxes.

DIRECT-USE RULE

Many goods, supplies, and much equipment are used in the production process but do not become an ingredient of the product. Some states try to exclude from tax a selected group of these, provided they are "used directly" in processing goods for sale. These states are said to follow the direct-use rule or the directly-dissipated rule. Like the component-part rule, the direct-use rule has many forms.

One common provision is the exclusion of materials and supplies which are directly dissipated in the process of production. Examples of directly dissipated items are grease and oil used by machinery, catalysts, fuel, electricity, cleaning agents, and solvents. These items do not become a physical part of the new product and cannot qualify for exclusion under a strict interpretation of the component or ingredient rule. Yet they are consumed in the process of production. This version of the direct-use rule widens the exclusion as compared with the component-part rule. Yet it restricts the concessions with regard to producer goods. To illustrate, a state may exclude fuel and electricity from sales tax but not tools, furnishings, machinery and equipment.[13]

A few states—most notably Ohio, Michigan, Connecticut, Oklahoma, Pennsylvania, South Carolina, and West Virginia—have instituted more complete direct-use rules. Alabama, Kentucky, North Carolina, Tennessee, and Mississippi have either somewhat similar exemptions or reduced rates. The general purpose of this convention is to exclude from tax liability the sales of tangible property *used directly* in manufacturing, mining, agricultural, and other processing. Under this approach the sales of tools, machinery, equipment, etc., are excluded, as well as fuel, electricity, catalysts, lubricants, and solvents.

Just what is used directly in processing is difficult to determine conceptually, but rulings and decisions delineate a fairly clear pattern. Generally, sales of property for use in nonfactory, nonmachine shop departments of a manufacturer are considered to be for "office" or "nonproduction" use. They are taxed. Sales to administrative, service, advertising, accounting, traffic, sales, and purchasing departments are usually in this category.

Fuel used for processing is generally exempt in direct-use states, but fuel for heating administrative offices and plants is taxed. Generally the sale of equipment for transportation is taxed—but the litigation is profuse.[14] Perhaps the principal difference in the tax schemes of Michigan and Ohio, the states which are most liberal with exclusions, is Ohio's greater leniency on purchases made for the purpose of merchandising. Ohio retailers are not required to pay a sales tax on a wide range of merchandising items: show cases, store fixtures and furniture, display shelves, equipment used to refrigerate perishable merchandise, and supplies and equipment used to consummate retail sales.[15]

This survey has been fairly brief and general. But it should suffice to demonstrate that the selection of items for tax or exclusion status is predicated on administrative and political considerations primarily, rather than on considerations of economic rationality.

Impact of Retail Sales Taxes on the Purchases of
Business Enterprises

If businesses pay a part of the yield of retail sales taxes through their purchases from other businesses, how important are these payments? The answer, of course, depends on the sales-tax law of the state we have in mind and on the law's administration. But we want to say something more than "it all depends." Perhaps the best approach to some meaningful answers is to assume a number of hypothetical tax plans and excellent administration of them. We will follow here my empirical work for the *Wisconsin's State and Local Tax Burden* study of 1958–59.[16]

The categories of businesses for which impact is analyzed are: *Industrial, Construction, Agricultural, Retail,* and *Wholesale.*[17]

HYPOTHETICAL TAX SCHEME FOR INDUSTRIAL
ESTABLISHMENTS (MANUFACTURING, MINING,
AND CONSTRUCTION ENTERPRISES)

Three hypothetical tax schemes are assumed for industrial firms. They correspond approximately with schemes now in effect in sales-tax states.

1. *HYPOTHETICAL TAX X*—represents a narrow component-part rule, with exemption only for purchases of items which become an actual physical part of the product being processed. This means that purchases of machinery, tools, equipment, construction materials, transportation equipment, and all other products not actually used directly in the production process are hypothetically taxed.

2. *HYPOTHETICAL TAX Y*—is a modified component-part rule, more liberal than Tax X in its exclusions and exemptions. It excludes or exempts other materials which become dissipated in the production process, such as fuel, lubricants, and catalysts. In addition, it is patterned after the old Illinois law in regard to construction materials. That is, most items used in construction are hypothetically excluded or exempted.

3. *HYPOTHETICAL TAX Z*—is patterned after the direct-use pattern of sales taxation. Tax Z excludes all items excluded under Tax Y,[18] and in addition excludes machines, tools, and equipment used "directly" in production. It follows the Ohio direct-use pattern in excluding display merchandise.

HYPOTHETICAL TAX SCHEMES FOR WHOLESALE
AND RETAIL ESTABLISHMENTS

For purchases by wholesalers and retailers, Tax X, Tax Y, and Tax Z are again assumed. But the distinctions are not as meaningful as they were for industrial concerns. Most purchases made by wholesalers and retailers are clearly sales for resale and therefore exempt.

An estimate is made for both wholesale and retail establishments of the percentage of purchases likely to be sales for resale. The tax rate is applied only to the taxable difference between total purchases and purchases for resale.

1. *HYPOTHETICAL TAX X*—assumes the entire difference between total purchases and purchases for resale to be taxable.
2. *HYPOTHETICAL TAX Y*—exempts the purchase of construction materials from a base otherwise the same as that of Tax X.
3. *HYPOTHETICAL TAX Z*—exempts, in addition to the exemptions of Tax Y, purchases of machinery and equipment.

HYPOTHETICAL TAX SCHEMES FOR AGRICULTURAL
ENTERPRISES (FARM PRODUCTION EXPENSE ONLY)

As applied to production purchases of farmers:

1. *HYPOTHETICAL TAX X*—taxes virtually all purchases of tangible goods used for production. (This is an unlikely base, but it is useful for testing the potential burden on farmers—as producers, not as consumers—should the logic of the ingredient rule be followed rigorously.)
2. *HYPOTHETICAL TAX Y*—exempts feed, seed, fertilizer, plants, trees, pesticides, and livestock for breeding and for dairying purposes. It also exempts construction materials and marketing containers. It taxes tools, supplies, tractors, engines, trucks, and automobiles (including their parts and supplies).
3. *HYPOTHETICAL TAX Z*—exempts all items exempt under Tax Y, plus all farm machinery, tools, and equipment used in production, except autos and trucks.

Taxes Y and Z, in other words, assume a very powerful farm lobby which is even more successful in pursuing agriculture's interests than farm lobbies have actually been in sales-tax states. Tax X assumes farmers to be politically impotent, which they have not been.

Table 2 summarizes broadly the taxable status of major industrial and agricultural purchases (sales) under the three hypothetical sales-tax plans.

Estimation of Taxable Purchases by Business Category

The author's Wisconsin study concludes that in Wisconsin in 1954 (a Census of Business year) under Hypothetical Tax X—the very strict component rule—all businesses in the state would have had combined taxable purchases of nearly $1.5 billion. Under Tax Y taxable purchases would have been $0.8 billion. Under Tax Z

TABLE 2

The Taxable Status of Major Industrial Purchases and
Principal Farm Production Expenditures under
Three Hypothetical Retail Sales
Tax Conventions

A. Industrial expenses				B. Agricultural expenses			
Item	X	Y	Z	Item	X	Y	Z
Groceries, confectionaries, meats	E	E	E	Livestock, animals, etc.	T	E	E
Industrial chemicals and explosives	T	E	E	Feed	T	E	E
Paint and varnish	T	T	T	Seeds, plants, trees	T	E	E
Furniture	T	T	T	Fertilizer	T	E	E
Stationery, office supplies	T	T	T	Fuel for:			
Coarse paper	T	E	E	Automobiles	T	T	T
Electrical appliances, radios, TV's	T	T	T	Motor trucks	T	T	T
Lumber and construction materials	T	E	E	Tractors	T	E	E
Industrial machinery and equipment	T	T	E	Other engines	T	E	E
Metals, bars, forgings, rods, sheets, rails	E	E	E	Nonmotor use	T	E	E
Fuel for processing	T	E	E	Lubricants	T	E	E
Fuel for other heating	T	T	T	Tires, inner tubes, chains for:			
Professional equipment and supplies	E	E	E	Automobiles	T	T	T
Hides, grains, skins, cotton	E	E	E	Motor trucks	T	T	T
Automobiles	T	T	T	Tractors	T	T	E
Motor trucks	T	T	T	Farm machinery, implements	T	T	E
Cranes, hoists, shovels, mining equipment	T	T	T	Antifreeze, batteries, spark plugs for:			
Supplies: barber, beauty, janitorial laundry, cleaning, shoe service	T	T	T	Automobiles	T	T	T
Amusement and sporting goods	T	T	T	Motor trucks	T	T	T
				Tractors	T	T	T
				Farm machinery	T	T	T
				Marketing containers	T	E	E
				Pesticide, fungicides, etc.	T	E	E
				Hand tools, supplies, etc.	T	T	E
				Construction materials for new construction, additions, fencing, land and water improvements, etc.:			
				Materials only	T	E	E
				Labor valued separately	E	E	E
				Labor and materials not reported separately	T	E	E
				Vehicle purchases (both old and new):			
				Automobiles	T	T	T
				Motor trucks	T	T	T
				Tractors	T	T	E
				Other machinery and implements	T	T	E

Key: E = Exempt; T = Taxable.

24

—the direct-use rule—taxable purchases would have been almost $0.4 billion.

The tax scheme most representative of actual state practice perhaps would be: Tax X applied to industrial firms, wholesalers, and retailers, and Tax Y applied to farmers. Under this "most rep-

TABLE 3

Percentage Distribution of Taxable Payments
under Alternative Tax Schemes, by Major
Category of Business, Wisconsin, 1954

Business category	Tax X	Tax Y	Tax Z	Most representative tax plan[a]
Industrial	49.0	62.5	59.3	69.7
Agricultural	46.1	31.1	25.5	23.3
Retail	3.6	4.7	11.2	5.1
Wholesale	1.3	1.7	4.0	1.9
Totals	100.0	100.0	100.0	100.0

For description of tax plans, see text and Table 2.

[a] "Most representative tax plan" is the tax scheme which is believed to most nearly approximate the norm among retail sales tax states. It is Tax X as applied to industrial, retail, and wholesale business, and Tax Y applied to agriculture.

resentative tax plan," just over $1 billion of purchases would have been taxable.

A percentage distribution of taxable purchases among the selected categories of businesses is given in Table 3. Clearly most of the impact of the business portion of the sales tax is on the industrial and agricultural sectors, especially on the industrial. Wholesalers and retailers through their *purchases* bear very little of it.

Included in the industrial category (following the Census of Business classification) is the construction industry. The study indicates that about half (by value) of the taxable purchases of industry under Tax X were composed of construction materials and items related to construction. In turn, over half (by value) of the construction materials purchased were used in connection with residential construction in Wisconsin in 1954. Because these totals are so large, there is obviously some truth to the allegation that the sales tax is a disguised tax on housing when construction materials are taxed, provided that there is validity to forward-shifting assumptions.

The Business Portion of the Sales Tax in Relation to Total Tax Yield

What we have said thus far gives no perspective for saying how significant the yield from the business portion of the sales tax is in relation to total yield. This, of course, depends on the tax plans in force. Suppose that we consider typical plans as they apply to transactions: (a) between household consumers and businesses; and (b) between businesses and other businesses. Table 4 does this. It reproduces the results of my study for Wisconsin.[19]

In the Household Sector of Table 4, Tax A is a hypothetical tax on most tangible goods (including food and gasoline), plus a few services. Tax B is the same as Tax A, except that home-consumed food is exempt. Tax C broadly taxes tangibles (food included) and services (household-operations services, clothing and personal-care services, etc.). In the Business Sector of Table 4, the only taxes applied are the direct-use tax (Tax Z in the text above) and the "most representative tax plan" (the typical component-part or physical-ingredient rule). In other words, one typical direct-use plan and one typical ingredient plan are assumed.

With the information given in Table 4, many sales-tax combination schemes may be formed by pairing business tax plans with household tax plans and by assuming various rates of tax. Table 5 is illustrative. It selects four plausible combinations and designates them Plans I through IV (see the footnotes to Table 5 for descriptions of the plans). With these plans we can gauge the importance of the business portion in relation to total sales-tax yield.

We see that the relative importance varies considerably, depending on the scope of the entire plan. Under the plans we have selected the business portion may constitute less than 7 per cent of total yield (Plan III) or more than 34 per cent (Plan IV). Under Plans I and II, over 21 per cent and 29 per cent of total yield, respectively, are estimated to be paid by businesses through their purchases from other businesses.

I believe that the following conclusions are warranted. If a state employs a very strict component-part convention and grants no reduction in rates for business items taxed under that convention, the business portion will probably yield about a third of total receipts from the sales tax. If a state operates under a very liberal direct-use convention, such as Ohio's, only 10 per cent or so will come from the business portion. The percentage of total yield from the business portion for most states is apt to fall between 15 and 25 per cent. The percentage is affected, of course, by what is taxed under the household sector of the given sales tax, such as whether it taxes food, tobacco products, services, etc.[20] The total sales-tax liability of business taken collectively may easily be halved by switching from a component convention to a direct-use convention. One convention is about as plausible as another from the standpoint of administration.

Allocation of Business Portion of Sales Taxes to Income Classes (Incidence)

We have said nothing up to this point about how the "ultimate burden" of the business portion of the sales tax is distributed among individuals, by income classes. We have talked, in other words, about a burden concept more akin to impact than to incidence. It is very difficult to reach conclusions about incidence, partly because what modern economic theory suggests about shifting is tenuous indeed. Nevertheless, Table 6 ventures to suggest the incidence pattern of the business portion.

Table 6 suggests that typical component-part rules are likely to take a larger percentage of current (adjusted gross) income of families in the lower income classes than of families in the higher classes. The direct-use rule is apt to be more nearly proportional in its burden on the various brackets of income classes. These conclusions may surprise many readers. The shifting assumptions used to derive them are critical in determining the results. They are therefore spelled out in detail in Table 6 beneath the findings.

As we elaborate the shifting assumptions, we realize how arbitrary our incidence conclusions really are. But this is simply another way of saying that we appreciate how uncertain it is who ultimately pays a sales tax. The sales tax is hardly unique because its incidence is uncertain. Still, most authorities feel that the personal income tax by comparison is considerably more predictable in its ef-

TABLE 4

Taxable Purchases under Hypothetical Tax Schemes,
Wisconsin Households and Businesses, 1956
(thousands of dollars)

Household Sector			Business Sector[a]				
Taxable expenditures				Taxable purchases			
Consumer group	Tax A	Per cent of total	Business category	Most representative tax plan (a component rule)	Per cent of total	A direct-use rule	Per cent of total
Wisconsin households	3,881,997	97.3					
Tourists, other visitors	108,300	2.7					
Totals	3,990,297	100.0	Industrial	384,972	34.9	184,190	59.3
			Construction	383,325	34.8		
	Tax B	Per cent of total	Farm	256,685	23.3	79,284	25.5
			Retail	55,699	5.1	34,961	11.2
Wisconsin households	2,621,150	97.8	Wholesale	21,083	1.9	12,349	4.0
Tourists, other visitors	58,300	2.2	Totals	1,101,764	100.0	310,784	100.0
Totals	2,679,450	100.0					
	Tax C	Per cent of total					
Wisconsin households	4,281,772	97.3					
Tourists, other visitors	119,053	2.7					
Totals	4,400,825	100.0					

[a] For discussion of taxable purchases of hypothetical tax schemes of Business Sector, see text.

Household Sector's Hypothetical Tax Schemes

Tax A

Tangible personal property assumed taxed:
1. Food and beverages: food prepared at home and food eaten away from home
2. Alcoholic beverages
3. Tobacco
4. Medicine and drugs
5. Household items: household operations items, textiles, floor coverings, furniture, equipment, other houseware
6. Clothing
7. Automobile: motor fuel, auto purchase, operation items (when they could be segregated)
8. Personal care: articles, preparations
9. Recreation and education: sports equipment, radios, TV's, musical instruments, books

Tangible personal property assumed exempt:
1. Sales to local, state, federal governments
2. Sales to educational, charitable, religious organizations
3. Direct sales, farm produce
4. Casual and isolated sales
5. Newspapers
6. Employees' free meals
7. School lunches

Services assumed taxed:
1. Gas and electric service
2. Admissions

Services assumed exempt: all other services

Tax B

Tax B is the same as Tax A except for the exemption of "food consumed off premises where purchased."

fects and incidence. If this is so we have with the income tax a more precise instrument for attaining any burden pattern we desire.[21] For many economists the difference in the degree of certainty of incidence is the decisive difference between the personal income tax and the retail sales tax. The critical factor is not that the business portion is regressive, but that no one really knows what the pattern is. And because of the way items are taxed, it is a near certainty that the incidence will be discriminatory.

Effects of the Analysis on the Rationale of Retail Sales Taxation

What is the effect on the rationale of the retail sales tax when it is realized that the tax is not exclusively a single-stage levy on final household expenditure?

So long as the sales tax is thought to be like a direct levy on family consumption expenditure, a formidable case on grounds of ability to pay can be marshaled for its neutrality aspects. Nicholas Kaldor has recently made such a case on neutrality grounds for an expenditure tax.[22] Kaldor argues that no form of personal income tax which is administratively feasible can measure taxable capacity with the degree of neutrality of a consumption tax. This is because in Kaldor's view no definition of income can be devised to equate relative capacities. Achieving a taxable capacity equivalence requires

---

[TABLE 4, continued]

Tax C

All items of Tax A assumed taxed, plus:

Services assumed taxed:
1. Admissions and amusements: movies, plays, concerts, sporting and other spectator events
2. Automobile servies: lubrication, repair, parking, garage, rent, insurance
3. Clothing services: dry cleaning, pressing, dyeing, shoe repair, shines, storage, dressmaker and tailor services, watch and jewelry repair
4. Communication services: telephone and telegraph
5. Household operation services: laundry, launderette, day nursery fees, child care centers, baby sitters service, repair and insurance of house furnishings and equipment, garbage collection, freight and express service, moving
6. Non-auto travel and transportation: streetcar, local bus and taxi fare, car pools, auto rentals, etc.
7. Personal care services: all barber and beauty parlor services
8. Utility services: gas and electricity service, water service

Services assumed exempt:
1. Most professional services
2. Education
3. Labor service other than those cited above.

TABLE 5

Impact of Four Hypothetical Combination Sales
Tax Plans, Wisconsin, 1956[a]

Taxpayer group	Plan I[b] (2 per cent)		Plan II[b] (3 per cent)	
	Amount	Per cent of total	Amount	Per cent of total
Wisconsin households	$ 77,639,942	76.24	$ 78,634,520	69.32
Tourists, visitors	2,166,000	2.13	1,749,000	1.54
Business:				
industrial	7,699,440	7.56	11,549,160	10.18
construction	7,666,508	7.53	11,499,762	10.18
farm	5,133,706	5.04	7,700,558	6.79
retail	1,113,981	1.09	1,670,972	1.47
wholesale	421,661	0.41	632,491	0.56
All business	22,035,296	21.63	33,052,943	29.14
Total, taxpayer group	$101,841,238	100.00	$113,436,463	100.00

Taxpayer group	Plan III[b] (2 per cent)		Plan IV[b] (3 per cent)	
	Amount	Per cent of total	Amount	Per cent of total
Wisconsin households	$ 85,635,436	90.88	$ 60,348,650	62.44
Tourists, visitors	2,381,057	2.53	3,249,000	3.36
Business:				
industrial	3,683,803	3.91	11,549,160	11.95
construction	—	—	11,499,762	11.90
farm	1,585,674	1.68	7,700,558	7.97
retail	699,226	0.74	1,670,972	1.73
wholesale	246,978	0.26	632,491	0.65
All business	6,215,681	6.59	33,052,943	34.20
Total, taxpayer group	$ 94,232,174	100.00	$ 96,650,593	100.00

Notes

[a] The impact concept used here is not the conventional definition of impact, as being on the party who makes the actual payment to the government. Rather, impact here is assumed to be on the purchaser, even though the seller may submit the tax to the government. This concept is sometimes called "first-round incidence." (Ursula Hicks' conception of "formal incidence" may also coincide with this idea. See "The Terminology of Tax Analysis," *Economic Journal*, LVI [March, 1956], 32–50.) No other shifting is assumed, however, and no allowance is made for offsets against federal income tax liability.

[b] The plans assumed are:

Plan I: Household Sector's Tax A combined with Business Sector's most representative tax plan (i.e., typical component-part rule), 2 per cent rate.

Plan II: Household Sector's Tax B combined with Business Sector's most representative tax, 3 per cent rate.

Plan III: Household Sector's Tax C combined with Business Sector's direct-use rule (Tax Z), 2 per cent rate.

Plan IV: Household Sector's Tax A, with $15 credit per resident, combined with most representative tax plan, 3 per cent rate. (This version is not shown in the Household Sector of Table 4.)

equating temporary and permanent sources of income and wealth, fluctuating and regular receipts, genuine and fictitious capital gains, and labor and property incomes. But individuals place themselves into equivalence—persons of differing income source, income regularity, age, and occupation—by the standard of living they support. They themselves sort the genuine from the fictitious gain. If the sales tax were a genuine consumption tax, this kind of argument might be advanced on its behalf.

A closely related argument is the familiar thesis of Irving Fisher to the effect that consumption is the only consistent definition of income. Any income concept except consumption, says Fisher, carries the error of combining discounted and undiscounted values. This is because income, to Fisher, is the net benefit from capital over a period of time. Saving or investment is not income because it enlarges the capital stock and therefore the future yield at the expense of present yield. To include saving or investment is to regard it as current yield. It is to add part of the discounted value of future income (i.e., part of capital) to the undiscounted present income.

These arguments are not directly applicable to a realistic picture of retail sales taxes. Actual retail sales taxes apply to investment goods as well as to consumption goods. And they are limited forms of multiple-stage or turnover taxes. Since the sales tax does not hit consistently and exclusively at final value of consumption (Fisher income), without extensive further investigation it cannot be claimed that it achieves the degree of neutrality (on grounds of ability to pay) which proponents claim for consumption-base taxation.

Consideration of Actual Retail Sales Taxes as Levies on Social Product (Income)

If the typical retail sales tax does not strike at a genuine consumption base, might it be thought to be a tax on final output (income)—in the social accounting sense of final value of consumption plus investment? The answer is clearly no: it taxes mainly tangible goods and neglects most services (and this is especially true of the business portion of the tax); it frequently taxes the same value more than once in the production-distribution process; it taxes transactions in used items; and it generally exempts some

TABLE 6

Percentage of Adjusted Gross Income Hypothetically Paid
under Alternative Retail Sales Tax Plans,
by Income Class, Wisconsin, 1956

Income class	Case A			Case B		
	Assuming all sales tax yield to be borne by Wisconsin residents			After federal tax offsets, and assuming some of tax yield to be "exported"		
	Portion (per cent)			Portion (per cent)		
	Business	Household	Total	Business	Household	Total
Plan I[a]						
$ 0– 999	1.26	3.66	4.92	0.88	3.66	4.54
1,000–1,999	0.62	1.79	2.41	0.44	1.74	2.18
2,000–2,999	0.48	1.53	2.01	0.33	1.46	1.79
3,000–3,999	0.41	1.41	1.82	0.27	1.32	1.59
4,000–4,999	0.37	1.36	1.73	0.23	1.26	1.49
5,000–5,999	0.34	1.32	1.66	0.21	1.19	1.40
6,000–7,499	0.32	1.23	1.55	0.20	1.10	1.30
7,500–9,999	0.30	1.12	1.42	0.19	1.00	1.19
10,000 and over	0.27	0.75	1.02	0.18	0.61	0.79
All clases	0.36	1.25	1.61	0.24	1.13	1.37
Plan II[a]						
$ 0– 999	1.89	2.91	4.80	1.32	2.91	4.23
1,000–1,999	0.94	1.54	2.48	0.67	1.50	2.17
2,000–2,999	0.72	1.40	2.12	0.50	1.34	1.84
3,000–3,999	0.61	1.34	1.95	0.41	1.26	1.67
4,000–4,999	0.55	1.33	1.88	0.35	1.23	1.58
5,000–5,999	0.51	1.34	1.85	0.32	1.21	1.53
6,000–7,499	0.49	1.32	1.81	0.30	1.17	1.47
7,500–9,999	0.45	1.21	1.66	0.29	1.08	1.37
10,000 and over	0.41	0.87	1.28	0.27	0.71	0.98
All classes	0.54	1.26	1.80	0.35	1.14	1.50
Plan III[a]						
$ 0– 999	0.27	4.03	4.30	0.12	4.03	4.15
1,000–1,999	0.15	1.96	2.11	0.08	1.91	1.99
2,000–2,999	0.13	1.67	1.80	0.06	1.59	1.65
3,000–3,999	0.11	1.53	1.64	0.05	1.44	1.49
4,000–4,999	0.10	1.47	1.57	0.04	1.36	1.40
5,000–5,999	0.09	1.44	1.53	0.04	1.30	1.34
6,000–7,499	0.09	1.35	1.44	0.04	1.20	1.24
7,500–9,999	0.08	1.25	1.33	0.04	1.12	1.16
10,000 and over	0.09	0.87	0.96	0.05	0.71	0.76
All classes	0.10	1.37	1.47	0.05	1.25	1.30

[a] Plans I, II, and III are the same as Plans I, II, and III of Table 5.

32

[TABLE 6, continued]

Notes

Shifting assumptions employed in deriving Table 6:

Case A: assumes a closed economy, pretending that all state taxes are borne by the residents of the state.

Case B: assumes that some of the burden of the state's taxes may be shifted to the residents of other states, i.e., exported.

Case A (No exporting):

Industry (manufacturing and mining)

Taxes paid by industry on purchases of items other than those related to construction are assumed to be shifted to consumers. They are allocated on the basis of consumer expenditures by income classes for total goods and services.

Construction materials purchases

Purchases of construction materials and supplies which are taxed by sales taxes are allocated to several kinds of users:

Industrial:

Whether the construction materials purchased by industry are for owner-occupied improvements or for tenant-occupied improvements, they are assumed to be shifted to consumers. They are allocated as under *Industry.*

Agricultural:

About 86 per cent of farm construction improvements (by value) in Wisconsin is estimated to be for owner-occupied farms. It is assumed that one half of such improvements expenditure is shifted forward to food purchasers. These are allocated on the basis of a percentage distribution of consumer expenditures on food products. One half is assumed to be absorbed by farm owners. This half is apportioned according to a distribution of farm income by income class.

Purchases of construction materials made on tenant-occupied farms are assumed to be shifted to the tenant farmer, who in turn shifts 50 per cent forward to consumers and absorbs 50 per cent. The shifted portion is allocated according to the distribution by income class of food expenditure. The absorbed portion is allocated to income classes according to a percentage distribution of farm income.

Wholesale and retail (mercantile):

Purchases of construction items for owner-occupied mercantile improvements are assumed to be 75 per cent forward-shifted to consumers and 25 per cent absorbed. The shifted part is allocated according to the distribution of consumer expenditures on all goods and services. The absorbed part is allocated on the basis of the distribution of business income by income classes.

Purchases for tenant-occupied mercantile improvements are assumed to be 75 per cent forward-shifted to consumers, and are allocated according to consumer expenditure by income class on all goods and services. The other 25 per cent is assumed to be absorbed. It is apportioned among income classes according to a distribution of rents and royalties.

Residential:

Purchases for construction or improvement of owner-occupied residences are allocated among income classes according to a distribution of house values by income class.

Purchases for tenant-occupied residences are assumed to be shifted to the tenant. They are distributed among income classes on the basis of consumer housing expenditure.

Public utility:

Materials purchases by public utilities for construction or improvement are assumed to be entirely forward-shifted to utility service consumers. They are allocated according to expenditure by income class for fuel, light, and refrigeration.

Agriculture

Purchases other than for construction materials made by farmers of both owner-occupied and tenant-occupied farms are assumed to be 50 per cent forward-shifted to consumers of food products and 50 per cent absorbed. The forward-shifted portion is allocated on the basis of consumer expenditures on food products, the absorbed portion according to the distribution of farm income by income classes. The reason that 100 per cent is not assumed to be shifted forward is the apparent inability or unwillingness of farmers to be mobile (elastic in supply of their services) in the face of declining income.

Wholesale and retail

All taxable purchases of wholesale and retail firms are allocated on the same basis as that described above for construction materials purchases by mercantile concerns.

(*continued on page 35*)

kinds of investment goods. Still, it should be said that in its business portion it does indeed levy on most transactions in new investment goods—industrial and agricultural machines, equipment and tools, construction materials and equipment, office equipment, supplies, furniture, and the like—at least in most component-part states.[23] So there are in fact grounds for contending that most actual retail sales taxes are as closely related to taxes on investment *and* consumption output as they are to taxes on merely consumption output alone.

One cannot infer from this, however, that the typical retail sales tax is equivalent to a factor-income tax.[24] While it is true that social product or social income is about the same in value as the payments to the factors of production—whether exactly the same depends on the particular concept of social income we have in mind—it need not follow that the sales tax therefore constitutes an indirect approach to factor-income taxation. The chance that the incidence of a tax on the sale of investment goods is just the same as a tax on savers is rather slight in today's noncompetive markets and in a state's open economy.

However, even if the typical sales tax were equivalent to a factor-earnings tax in its incidence, such a tax is deficient if it is to be rationalized on grounds of ability to pay. This is because social income, which equals factor earnings, does not constitute an adequate barometer of relative capacities of individuals or families to pay taxes. Social income is an estimate of the value which is generated in the production process from a social aggregate perspective. Measuring the relative capacities of individuals to pay taxes requires a different yardstick. Most tax authorities adhere to the idea that total accretion is the best measure of capacity. This is the so-called Haig-Simons approach: income from an ability-to-pay viewpoint is one's rights exercised in consumption during a period of time, *plus* one's increase in net worth.[25]

Under this approach, income as taxable capacity includes all accretions to wealth—power to command all resources—no matter in what form the wealth happens to accrue. Windfalls and transfers provide no less tax-paying ability than income earned in production. In theory at least all accretions should count: not merely earned income of the factors of production but also transfer payments, gifts, inheritances, gambling winnings, or any other kind of windfall. It does not matter under the Haig-Simons approach whether these accretions are regular or irregular, expected or unexpected, realized or unrealized. Administrative difficulties may not allow taxation of all such accretions. But income taxation designed to tax according to relative ability to pay may at least aim at it. Taxation of *social income* would not aim at it, however. To repeat, windfall or transfer receipts provide at least as much paying capacity as factor receipts and they should not be omitted from taxation. There is no proscription against taxing some receipts twice, for example, once to the "earner" and again to the windfall recipient. This is not analogous to taxing the same value twice in the production-distribution process.[26]

The crux of the difficulty is this. If the index of ability is taken to be consumption, sales transactions between businesses and final consumers suffice as a barometer. One demonstrates capacity by one's nonbusiness purchase transactions. But if the index of ability is taken to be income, purchase transactions will not suffice; more information is required.

[TABLE 6, continued]

CASE B (EXPORTING):

Federal tax offsets

When we consider the interrelationship between state and federal tax systems, we recognize that not all of the sales tax burden of a state is borne by residents of the state. Part is borne by all United States citizens because sales taxes are deductible from income (corporate and personal). The burden of state residents is only the net additional amount of taxes that must be paid because of the tax.

For taxes assumed to be absorbed by owners of incorporated businesses, the average 1956 federal corporation income tax rate (45.6 per cent in Wisconsin) is offset against the total estimated sales tax liability.

For taxes assumed to be absorbed by unincorporated taxpayers (individuals or business owners), sales taxes are offset against the federal personal income tax. The amount of the offset depends on the marginal tax rate and the type of return filed. Those employing the standard deduction are unable to offset additional amounts because of the sales taxes they pay. For "itemizers" the deductibility enables an offset. The federal tax offset is equal to the product of the marginal tax rate and the sales tax liability. The offset is estimated on the basis of the table of average marginal federal income tax rates by income class.

Out-of-state buyers of state's products

Manufacturing output:

From a sample, 80 per cent of Wisconsin's manufacturing output is estimated to be sold to nonresident buyers. Therefore 80 per cent of sales taxes which would be paid initially by manufacturers, but assumed ultimately to be shifted to consumers of manufacturing output, is assumed to be exported to nonresident buyers.

Agricultural produce:

About 50 per cent of Wisconsin's farm output is estimated to be sold outside Wisconsin. Therefore, half of all sales taxes the impact of which is on farmers but is assumed to be shifted to consumers of farm produce is assumed to be exported from the state.

Retail sales:

About 5 per cent of taxes paid initially by wholesalers and retailers but assumed to be shifted to consumers is treated as being exported to nonresidents. This does not account for retail purchases within the state of tourists, conventioners, businessmen, students, and other visitors. These purchases are estimated separately, but are not included in the distribution of taxes by income classes.

We conclude that actual American retail sales taxes are corruptions of taxes on either consumption or consumption plus investment. As they now exist they are not rational ability-to-pay levies, whether consumption or whether income is taken to constitute the index of taxable capacity.

III

CONSUMER-BEHAVIOR HYPOTHESES
AND RETAIL SALES TAXES

Are retail sales taxes regressive? Should they be? Do they exempt some level of income from tax? Do they tax equally circumstanced families equally? Is a tax on consumption better than a tax on income? These are some of the important questions in sales-tax appraisal. To each question there is not one but many answers. Strange as it may sound, in our present state of knowledge each answer depends in part on the particular theory of consumer behavior we accept. In this chapter and the following one we shall see why this is so.

Suppose we want to know how progressive (or regressive) a retail sales tax is. We get a different answer as we change the inclusiveness of the tax, the definition of progressiveness, and the incidence assumptions. This much is widely understood. Perhaps less well understood is the fact that the progressiveness of a sales tax is affected as we vary the definitions of income and consumption, the time period of receipt and expenditure, the receiver-unit concept, and the status rankings. The time period is especially important. We would like to be able to make a study of the progressiveness of a given sales tax by varying the time period, say, from six months to several years. Unfortunately, the necessary long-period data do not exist. Our studies of sales-tax progressiveness are of necessity based on cross-section budget data covering the conventional time period of one year.

Lacking the long-period data, we form our expectations about the progressiveness of a retail sales tax by the particular theory of consumer behavior we accept. There are many theories of household consumer behavior which underlie the competing theories of the aggregate consumption function. The theory we explicitly or implicitly espouse shapes our views about the burden pattern we expect from a sales tax.

Consider three basic theories of the consumption function: the absolute-income hypothesis, the relative-income hypothesis, and the permanent-income hypothesis. Most versions of the absolute hypothesis and the relative hypothesis lead us to expect the percentage of income saved by a consumer unit to rise as the income of the unit rises—either absolutely or relative to others, respectively. The absolute-income hypothesis leads us to expect the saving-income ratio to rise as the absolute, real level of income rises. The relative-income hypothesis posits that the units which are high in income relative to others will have the high saving-income ratios; the saving-income ratio depends on a unit's relative position in the income scale, and not on its absolute level of income. Whether one accepts the absolute hypothesis or the relative hypothesis, one expects a tax at a proportional rate on total consumption expenditure to be regressive with respect to income. Under each hypothesis one expects a smaller percentage of income to be subject to tax as we ascend the income scale. But under a leading version of the permanent-income hypothesis, one expects the same tax to be proportional, not regressive. The permanent hypothesis posits that if the time period of income receipt and expenditure is sufficiently long, and if we define consumption and income correctly, the consumer unit will spend the same portion of its income regardless of the size of the income. If empirical studies seem to contradict the hypothesis, it is because their brief (one-year) time period distorts the true consumption-income relationship.

Sophisticated versions of the absolute, relative, and permanent hypothesis probably explain and forecast aggregate consumption expenditure about equally well. But the simple behavior assumptions which underlie them are contradictory. If tax policy is formulated on the basis of the behavior assumptions, as it is likely to be, policy conclusions will be contradictory given our disposition to reason from simple theories. To illustrate, suppose we agree that at the state level of government taxes should be effectively proportional to income. The typical retail sales tax receives a high grade if one accepts the permanent-income hypothesis and a low grade if one accepts the absolute-income hypothesis.

Welfare and policy conclusions need not follow from propositions about how people actually behave, and certainly not from how they behave in spending their incomes. Yet social ethics are often derived from behavior hypotheses, and this has been a venerable approach in the economics of public finance. So we intend to examine the absolute-income, the permanent-income, and the relative-income hypotheses with two purposes in mind. One is to draw out the differences in behavior which are posited by the competing theories of the consumer. The other is to investigate whether any welfare and tax policy norms follow if one accepts as representative the behavior posited.

In this chapter we accept the conventional doctrine that sales taxes are consumer-burden taxes. In Chapter II we qualified this doctrine by pointing to the importance of what we called the business portion of the retail sales tax, and in Chapter VI we examine Earl Rolph's theory which denies that sales taxes are actually taxes on consumers. But in this chapter we reason along the lines of the public's intuition. The popular view would have it that under a 2 per cent sales tax the family with $1,000 of taxable expenditures bears a money burden of $20. We know, of course, that this may be a naïve view of sales-tax incidence. Even so it seems fruitful to explore the effects of the retail sales tax in this way, as if it were like a proportional personal income tax, except that we apply it to consumer expenditure rather than to income.

A Brief Survey of Alternative Formulations of the Consumption Function

What we want to examine are the behavioral theories for individual consumer units which underlie alternative theories of the consumption function. The term "consumption function" actually applies to aggregates. It is the relationship between aggregate consumption and aggregate income.

The consumption function has occupied a major role in economics since Keynes made it the touchstone of his theoretical structure in his *General Theory of Employment, Interest and Money*. It is Keynes' formulation and some modern variations of it which we refer to as the absolute-income hypothesis. Keynes thought that the level of current consumption expenditure depends on the absolute level of real, current income. He probably thought that the proportion of aggregate income which is saved rises as the real level of aggregate income increases.

Keynes' absolute-income formulation—the view that consumption depends on, and is a decreasing function of, the absolute, real level of income—began to be questioned as evidence accumulated that, despite marked increases in real income (aggregate and per capita) over time, the ratio of aggregate consumption to aggregate income remained approximately constant. Alternative hypotheses began to appear. Dorothy Brady and Rose Friedman advanced the relative-income hypothesis,[1] contending that a consumer unit's consumption depends on its position in its community's distribution of income. James Duesenberry seconded this hypothesis and tied it to sociological behavior assumptions.[2] It is Duesenberry's version that we examine—an approach especially fruitful for our purposes. Several prominent economists have continued to believe that the absolute hypothesis is more consistent with available data if we modify it slightly.[3] They suggest that taking account of changes in wealth and allowing for the introduction of new goods may explain the constancy over time of the fraction of income saved. In recent years a great deal of attention has been given to the role of assets as well as income in explaining consumption.[4]

Milton Friedman, following the lead of Franco Modigliani and Richard Brumberg,[5] has advanced the permanent-income hypothesis,[6] which he contends incorporates a wealth-income effect. Friedman sees the relative-income hypothesis as something of a special case under his more general theory. He argues that proper concepts of income and consumption would result in a consumption-income ratio for any unit that would be invariant with respect to income. The ratio will of course differ between individual units. What the ratio is will depend on the rate of interest, the unit's assets-to-income ratio, its income variability, and its time preference. But whatever the ratio, it will be the same at all levels of income that the individual might experience. The level of income per se does not influence the consumption-income ratio of any individual unit. Further, under certain simplifying assumptions we expect the aggregate consumption-income ratio to be the same at all levels of income. Extensive statistical tests of this hypothesis have been performed and several are in process (see the last section of Chaper IV).

Behavioral Assumptions Underlying Consumption-Function Hypotheses

With this introduction let us examine the theories of consumer behavior that underlie the competing hypotheses of the consumption function. Keep in mind that we want to note their implications for progressivity measurement and for the formulation of tax policy.

The Friedman permanent-income hypothesis and the (Keynes, *et al.*) absolute-income hypothesis may both be interpreted as special cases of what was once the received theory of consumer behavior. Suppose we take the approach of J. R. Hicks in his *Value and Capital* as the received doctrine. First, we review Friedman's approach, by which he concludes that the received ("pure") theory of consumer behavior most reasonably implies proportionality of consumption-to-income as income increases. Next, we criticize Friedman from the orthodox Keynesian point of view, which infers from the received theory that the consumption-income ratio is apt to decline as the absolute level of income rises. Finally, we evaluate all of this with the perspective of Duesenberry's revision of the received theory of consumer behavior.

FRIEDMAN'S VERSION OF THE "PURE THEORY" OF CONSUMER BEHAVIOR

Friedman counters the orthodox view of time preference which holds that there will be greater urgency at lowest levels of income. Under conditions of certainty, with only two income periods, and employing the traditional ordinal indifference map approach, Friedman's formulation runs as follows.[7]

The consumer unit, knowing in advance its receipts in each period—call these R_1 and R_2—and the prices which will prevail, including the interest rate i, will have only two reasons for consuming more or less than its receipts in either period:

1. To eliminate fluctuations in its expenditure stream. It can do this by borrowing and lending.

2. To gain interest i by loaning, assuming that i is positive.

It is the unit's total resources (wealth) over the period that determined its consumption, and not its actual receipts in either period. If we assume that all resources are depleted by the end of the second period, the maximum that can be consumed in period 1 is R_1 plus the maximum loan that can be repaid in period 2. The unit can borrow on the basis of certain receipts R_2. So the maximum that can be consumed in period 1 is $R_1 + R_2/(1 + i)$. If nothing is consumed

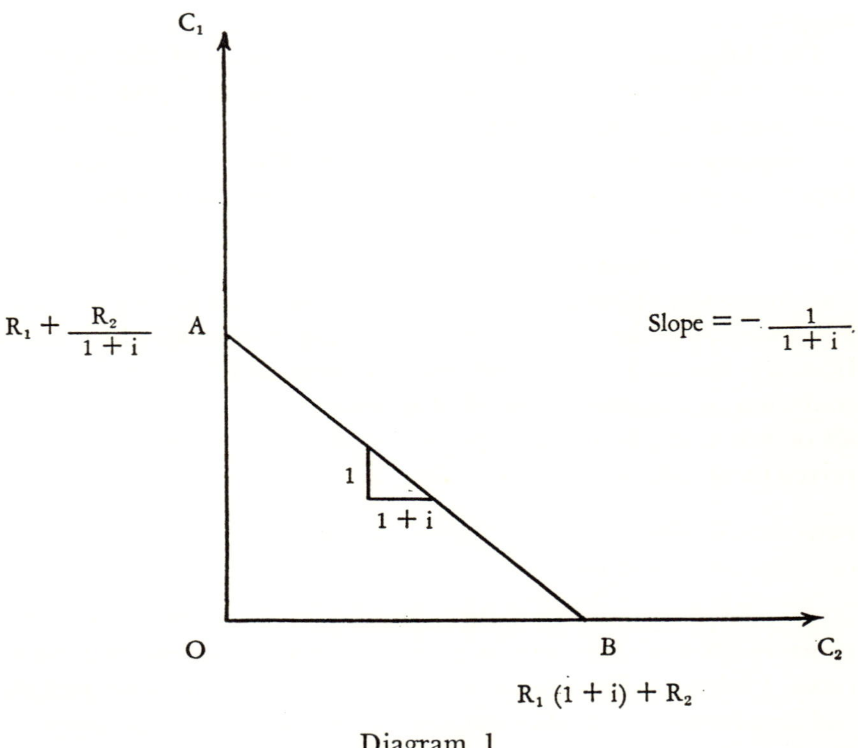

Diagram 1

in period 1 the maximum that can be consumed in period 2 is $R_1(1 + i) + R_2$. On the traditional diagram this will appear as in Diagram 1. Notice that what can be consumed in period 1 or in period 2 depends on two variables:

1. The position of the budget line.
2. The slope of the line.

The slope is determined by the interest rate i. By giving up one dollar in consumption in period 1 the unit can get one dollar $+ i$ in period 2. OA represents the maximum that can be consumed in period 1 if nothing is considered in period 2. OB represents the maximum that can be consumed in period 2 if nothing is consumed in period 1.

Thus, how much can be consumed in period 1 does not depend at all on $R_{1'}$ but on wealth in period 1. A change in R_1 will affect consumption only through its effect on wealth. Notice that it is receipts, such as R_1, that we usually take to be income. But one period's receipts are not income at all, properly considered.

Budget line AB in Diagram 1 represents the maximum possible

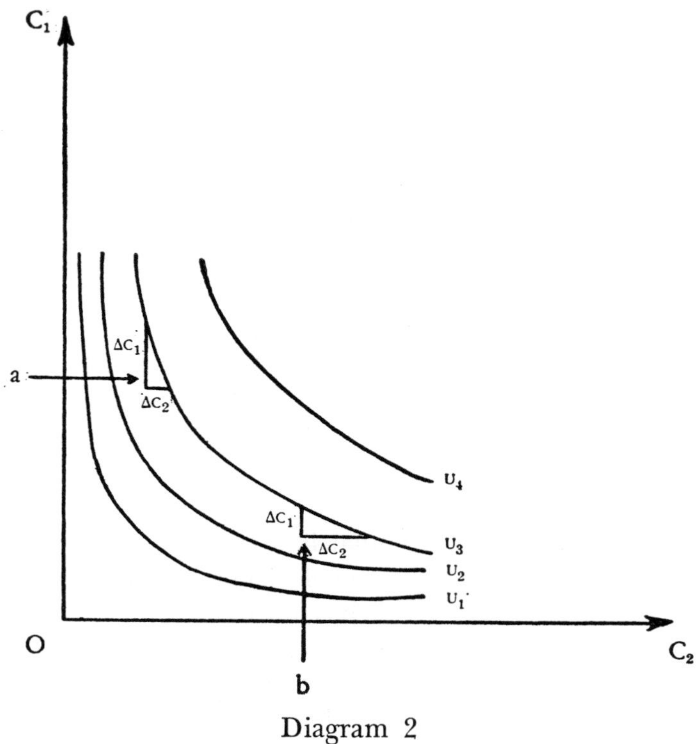

Diagram 2

combinations of consumption in periods 1 and 2. The combination that the consumer unit actually chooses depends on its tastes—time preference, etc.—as well as on the budget line and i. Tastes can be depicted with ordinal indifference curves in the usual way, with U_3 representing a higher level of satisfaction than U_2, U_2 than U_1, etc., as in Diagram 2. The indifference curves represent the rates at which the consumer unit would be willing to exchange consumption in period 1 for consumption in period 2. This is called the marginal rate of substitution between consumption in period 1 and period 2.

In Diagram 2, *a* represents a high marginal rate of substitution of period 1 for period 2 consumption; *b* represents a low rate. At combination levels represented by *a*, a unit would be willing to give up a considerable amount of consumption in period 1 for a little more consumption in period 2. But at levels represented by *b*, the unit is in the reverse position, willing to give up much consumption in period 2 for a little more in period 1. Thus the marginal rate of substitution varies positively with the C_1/C_2 ratio. High on the indifference curve when the unit is long on C_1, it takes much C_1 to compensate for a little C_2. When long on C_2, it takes much C_2 to compensate for a little C_1. The marginal rates of substitution may be said to reflect the relative urgencies of present and future consumption.

What combination does the consumer unit actually choose? The familiar maximizing answer is that it goes to the highest possible indifference level consistent with its budget (wealth) constraint, which is the point of tangency between budget and indifference lines (point X in Diagram 3).

All of this is agreed upon by those who are happy in this medium of the theory of consumer behavior. The key question, however, is—what happens to this equilibrium position when the unit's level of wealth changes? Suppose the level is doubled while i remains constant. Where will the new equilibrium be?

What we are concerned about is the ratio of C_1/C_2 at the higher level. Friedman's contention is that it is constant. A constant C_1/C_2 ratio is represented on the traditional diagram by a straight line. In Diagram 4 ray OA is a high and constant C_1/C_2 ratio; OB is low and constant. In each case if wealth is doubled the unit simply doubles consumption in each period, leaving the C_1/C_2 ratio constant.

Friedman argues that while a change in i will alter the C_1/C_2 ratio, a change in wealth will not. The rate at which a consumer unit will be willing to substitute consumption in two periods does not depend on absolute level of consumption, he says. He contends:

Doubling the level of consumption in Year 1 may diminish the urgency of additional consumption in Year 1 relative to consumption in Year 2, which, by itself, would tend to lower the additional Year 2 consumption required to compensate the consumer unit for giving up one dollar of Year 1 consumption; however, if the level of consumption in Year 2 is simultaneously doubled, this would have the opposite effect, diminishing the urgency of additional consumption in Year 2 relative to consumption in Year 1, and so, by itself, tending to raise the amount of Year 2 consumption required to compensate the consumer unit for giving up one dollar in Year 1 consumption.[8]

The two effects need not offset each other. But Friedman sees no a priori reason why the first should systematically or generally tend to exceed the second, or conversely. So he assumes the simplest hypothesis: they offset each other.

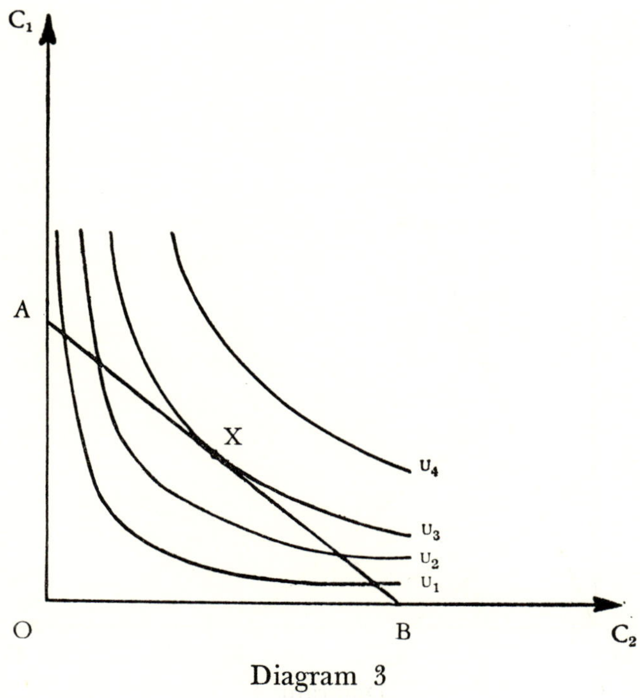

Diagram 3

Moving from conditions of certainty to uncertainty, Friedman concludes that there is no way to say whether uncertainty would tend to make consumption a larger or a smaller fraction of wealth the higher the level of wealth. In discussing uncertainty he does argue, however, that the ratio of nonhuman wealth to permanent income is an important variable. Nonhuman wealth provides a reserve for emergency and lowers the necessity for saving. Therefore, the higher the ratio of nonhuman wealth to permanent income, the higher consumption is expected to be. It is the ratio of assets to permanent income that counts and not the absolute amount of assets. A proportional increase in both nonhuman assets and permanent income increases both the reserve available and the level of consumption to be protected. It constitutes merely a change in scale.

Uncertainty about future income and needs influences Friedman's k, the relationship between permanent consumption and permanent income. But it does not alter the consumption-income ratio as between different income levels.

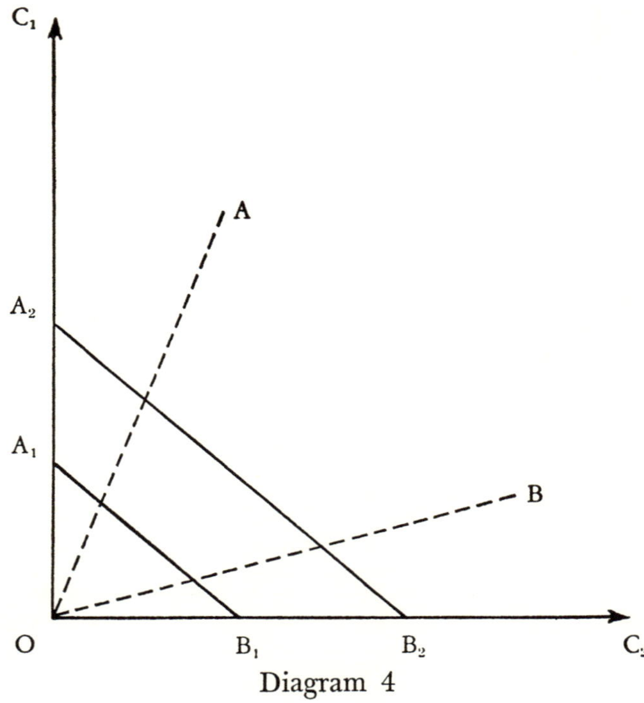

Diagram 4

Friedman's conclusion that units with low permanent income will have no greater preference for present over future consumption than units with high permanent income is at odds with the more conventional conclusion.

ORTHODOXY'S "PURE THEORY" OF
CONSUMER BEHAVIOR

The more conventional view, associated with the names of Irving Fisher, J. R. Hicks, and J. M. Keynes, is that there are pressures and motivations which keep the consumption-income ratio of low-income receivers high and of high-income receivers low. Presumably the conclusion applies to permanent income as well as to current receipts.

First, there are the pressures on the low-income groups. We hold in abeyance Duesenberry's idea that the lowest income units are under sociopsychological pressure to "keep up." Besides this there is the fact that some physiological minimum is essential. The physiological minimum destroys the universality of Friedman's proportionality assumption. At some low level of income all or more than all must be spent. Higher income units are in a position to exercise discretion. Friedman's proportionality proposition might apply so long as income exceeds the minimum, but it cannot apply when income falls below it.[9]

Irving Fisher argues in a classic passage that the absolute size of income affects time preference. He states that there is an

inverse relationship between the absolute size of income and the degree of time preference. The poor man—pressed with the need for providing day-to-day necessities—will place a very high value on present v. future consumption. An affluent individual can relax the vigil.[10]

Irwin Friend and Irving Kravis argue in an orthodox vein against Friedman, to the effect that uncertainty enhances the preference for present over future consumption of lower-income families as compared with higher-income families.[11] When the future is clouded by uncertainty, the low-income family trusts to better luck to provide. It yields to the pressure of immediate needs, probably more than it would if the future were known with certainty. As income rises, less urgent wants are satisfied and the family is better able to allocate present resources for future needs even when future needs and income are uncertain.

Now let us look at the highest end of the income scale. Concerning the top of the income distribution, Friedman's time-preference discussion seems to say that accumulated wealth has little if any utility apart from that of future consumption for the family and heirs. Friedman neglects motives such as power, prestige, and independence. Again this is unorthodox. Friedman thinks, for example, that self-employed entrepreneurs have higher saving-income ratios than other occupation groups because they have greater vari-

ation in income. This is his only explanation. He gives no attention to motives of power, prestige, acquisition, or independence.[12]
Orthodoxy would stress these motives. It would say that they may
be increasingly important as income and wealth rise, once the more
urgent consumption needs or wants have been met.[13]

So it seems that Friedman's theory is not simply the logical in-
ference from the "pure theory" of the consumer, as he indicates.
On the contrary, it is a very radical aberration.

DUESENBERRY'S VERSION OF THE RELATIVE-
INCOME HYPOTHESIS

As the reader knows very well, there is no orthodox or pure
theory of consumer behavior today, in the sense that nearly everyone agrees on what motivates consumers. Part of our uncertainty is
the doing of James Duesenberry and his provocative hypothesis.

Duensenberry formulated his departure from orthodoxy[14] in an
effort to explain the apparent contradiction between budget-study
data and secular data regarding consumption and saving. Budget
studies indicate that family saving is a rising function of income. A
family with $1,500 income will dissave; one with $20,000 will have
significant positive saving. At least, in each case this is true for a
period of one year. Secular aggregate data indicate that over long
spans of time there has been no particular tendency for saving as a
percentage of income to rise, despite the fact that aggregate and
per capita real income have risen markedly. The budget data would
lead us to expect saving to rise as a percentage as income increases
in absolute real value, or so it would seem. Is there a contradiction?

Duesenberry argues that there is no real contradiction. There appears to be one because of the implicit assumptions of the orthodox
theory of consumer behavior. Orthodoxy says implicitly that every
individual's consumption is independent of the consumption of
every other individual. If in fact one's consumption is independent
of the consumption of others in his society, then we probably would
expect his saving ratio to rise as his income rises. At least this
would seem plausible if we reason from cross-section budget data.
Budget studies show that higher-income groups save much higher
percentages of their income than do lower groups. So, over time,
as the $2,000-income family moves to the $6,000 bracket, say, we
would expect it to act like the $6,000 family now acts and save a

higher portion of its income. To repeat, this is what we would expect if consumer behavior is in fact independent of the consumption of others. As we raise the real per capita income level over time we would expect the real per capita saving ratio to rise.

But, says Duesenberry, there are many sociological and psychological reasons for supposing that consumer preferences are interdependent rather than independent. Once we grasp this simple idea we are prepared for his theorem:

For any given relative income distribution, the percentage of income saved by a family will tend to be a unique, invariant, and increasing function of its percentile position in the income distribution. The percentage saved will be independent of the level of income.[15]

How much a unit saves depends largely on its position in the income distribution scale. That is, its saving depends on its income relative to the income of others—thus the designation *relative*-income hypothesis. Over a long span of time, even if aggregate income rises, if the distribution remains the same and there is no shifting of the percentile positions, there is no reason to expect a rise in the aggregate saving ratio, *ceteris paribus*. (The other things assumed equal or offsetting may be other factors influencing the saving ratio, such as interest rates, relation between current and expected future incomes, age distribution of the population, and rate of growth of income.) Thus Duesenberry reconciles the findings of the budget data and the secular data.

Consumption wants are highly interdependent, says Duesenberry. The strength of an individual's impulse to increase his consumer expenditure depends almost exclusively on the relationship between his expenditures and the expenditures of others with whom he associates most closely. One reason for this is the "demonstration effect." An individual comes into contact with goods of superior quality and becomes dissatisfied with his own inferior products. Perhaps a higher standard of living per se seems to be prized. But this is very much because one's own standard is judged in comparison with the living standards of others.

So preferences are interdependent and welfare is relative. More formally, Duesenberry posits that the satisfaction obtained by the i'th individual from consumption depends not on his absolute consumption C_i, but on his relative consumption $C_i / \Sigma a_{ij} C_j$, where C_j

is the quantity consumed by the j'th individual and aij measures the importance attached by the i'th individual to that quantity.

In our society the coefficient attached by the typical i'th individual to the consumption of individuals with higher consumption than his own is greater than the coefficient he attaches to the consumption of individuals with less than his own. That is, the type of consumer-preference interdependence which is characteristic of our society is that of emulation or keeping up with the Joneses—greater valuation attached to consumption of one's superiors than to consumption of one's inferiors. This is contrasted with the preference system which may characterize some European and other societies, so-called "superiority" or keeping ahead of the Smiths. With presumed superiority, the typical individual is anxious to consume goods in greater quantity and quality than those consumed by presumed inferiors. He attaches a relatively high valuation to consumption lower than his own and a relatively low valuation to consumption greater than his own.[16]

Utility is not derived exclusively from consumption, however. If it were, with emulative behavior prevalent, everyone except the highest individual might spend all his income in the effort to keep up with his superiors. Duesenberry posits that one's utility index is a function of one's consumption and asset holdings. Choice between consumption and saving is the result of the struggle between invidious motives leading to expenditure, and asset-accumulation motives leading to saving. But consumption goods are more directly observable than are most asset holdings for purposes of invidious comparison. So it is not unreasonable to say that one's utility index varies with the ratio of one's consumption to a weighted average of other people's consumption.

Duesenberry seems to be saying that, as one rises in income relative to others, the pressure to keep up by means of consumption abates and that asset accumulation motives assume increasing importance. The theory is completely general as to why asset accumulation gives utility. People may save to acquire assets because of their desire for future consumption—retirement or contingency, for example. But they may also accumulate for reasons of power and prestige and to leave an inheritance. Or they may save for irrational reasons, such as simply liking to have a large bank account.

Normative Implications of Consumption Hypotheses for Tax Policy

These consumer-behavior hypotheses are interesting. But have they any significance for the formulation of equitable tax policy? More specifically, how can they help us to assess the consequences of retail sales taxes? We suggested at the outset of the chapter that they may shape our expectations about whether sales taxes are regressive, and we suggested that they may have welfare implications. Can they, for example, shed any light on the age-old question of whether taxes should be regressive or progressive or proportional, a question central to an appraisal of retail sales taxation. Can they give us any guide on the question of what form exemption policy should take?

Consumption hypotheses may be irrelevant or inconsequential on normative issues. But we should not like to come to this conclusion without investigation. At the conclusion of the chapter we return to this question of the advisability of drawing conclusions about normative issues from statements about the way people spend their incomes.

THE PERMANENT-INCOME HYPOTHESIS

The impact of the Friedman permanent-income hypothesis is discussed more fully in the following chapter. Here we simply mention a few of the possible implications.

Friedman himself stoutly denies that there are any normative implications in his theory of consumer behavior. As a "positive" economist he feels that how people actually behave need not imply anything as to how they ought to behave. Nor need it imply anything about what social policy should be with regard to their behavior. The concept that is appropriate for welfare need not be the same as is empirically relevant in explaining behavior.[17] Whether taxes ought to be progressive, proportional, or regressive may be decided better by other criteria than those of how consumers behave.

However, readers of Friedman's theory may be disposed to make normative inferences. The following three are illustrative.

1. If permanent consumption is proportional to permanent income, proportional taxes on a broad consumption base will not be regressive. Many people—those who favor proportional taxes in principle—will conclude that such taxes deserve a high equity rating. Chapter IV analyzes this idea.

2. Several conventional views are altered if, as Friedman's theory suggests, one year's income and consumption statistics are misleading, and if this is true for the reasons he suggests. Income inequality as portrayed by one-year distributions of income is apt to be overstated. The severity of the true or permanent low-income problem is overstated because many with low receipts (income) in any given year have them only temporarily. The burden of consumption taxes on the low-income population is severely exaggerated by most of our studies. From this many people will infer that proportional consumption taxes are not so oppressive after all. Chapters IV and V evaluate these ideas.

3. If consumer units behave as Friedman posits, there is a presumption against diminishing marginal utility of income, and, what is more, against diminishing marginal utility of consumption. The utilitarian or sacrifice case for progressivity in taxation has turned on the conjectured nature of the marginal utility of income—whether it declines, and if so at what rate.[18] Friedman's behavioral assumptions question or deny that even the marginal utility of (total) consumption declines. The sacrifice argument for progressivity would therefore find no support from this hypothesis.

THE ABSOLUTE-INCOME HYPOTHESIS

The absolute-income hypothesis has no inherent policy imperative. But again the behavior assumptions underlying it may condition us to approve certain policy norms. Consider, for example, the idea that lowest-income groups will have the highest consumption-income ratios because of minimum physiological needs, most urgent needs being first satisfied: acceptance of this partial explanation for the high consumption-to-income relationship which we find for low-income classes in one-year budget studies disposes us to view favorably a minimum exemption of income from taxation,[19] though of course it gives us no criterion for establishing the size of the exemption.

THE RELATIVE-INCOME HYPOTHESIS

The sociological motives on which Duesenberry bases his hypothesis have normative implications. Duesenberry himself derives some sophisticated inferences within the framework of modern "welfare economics." It is easy to draw other inferences as well.

Possible Inferences from Duesenberry's Hypothesis. One could, for example, on one interpretation of Duesenberry's theory, reach the bizarre conclusion that proportional taxes are "burdenless"! If we should take the view that utility is almost exclusively a relative matter, tax rates which leave the status ranks in precisely their pretax relative position may be said to create no sacrifice. Proportional taxes accomplish this trick. Admittedly this is a bit farfetched, and though it may be in the spirit of his hypothesis, Duesenberry himself does not go this far.

Paradoxically, Duesenberry's relative hypothesis shatters Pigou's effort to revive the case for progressivity on utilitarian or "sacrifice" grounds; yet Duesenberry employs his theory to construct his own case for progressivity (on "welfare" grounds). Pigou has attempted to revive the flagging utilitarian (sacrifice) case for progressivity by intuitively constructing a marginal utility of income curve.[20] He argues that the curve surely falls at a faster rate than that of a rectangular hyperbola. A marginal utility of income curve steeper than a rectangular hyperbola demands progressivity whether "equal," "proportional," or "minimum" sacrifice is the equity criterion (see note 18). Pigou reaches his conclusion by reasoning that at high levels of income the utility from additional income is based on invidious comparison of one's income with the incomes of one's social and business rivals. If large amounts of income are taken from these higher-income groups, there is little loss of utility: rivals have suffered the same fate, and with such groups everything is relative.

Duesenberry's hypothesis is bad medicine for Pigou. Like Veblen, Duesenberry contends that invidious comparison is not confined to the wealthy; it pervades all classes. If it does, the marginal utility of income curve cannot take the shape suggested by Pigou, and once again the case founders for progressivity on sacrifice grounds.

Duesenberry's Application of His Hypothesis. Duesenberry does conclude, however, that progressive taxes, and income taxes, are required by his theory of interdependence if welfare is to be maximized. In reaching these conclusions he operates within the framework of modern ("new") welfare economics. New welfare economics sanctions against interpersonal utility comparisons (comparisons of satisfaction or happiness between different persons). And new welfare economics is dubious that utility can be measured "cardinally." (We may talk about "ordinal" utility but not about "cardinal" utility. That is, we may say that one thing induces more utility than another—ordinal—but not precisely how much more—cardinal.) Cardinal-utility comparisons were the foundation of utilitarian or "old" welfare economics, from which sprang the debates over justification of progressive taxes on sacrifice grounds.

If we cannot compare utility between persons, agnosticism on the part of the economist ("*qua* scientist") is said to be required on most policies which make some persons better off while making others worse off. Progressive versus regressive taxes (and progressive versus regressive government benefits) are largely policy questions of this kind; so this doctrine, if adhered to by economists, would represent professional self-emasculation. Old welfare economics, by contrast, was based on the utilitarian welfare objective of the maximization of a sum of individual, cardinal-utility indexes.

For some time new welfare economics has dominated the economic stage. Its goal is the maximization of a "social welfare function," which is itself a function of the utility indexes of individuals. But these indexes are ordinal only, not cardinal; and if one individual's welfare index increases while another's decreases, new welfare economics says that the sign of the social welfare function cannot be specified. Finally, as Duesenberry clearly shows, new welfare economics posits implicitly that only goods and services received (and supplied) by an individual himself affect his utility index; the goods and services of others do not affect it. This is the implicit "independence postulate" which Duesenberry supplants with his interdependence postulate.

Disenchantment with the cardinal approach of old welfare economics resulted in part from skepticism that utility comparisons could be made interpersonally or in a scientific way. The importation of logical positivist philosophy to economics suggested that if no operational test could be performed to quantify "utility," statements about it were merely ethical expressions of the speaker's personal preferences.[21]

If interpersonal utility comparisons are forbidden, one can make few statements about matters such as what constitutes the "best" distribution of income for society. Conclusions about "optimum" rates of tax progressivity, so far as they affect the distribution of income, are said to be on a par with aesthetics—"nonverifiable" value judgments or, more provocatively, "nonsense statements." But within any *given* income distribution certain kinds of taxes and rates of progressivity can be said to foster optimum conditions of production and exchange, conditions which will make some better off without making anyone worse off.

Before Duesenberry, the orthodox view took somewhat the following line: We may wish for ethical or aesthetic reasons to specify a social welfare function such that inequality be reduced. This probably calls for progressive taxes. But progressive taxes interfere with choices between work and leisure. Therefore, egalitarian reform is attainable only at the expense of allocation efficiency.[22] Duesenberry reverses this conclusion while continuing to operate within the confines of welfare economics. It is his injection of "interdependence" which leads to the conclusion.

Duesenberry shows that the conclusions of welfare economics are reached on the implicit assumption that each individual's preferences are independent not only of the preferences of others but of the amounts of goods and services consumed by others. Under this assumption an individual's utility depends only on the size of his own income, not on the size of others' income. An individual's marginal rate of substitution between work and leisure under these assumptions is a simple matter. To perform an increment of labor, he must acquire just enough additional income to compensate him for his additional disutility resulting from the labor.

With interdependence, optimum conditions become difficult to analyze. The social welfare function to be maximized requires that we attain a position at which the utility of one individual cannot be increased without decreasing that of another. If one person works more and acquires more income, he adversely affects the utility of others. Each person's utility index depends on the amount of income he receives and *also* on the amount received by others. If one is to opt to work for more income, he must not only produce enough more to compensate himself for his own increment of disutility, but he must produce enough more to compensate others for the fact that he has obtained more income. Recall Duesenberry's sociological assumptions: "emulation" is strong, "superiority" is weak; low-income groups are affected by the consumption of higher-income groups, but not so much vice versa. (To make a strong case, assume that each group in an income distribution is affected by all the groups above it, but not at all by the groups beneath it.)

If wage rates must equal marginal productivities (for optimum "allocation"), an income tax is necessary. And, further, the income tax should have a progressive rate. Each person undertaking marginal effort must produce enough to compensate others for the fact that he is gaining income and consumption relative to them. The very lowest income group should have a marginal rate of zero, and the rate should rise as we ascend the income scale.[23] The assumption is that the proceeds of the taxes, or the services these taxes enable, bring utility to the individual members of society. (Recall that utility is derived from both absolute income, or consumption, *and* from one's relative standing in the income, or consumption, scale.[24])

The significance of Duesenberry's approach is that it overturns a conventional bias against progressive taxes. As we noted, welfare economics had reached the conclusion that inequality could be reduced only with a loss of allocational efficiency. By introducing interdependence Duesenberry concludes that progressive taxes, and income taxes, are required for allocation efficiency.

Digression on "New" and "Old" Welfare Economics and Their Relationship to Tax Policy and Income Distribution. Duesenberry's conclusion is surely plausible, given his framework and his assumptions—those of new welfare economics. One can hardly escape the observation, however, that the perspective of new welfare economics is needlessly sterile in its agnosticism. New welfare economics arose, recall, because of skepticism that utility could be scientifically measured, either interpersonally or cardinally. Gradually, however, economists are swinging back to the view that it is possible to frame hypotheses about utility in such a way that they are susceptible to objective test and are therefore verifiable. The important distinction between recent operational definitions of utility and those of welfare economics is that with the former we need empirical investigation of the causes of welfare in order to determine optimal arrangements.[25] We are getting ahead of ourselves, however. Let us backtrack for a brief digression on why it now appears that new welfare economics has been unduly pessimistic and agnostic on important issues of welfare—for example, on issues such as what constitutes the "best" distribution of income and what constitutes the optimum rate of progressivity in taxation.

New welfare economics is an approach to determining how far we can go in reaching conclusions about optimum conditions without making interpersonal or cardinal utility judgments. It was demonstrated several years ago, however, that a statement such as "A is happier than B" is clearly not a nonverifiable proposition analogous to aesthetic judgments, as it has been taken to be.[26] True, one's happiness or utility, a mental state experienced introspectively, may not be susceptible to *direct* measurement (whatever that may mean). What is required, however, is an *indirect,* objective criterion.[27] A may not be able to feel exactly how feverish he is. A and B surely cannot say between them which feels more feverish and by how much. But they can agree on an indirect criterion of comparison, for example, by means of a thermometer placed in the mouth of each and the resulting rise in the mercury. Just as we turn to an indirect convention for making interpersonal comparisons of body temperature, we can agree on indirect, objective tests of different capacities for satisfaction ("utility," "happiness," and so forth) between different people. Then we try to establish how alternative arrangements—distribution of income, rate of tax progressivity, etc.—affect the criteria. A large number of criteria are available. We are by no means confined to conventions which measure marginal utility by the way in which people spend their incomes.[28]

This line of thought leads to another fundamental deficiency of welfare economics, especially old welfare economics in this case. Even if interpersonal comparisons of utility can be made, these comparisons need not be decisive in formulating conclusions about how income ought to be distributed and therefore what the rates of tax progressivity should be. Interpersonal utility, or capacity for happiness, may indicate nothing about interpersonal comparisons of need or worth:

> See how the fates their gifts allot,
> For A is happy,—B is not.

> Yet B is worthy I dare say,
> Of more prosperity than A!
> Yet A is happy . . .
> Ever joyous, ever gay,
> Happy, undeserving A.
> If I were fortune—which I'm not—
> B should enjoy A's happy lot.
>   W. S. Gilbert, *The Mikado*.[29]

Again, what is needed is an indirect, objective indicator, not of interpersonal capacity for happiness, but of interpersonal need or worth, that is, an indicator of social utility.[30] "Welfare budgets" are but one example of the application of this idea (see Chapter VII for an example of their use in formulation of tax policy). As Fagan has said, the question of progressive versus proportional or regressive taxation is one which must be decided by ethical judgment rather than by psychological measurement. Given the objective, measurable indicator, we try to derive the effects on the indicator of various rates of tax progressivity.

It follows from the last remarks that much of the effort of this chapter has probably been misdirected. That is, the attempt to draw inferences about whether taxes should be progressive, regressive, or proportional might be pursued more fruitfully in directions other than the analysis of consumption-behavior hypotheses. We cautioned as much at the outset, but we set out hopefully, following an approved tradition. Perhaps something is gained from the pursuit. But the principal gain, perhaps, is a conditioned wariness of norms derived from study of how people spend and save from income. Such norms are at best only suggestive, yet they have played a very important role in the theorizing of economists.

Of the norms derived from this chapter, perhaps the following stand out:

Duesenberry's relative-income hypothesis leads to the conclusion that progressive income taxes are required for maximizing "welfare." Friedman's permanent-income hypothesis, however, contradicts Duesenberry's "interdependence" consumption-behavior thesis, and therefore his welfare conclusion. And in apparently denying the doctrine of diminishing marginal utility of income, Friedman's hypothesis opposes the sacrifice case for progressivity. Perhaps the principal normative impact of the absolute-income hypothesis, if it has one, is simply to buttress the case for exemption of some minimal income or consumption from taxation.

What is likely to be of greater importance, especially for retail sales-tax analysis, is the more "positive" implications of the consumer-behavior assumptions we have been analyzing, especially as to what they imply about the relative burden which consumption taxes place on income classes. Absolute and relative hypotheses imply that consumption taxes will be regressive according to income, while the permanent hypothesis challenges this idea and conditions us to think of such taxes as proportional levies with respect to "income," properly conceived.

The Friedman permanent-income hypothesis stresses that one year's income and consumption data may be very poor indicators of the true relative economic positions of families. This hypothesis raises several interesting conjectures about the "true" neutrality and progressivity of both sales and income taxes. There is hardly an orthodox conclusion about the relative effects of sales and income taxes which this hypothesis does not make suspect. We turn to an examination of some of these.

IV

SALES TAX OR INCOME TAX: THE SIGNIFICANCE OF THE PERMANENT-INCOME HYPOTHESIS

Has the permanent-income hypothesis any startling implications for an evaluation of the retail sales tax? Current discussion would seem to suggest that it has. It would seem to suggest that sales-tax advocacy is given a boost by the hypothesis. Perhaps the retail sales tax is more equitable than we have thought, relative to the personal income tax, for example.

There are two lines of reasoning which have led to the conclusion that if the permanent-income hypothesis were valid it would improve the equity rating of the sales tax. One is that sales taxes are more progressive if permanent income is the base used for computation instead of the conventional current-income base. The other is that sales taxes may be more "neutral" (in some important senses of the term) than are income taxes according to permanent income.

What are these new arguments? Are the inferences about higher equity rating for the sales tax warranted? Can we accept the permanent-income hypothesis and its implications?

The Friedman Permanent-Income Hypothesis

The basis for most of the new speculation is the Friedman version of the permanent-income hypothesis rather than the Modigliani-Brumberg[1] or other versions. We began our exposition of Friedman's hypothesis in Chapter III. Recall that Friedman rejects the idea that consumer expenditure is a declining function of the absolute real level of income. We should not expect the fraction of (permanent) income saved to increase as income increases, either for an individual consumer unit or for an aggregate economy. Friedman distinguishes between permanent and transitory components of both income and consumption. For an individual consumer unit, consumption is a constant, k, times permanent income. Whatever the ratio k, it is likely to be the same at all levels of permanent income.

The basic idea is simple enough. Consumer units do not spend for consumer goods on the basis of current, absolute income. They spend on the basis of what they consider to be normal or permanent income. If one period's receipts are abnormally high, consumer units show temporarily high saving-income ratios. If receipts are abnormally low, they have temporarily low saving-income ratios, or they dissave. The saving-income ratio (or, alternatively, the consumption-income ratio, k) does not depend on the level of income. It will be the same, *ceteris paribus*, no matter the level of permanent income.

Permanent income, roughly, is the annual equivalent of the revenues which a person expects to get over a long period of time. How long? The period will differ among consumer units. It depends on the unit's "horizon and farsightedness." The period is surely longer than a year, but it might be only a few years. It need not be a lifetime, as under one version of the Modigliani-Brumberg permanent-income hypothesis. In theory the time span which is relevant for permanent income is the minimum period over which income influences must persist before the consumer unit regards them as permanent. The actual length of time, says Friedman, will depend on the unit's occupation, its environment, its inherited capital, and other factors.

If the ratio between permanent consumption and permanent income k is independent of the level of permanent income, what determines k? Friedman says that for an individual consumer unit, k is a function of: the interest rate i, the unit's ratio of assets to permanent income w, and its preferences between present and future consumption u (which can be affected by age, family composition, and income variability).

Even if k is the same at all levels of permanent income for each individual consumer unit, it need not follow that for the aggregate the consumption-income ratio is the same at all levels of permanent income. There are differences between units in the values of i, w, and u. In order to facilitate testing, Friedman assumes that the distribution of consumer units by income is independent of their distribution by i, w, and u. So aggregate permanent consumption $C_p{}^*$ is the same proportion k^* of aggregate permanent income $Y_p{}^*$ at all levels of permanent income. Thus $C_p{}^* = k^*(\quad)Y_p{}^*$. The value of k^*, roughly, is the mean values of i, w, and u, their variances and covariances.[2]

A critical assumption of Friedman is that transitory components of income have no effect on consumption. Transitory income is unexpected additions to or deductions from expected income; it is income or loss of income which is not expected to persist. Friedman posits the very bold hypothesis that the transitory component of consumption will be uncorrelated with the transitory component of income. The marginal propensity to consume out of transitory income, therefore, is zero.

But is not the assumption of a zero marginal propensity to consume from transitory income absurd on the face of it? If a man receives a windfall, will he spend none of it? Does not the man who wins at the track during the day spend at least part of it that very night—easy come, easy go? Friedman's answer is that we should not define all spending by an individual as consumption. Consumption is a flow of services or a flow of satisfactions. The purchase of durable goods should not be thought of as consumption during the year of purchase any more than the purchase of a house should be thought of as consumption in the purchase year. Only the use or depreciation value of consumer durables should be considered to be consumption. In the year of purchase most of the value of consumer durables should be counted as saving rather than as consumption. So if the marginal propensity to consume from transitory income is zero, it means that the consumer unit either will not spend the transitory income or will spend it for consumer durables or housing or will do some of each. Friedman's proposition might be simply that purchase of consumer durables coincides with windfalls.

In résumé, the two most important assumptions to keep in mind for our purposes are (1) that the transitory components of a consumer unit's income have no effect on its consumption: they show up in changes in its assets and liabilities; (2) that the ratio between permanent consumption and permanent income is the same for all income levels. The second assumption we call the proportionality assumption.

Friedman states his hypothesis formally in three basic equations:

$$C_p = k(i,w,u)Y_p \tag{1}$$
$$Y = Y_p + Y_t \tag{2}$$
$$C = C_p + C_t. \tag{3}$$

Equation (1) is the substantive one. It says that permanent consumption is a proportion k of permanent income, and that the proportion is invariant with respect to the size of permanent income. Proportion k depends on: i, "the" interest rate; w, the ratio of non-human wealth to permanent income; and u, utility or time-preference factors. Equations (2) and (3) are definitional: they say that current income and current consumption are each composed of both permanent and transitory components. Friedman assumes no correlation between transitory and permanent income, no correlation between transitory and permanent consumption, and no correlation between transitory consumption and transitory income. That is, he assumes:

$$rY_tY_p = rC_tC_p = rY_tC_t = 0$$

(with r as the coefficient of correlation).

The Argument that the Permanent-Income Hypothesis Makes Sales Taxes More Progressive

Does this hypothesis modify our appraisal of state retail sales taxes vis-à-vis other taxes—state income taxes, for example? If we say with Friedman that cross-section budget data for only one year characteristically pervert the true or permanent consumption-income relationship, and that if we had data for a sufficient period of time the consumption-income ratio would be the same for all levels of income, we introduce the possibility that sales-tax regressivity is apparent rather than real.

David Davies has stressed this idea: that while typical sales taxes are regressive according to current income (gross and disposable), they are often progressive according to Friedman permanent income.[3] Permanent income seems to connote something more reliable than current income with its transitory elements. So it is easy to conclude that the permanent-income hypothesis has improved the equity rating of the sales tax. It has slain regressivity—the sales tax albatross.

Typical state sales taxes do indeed appear to be far more progressive (or less regressive) under this hypothesis. Table 8 demonstrates this clearly, corroborating Davies' empirical results; it indicates that hypothetical Sales Tax A, a typical retail sales tax which levies on tangibles and a few services, takes over 4.5 per cent of the (current) gross income of the lowest income class. It takes a progressively smaller percentage as we climb to higher income brackets, and in the highest bracket it takes only ¾ per cent. Sales Tax B hypothetically taxes the same items, except that it exempts home-consumed food. Its rates are higher so that its yield will be comparable to that of Sales Tax A. (For taxable expenditures, taxable income, and rates, see Table 7; for yields see the notes beneath Table 8.) Over some ranges the food-exemption tax, Sales Tax B, is nearly proportional, but over all ranges it is somewhat regressive. This is a well-precedented conclusion as to the incidence of food-exempt sales taxes.[4]

With respect to permanent income, however, under the Friedman hypothesis Sales Tax A is approximately proportional (Table 8). And Sales Tax B is even slightly progressive.

Higher Equity Rating for Sales Taxes?

Is it correct to infer that if this hypothesis should be valid it would mean that sales taxes are more progressive than we have thought and that they are therefore entitled to higher relative equity rating? There are several strong caveats to consider before we reach this conclusion.

1. Nothing has been said about the effect of this hypothesis on the progressivity of other taxes. The progressivity of any tax is altered when we shift from a current-income base to a permanent-income base. Not only the sales tax but also the income tax and other taxes are more progressive according to permanent income then they are according to current income. Table 8 illustrates this "empirically" for the Wisconsin income tax. The Wisconsin income tax is far more progressive with respect to permanent income than with respect to current income (one year's adjusted gross income in this case), computed according to the Friedman hypothesis.

2. The application of the Friedman hypothesis to analysis of sales-tax burden may involve unwarranted assumptions. In the first place, permanent income is an expectational (ex-ante) concept.

Who wants to advocate taxing a man on the income or wealth he anticipates? In a more technical vein, consider the following. In order to compute the relationship between taxes paid under a sales tax and under permanent income, we must assume that permanent

TABLE 7

Income and Sales Taxes Assumed
in Computing Tables 8 and 9

A. WISCONSIN INCOME TAX, 1960 RATES

Net taxable income brackets	Rates, Wisconsin income tax[a] (per cent)	Credits: $7/person
$ 0– 999	1.0	*Taxable income:*
1,000– 1,999	1.25	
2,000– 2,999	1.5	Wages, salaries, fees, commissions, bonuses
3,000– 3,999	2.5	Interest, except on U.S. bonds
		Ordinary dividends (fully)
4,000– 4,999	3.0	Capital gains (fully, all varieties)
5,000– 5,999	3.5	Fiduciary income
6,000– 6,999	4.0	Rent from Wisconsin real estate
7,000– 7,999	5.0	Royalties, from state property
		Maintenance received
8,000– 8,999	5.5	Retirement benefits (in part)
9,000– 9,999	6.0	
10,000–10,999	6.5	*Deductibility of U.S. tax:*
11,000–11,999	7.0	
		Federal income tax deductibility limited to 3 per cent of
12,000–12,999	7.5	adjusted gross income after all deductions, except
13,000–13,999	8.0	donations and federal income taxes.
14,000–14,999	8.5	

B. HYPOTHETICAL RETAIL SALES TAXES[b]

Plan	Rate (per cent)	Taxable Expenditures
A	2.5	All tangible commodities, including food and motor fuel. All services are exempt, except gas, electricity, admissions, communications.
B	4.0	Same as A, except "food consumed off premises" exempt.

[a] Add 20 per cent surtax to all rates listed.
[b] For a detailed breakdown of Retail Sales Tax Plans, see footnotes to Table 4.

income can be taken to mean the same thing for the different categories of consumption as it means for total consumption.[5] Sales taxes do not apply to the total range of Friedman consumption. They are primarily taxes on tangible goods with extensions to a limited range of services. There is no assurance that permanent consumption and permanent income mean the same for the individual categories of consumption as they mean for total consumption. The consumer unit's permanent consumption horizon will differ for individual consumption categories. The horizon for total consumption is only an average of the longer and the shorter individual horizons. Therefore, ambiguity results when we talk, as Davies is fond of doing, about the progressivity according to permanent income of various sales taxes which differ in their inclusiveness. For example, what if "housing" is exempt under a given tax while food is taxed? A unit's permanent consumption horizon for housing is surely longer than his horizon for food. Under another tax plan, what if both food and housing are exempt?

3. Despite our warnings about using Friedman's permanent income as a base for computing the progressiveness of taxes, we should not wish to deny that sales taxes look more progressive as we lengthen the period of income receipt and expenditure. But varying the income period is not the only way to affect the measure of progressivity of a tax.

Before we can talk about progressivity and narrowing inequality, we must be sure that we have people ranked correctly to begin with. Our conclusion about the equalization effect (progressivity) of a tax is shaped by our initial statement of pretax inequality. The degree of inequality shown in a size distribution of income depends in large part on the following: (a) the definition of income employed; (b) the income period employed; (c) the income-receiving unit; and (d) the initial status rankings. If the initial size distribution overstates "true" inequality, our progressivity measure will understate the true equalizing effect of the tax. If the distribution understates true inequality, our measure overstates the equalizing effect. Since the degree of inequality in a size distribution of income depends on the definition of income, the income period, the receiver unit, and the original status rankings, it is possible to affect our progressivity results by varying any or all of these.

The Friedman hypothesis criticizes the one-year period of conven-

TABLE 8

Effective Tax Rates of Wisconsin Income Tax and Two Hypothetical Sales Taxes,
According to Adjusted-gross-income and "Permanent-income" Bases

Income class	Effective rate of tax as percentage of ("current") adjusted gross income			Effective rate of tax as percentage of "permanent income"		
	Wisconsin income tax	Sales Tax A	Sales Tax B	Wisconsin income tax	Sales Tax A	Sales Tax B
$ 0– 999	0.05	4.57	3.89	0.01	1.55	1.32
1,000–1,999	0.35	2.17	2.00	0.27	1.67	1.53
2,000–2,999	0.52	1.83	1.78	0.48	1.69	1.64
3,000–3,999	0.75	1.65	1.68	0.76	1.68	1.71
4,000–4,999	0.95	1.57	1.64	1.01	1.67	1.74
5,000–5,999	1.17	1.49	1.61	1.28	1.63	1.76
6,000–7,499	1.39	1.37	1.60	1.61	1.59	1.86
7,500–9,999	1.69	1.24	1.44	2.11	1.55	1.80
10,000 and over	3.83	0.76	0.93	6.62	1.32	1.60

Basis for Calculation

Based on the work sheets of the Tax Impact Study Committee Research Staff (Wisconsin Department of Taxation) for Wisconsin residents, 1956. See University of Wisconsin Tax Study Committee, *Wisconsin's State and Local Tax Burden, 1959.*

Computations for permanent income are based on the reasoning of note 5 of this chapter.

"Adjusted Gross Income" is essentially a money-income concept. (See Appendix II-G of *Wisconsin's State and Local Tax Burden*, available on request, Department of Taxation, Madison, Wisconsin.) Money income is a deficient measure of economic well-being, mainly because it omits several imputed and "in kind" components. It is employed here because it coincides most nearly with the Bureau of Labor Statistics income concept used in establishing the BLS City Worker's Family Budget (referred to shortly in the text), and with the BLS–Wharton gross income concept used in the *1950 Study of Consumer Expenditures*, used here to derive Table 9.

"Consumption," as employed in computing the table, includes durable goods purchases (entire value in year of purchase) and so does not conicide with the Friedman consumption, which includes only depreciation value of durables.

The 1956 Wisconsin Income Tax assumed in the table yields $110.2 million. About $15 million is assumed to be offset against federal income tax liability.

Sales Tax A, at a rate of 2.5 per cent, hypothetically yields $95 million from individuals, ignoring the portion paid by business units through their purchases, some of which surely would be borne ultimately by Wisconsin income recipients. (The business portion of the sales tax simply is not amenable to analysis under the permanent-income hypothesis, and therefore several problems are created for the present purpose of yield comparability between retail sales taxes and income taxes.) Of the $95 million, $82.7 million is assumed to be borne by Wisconsin residents; $8.3 million is assumed to be offset against federal income taxes; $4 million is assumed to be borne by nonresident tourists, visitors, businessmen, convention goers, sports enthusiasts, and so forth.

Sales Tax B, at a rate of 4.0 per cent, yields $102.5 million, plus the business portion. Of this amount $89 million is assumed to be borne by Wisconsin residents; $4.5 million is assumed paid by nonresident tourists, and so forth.

For tax schemes, see Table 7.

67

tional studies. A one-year distribution overstates inequality and understates the true progressiveness of a tax. We get a different size distribution of income with each time period we select. This means that we will get different measures of progressivity for a tax as we vary the income period from a day, to a month, to a year, to five years, to a lifetime. Most of our estimates of the share of income paid in taxes by income classes have been based on a one-year time period. We are quite right to want a longer period.

Since we do not now have long-period data, and until we have, there may be some sense in using Friedman permanent income as a short-cut approach or proxy for a long period. But we should keep in mind that Friedman's permanent-income hypothesis is tied to two very dubious theories: (1) the relationship between long-period consumption and income is invariant with respect to the level of income; and (2) the marginal propensity to consume from transitory or windfall income is zero. These are both very strong assumptions. The empirical support for both—especially the first—is weak in my opinion, as I shall develop shortly. The basic insight and usefulness of the permanent-income idea does not depend on either assumption. But a measure of sales-tax progressiveness according to Friedman permanent income is inextricably enmeshed with both assumptions.

Tax Burdens According to "Equivalent Income": A Digression

There are many deficiencies in the conventional measures of tax progressivity, such as the measures which we present in Table 8. The deficiency which we have been discussing, that which results from employing a too-brief time period (one year), is only one of the deficiencies. Another very serious deficiency results from the conventional method of designating the status ranks—the matter of who shall be considered to be equals in the vertical line-up.

To illustrate, the pattern of progressivity which we reported in Table 8 may be mixed with a family-size effect. The money income of all families with income falling in the specified ranges ($0–$1,000, $1,000–$2,000, . . . , $5,000–6,000, etc.) is grouped, despite the size of the family. Median income rises with family size; the principal reason probably is that there is a concentration of "unattached" persons in the lower brackets. This signifies that a distribution of the kind employed to derive Table 8 may overstate the "true" inequality between families.

Should all families with comparable income be put in the same money bracket despite the size of the family? To say so is tantamount to saying that, despite size, families with the same money income have the same welfare or ability to pay taxes. Most students of the subject agree, however, that it takes more income for a family to attain a specified level of welfare as the family's size increases. The recent revision of the Bureau of Labor Statistics' City Worker's Family Budget concludes that a typical urban family of two needs only 66 per cent of the (gross) money income of a family of four in order to attain their "modest but adequate" budget standard, while a family of five requires about 120 per cent as much.[6]

Suppose we accept the BLS study as a basis for establishing equivalent status of families before taxes. That is, suppose we say that, in order to have equal welfare or ability-to-pay taxes, a family of two needs 66 per cent of the income required for a family of four; a family of three needs 87 per cent as much; a family of five needs 120 per cent as much, etc.[7] It is then possible, following the method proposed by Lampman,[8] to construct a table which shows the hypothetical effective rates of taxes for "equivalent incomes" of various family sizes. This is done in Table 9. The effective rates for equivalent incomes are computed for income taxes and sales taxes which yield approximately the same revenue. The Wisconsin income tax is compared again with Sales Tax A and Sales Tax B.

In Group I of Table 9, we equate as equivalent income before taxes an income of $920 for a single individual, $1,680 for a three-person family, $2,560 for a six-person family, etc. Similarly, for Groups II through VI, equivalent incomes are established for the various family sizes on the basis of the BLS equivalence ratios. The base incomes selected for the family of four are $2,000, $3,000, $4,000, $6,000, $9,000 and $12,000, which are 33 per cent, 50 per cent, 67 per cent, 100 per cent, 150 per cent, and 200 per cent, respectively, of the approximate annual cost of the City Worker's Family Budget in twenty large cities.[9] (The cost is approximately $6,000.)

Reading down Table 9 under any family size suggests the progressivity of any tax, without a family-size effect. That is, it gives in-

TABLE 9

Effective Tax Rates for "Equivalent (Current) Income" Groups of Various Family
Sizes, for the Wisconsin Income Tax and Two Hypothetical Sales Taxes

Equivalent income group	Number of persons in family						
	1	2	3	4	5	6	7
GROUP I							
Adjusted gross income	920	1,300	1,680	2,000	2,300	2,560	2,980
Effective rates							
Wisconsin income tax	0.0	0.0	0.0	0.0	0.0	0.0	0.0
Sales tax A	2.5	2.0	2.0	2.1	2.2	2.5	2.5
Sales tax B	2.4	1.6	2.0	1.6	2.6	1.7	1.8
GROUP II							
Adjusted gross income	1,380	1,950	2,520	3,000	3,450	3,840	4,470
Effective rates							
Wisconsin income tax	0.0	0.1	0.2	0.2	0.2	0.2	0.3
Sales tax A	1.6	2.0	2.0	2.0	2.0	2.1	2.1
Sales tax B	1.9	1.6	1.9	1.7	1.7	1.7	1.8
GROUP III							
Adjusted gross income	1,840	2,600	3,360	4,000	4,600	5,120	5,960
Effective rates							
Wisconsin income tax	0.2	0.5	0.6	0.7	0.8	0.9	1.1
Sales tax A	1.6	1.7	1.8	1.8	1.9	2.0	2.0
Sales tax B	1.9	1.6	1.7	1.7	1.9	2.0	2.0
GROUP IV							
Adjusted gross income	2,760	3,900	5,040	6,000	6,900	7,680	8,940
Effective rates							
Wisconsin income tax	0.9	1.1	1.3	1.5	1.7	1.9	2.2
Sales tax A	1.4	1.6	1.6	1.7	1.7	1.6	1.6
Sales tax B	1.9	1.6	1.7	1.7	1.8	1.8	1.7
GROUP V							
Adjusted gross income	4,140	5,850	7,560	9,000	10,350	11,520	13,410
Effective rates							
Wisconsin income tax	1.4	1.7	2.3	2.4	2.8	3.0	3.4
Sales tax A	1.3	1.8	1.5	1.4	1.5	1.4	1.4
Sales tax B	1.9	1.8	1.7	1.6	1.6	1.7	1.7
GROUP VI							
Adjusted gross income	5,520	7,800	10,080	12,000	13,800	15,360	17,800
Effective rates							
Wisconsin income tax	1.8	2.3	2.8	3.4	3.8	4.2	4.7
Sales tax A	1.1	1.4	1.4	1.4	1.2	1.4	1.4
Sales tax B	1.6	1.6	1.7	1.2	1.4	1.4	1.4

sight into the pure vertical redistribution effected by the tax. Reading across Table 9 suggests the horizontal neutrality of the tax by family size. Taxes may be said to have horizontal as well as vertical redistribution effects. A true vertical equalization effect requires (1) that units in a distribution having equal status before tax also have equal status after tax, and (2) that the higher-lower ranking of the units be narrowed but not altered by the tax. Obviously, however, taxes may alter initial rankings. There may be, for example, a redistribution from purchasers to nonpurchasers effected by excises, or a redistribution from irregular to regular income recipients effected by progressive income taxes; etc. These are what we mean by horizontal effects.

As we would expect, income taxes are clearly more progressive than sales taxes, even with respect to equivalent income (read down Table 9).

By comparing horizontally we might conclude that sales taxes are more neutral than income taxes. On the average, equivalent-income families pay more nearly a constant percentage of equivalent income under our hypothetical retail sales taxes than under the Wisconsin income tax.

Table 9 is based on current data (i.e., "measured" or one-year data) rather than on permanent-income and consumption data.

[TABLE 9, continued]

Basis for Computation

Based on interpolations from the BLS–Wharton *1950 Study of Consumer Expenditures,* income and consumption estimates for "large northern cities," vols. I–V, VII–XI.

Equivalent incomes are established according to the BLS City Worker's Budget scales for estimating relative costs of "the budget" for various family sizes. With the budget cost for a family of four=100, the recent revision established the following for the other family sizes: 2=66; 3=87; 5=120 (see note 6 for reference). For sizes 1, 6, and 7, the earlier BLS estimates are employed: 1=46; 6=128; 7=149. See *Monthly Labor Review,* LXVII (February, 1948), 179.

The City Worker's Budget needs are established on the assumption of only one income earner in the family. Similarly, Table 9 assumes only one taxpayer per family. The City Worker's Budget is inclusive of personal taxes. Similarly, income- and sales-tax liabilities are based on gross income: i.e., "money income before taxes" in the BLS–Wharton *1950 Study of Consumer Expenditures.*

The tax rates of Table 7 are also assumed here, although here no reduction of tax liability is computed for the offset against federal income taxes.

For the sales taxes, no consideration is given to the portion of the sales tax paid by business units or by nonresident tourists and visitors.

What conclusion would we reach regarding neutrality if we accept and employ the Friedman permanent-income hypothesis? This brings us to an evaluation of the second line of reasoning mentioned at the outset of the chapter, wherein it has been contended that the permanent-income hypothesis improves the relative rating of retail sales taxes. This is the idea that sales taxes may be more neutral than income taxes with respect to permanent income.

Are Sales Taxes More Neutral Than Income Taxes With Respect to Permanent Income?

Suppose that we want taxes to fall with neutrality not according to income of one year but according to income of several years, something comparable to Friedman permanent income. Suppose initially that we take this to mean that we want families with equal permanent incomes, despite size, to be taxed equally. It has been said that taxes on current consumption may be more neutral with respect to something akin to permanent income than are taxes on current income.[10] Is this true? If it is, does the reasoning carry over to state retail sales taxes versus state income taxes?

First, does the Friedman permanent-income hypothesis, if valid, suggest that neutrality among taxpayers according to permanent income is better achieved by taxing current consumption rather than by taxing current income?

The answer is in the affirmative only under certain stipulations: (1) that the consumption and income taxes under consideration are progressive taxes; (2) that anticipations of income are actually realized, so that notions of permanent income are not undergoing continuous revision and so that in taxing people's consumption expenditures we are not simply taxing people on their anticipations of income rather than on their realizations; (3) that the graduated income tax has no averaging scheme in operation; (4) that consumption is defined in Friedman's way, to include only the use value of durables; (5) that the persons or classes of differing levels of income are similar in their distribution of (a) assets to (permanent) income ratios—w and (b) the factors which influence time preference—u.

Suppose that persons do as Friedman suggests and spend and save on the basis of permanent income. Suppose further that tax rates are proportional, that consumer units are similar in their distributions of w and u, and that they do in fact realize their income expectations over the relevant period of years (i.e., over the permanent-income period). Over the period—uncertain in length but longer than a year—a proportional tax on current income will achieve the same neutrality as a proportional tax on current consumption. If the proportional rates are set so that the tax on current consumption yields the same total revenue as the tax on current income, both taxes exact the same nominal toll over the permanent-income period. That is, two individuals with the same permanent income, one with regular receipts, the other with irregular receipt, are taxed about the same over an entire permanent-income period. The important consideration is timing, including the matter of interest on taxes which the government collects either prematurely or belatedly in relation to what it would collect if taxes could actually be assessed according to permanent income.

Therefore, if the tax system is proportional and if we should want the base to be permanent income rather than permanent consumption, we should select current income rather than current consumption as the base on which to levy. The reason for this is that anticipations are not in fact realized. The proportional income tax is a tax on realization. Taxing current consumption to get at permanent income is effectively taxing anticipation rather than the realization of income under the Friedman hypothesis. This is because under the permanent-income hypothesis the presumption is that consumer units spend in accordance with the income they expect to receive over a future period. The hypothesis is expectational. But the unit may be favorably surprised, or it may be disappointed. In either case it alters its permanent-income conception—that is, its expectation—and therefore alters its consumption as well. Since anticipations are not in fact realized, there is more wisdom in basing a tax on realization than there is in basing it on expectation. With proportional taxes, therefore, current income is preferable to current consumption as a basis for taxing permanent income.

But if taxes are progressive, this conclusion can be reversed if the income tax has no viable income-averaging device. Without averaging, neutrality may be more nearly achieved by taxing current consumption rather than current income, even though it is permanent income that we want to reach. The reasoning is as follows.

In the absence of averaging under a progressive income tax, persons with fluctuating receipts pay more than persons with regular receipts. A distribution of persons according to their current income (receipts) does not rank them according to their permanent or true position in the economic scale. Thus a ranking by current receipts fails to rank properly for application of progressive tax rates. Serious tax differentials—unneutralities—can result between regular and irregular income receivers.[11] But with the Friedman hypothesis, persons rank themselves properly according to permanent income by their consumption. Permanent consumption is based on permanent income rather than on current income. If the transitory component of consumption is less than the transitory component of income and is uncorrelated with it (as Friedman assumes), a ranking according to current consumption expenditure will put persons with fluctuating receipts approximately in their proper rank for the application of progressive rates.[12] If the relevant income period should be an entire lifetime, persons of different age are more neutrally taxed by current consumption than by current income. The assumption is that they even out expenditures over a lifetime by consuming high in relation to current income in early and late years of life when current income is below the lifetime average income.

Perhaps this line of analysis does not so much support the desirability of taxing current consumption to achieve neutrality according to permanent income as it supports the case for an income-averaging technique when income taxes are progressive. The welfare conclusion for taxation which seems to follow from the permanent-income hypothesis is that permanent income, or in any event receipt for a period longer than one year, is a better indicator of ability to pay taxes than is current income (or simply one year's receipts).

If this conclusion is acceptable, one of the principal objections to several techniques of income averaging loses its force. This is the objection which arises from the fact that many averaging proposals allow a large liability to be incurred when one's current income, and presumably one's ability to pay taxes, is low. Under the permanent-income hypothesis, temporarily low current income (receipts) does not indicate low tax-paying capacity. A family's consumption reflects its assessment of its welfare and, we may infer, its taxable capacity as well. Perhaps, then, most income-averaging devices are not too objectionable even if they should impose a heavy levy in years of low receipts. And if the relevant permanent-income period is an entire lifetime, perhaps the Vickrey lifetime averaging proposal is in order.[13]

The Friedman hypothesis is relevant to the analysis of sales-tax neutrality in another way. One of the arguments against the typical retail sales tax is that it is "perverse" and "capricious." Harold M. Groves presents this case effectively in his oral tradition at the University of Wisconsin. Groves' former student, Reed R. Hansen, has established an empirical foundation for the argument.[14]

Hansen and Groves contend that under most retail sales taxes, the tax burden increases with family size at comparable income levels. They call this characteristic "perversity." Even families of the same size and income and with the same total expenditures can bear rather different tax burdens because their preferences between taxed and exempt items differ. This they call the "capriciousness" of the sales tax. Hansen points to other unneutralities of sales taxes: at the same level of income urbanites pay more than rural dwellers and whites pay more than Negroes.[15] Other writers have argued on similar grounds that at the same income levels the young and the old pay more than middle-aged families, and persons with manual, clerical, and service occupations pay more than professional, managerial, and self-employed persons.

Criticism of the Groves-Hansen "perversity-capriciousness" case against the sales tax can take several forms. One is to contend against their index of equality. They use income as their index. The sales-tax advocate will usually argue for consumer expenditure in preference to income. He doubts that the evidence shows that sales-tax burdens borne by families of the same size and expenditure really differ significantly.

The Friedman permanent-income hypothesis suggests that Hansen's empirical evidence of discrimination attributable to the sales tax may be more apparent than real. Hansen's method, basically, is to run regressions of sales-taxable consumption expenditure on income. The results indicate that under most sales taxes at the same income level large-family sizes pay more than small-family sizes, urbanites pay more than rural dwellers, whites pay more than Negroes, etc. But Friedman would say that what is being held constant in these regressions is one year's receipts—"measured income"—and not genuine or permanent income. He shows how equal measured income for the groups being compared can correspond to unequal permanent income.[16] For example, Negroes as a group have a lower mean income than whites. Any given level of measured income for a group of Negroes corresponds on the average to a lower permanent income than it does for a group of whites. Our regressions of measured consumption on measured income may appear to show that Negroes are more parsimonious than whites. But what the regressions really show is simply that one year's income is an inappropriate measure of true income.

If one-year data are not indicative of normal relationships, what empirical difference does it make if we reject measured data and employ instead synthetic permanent-income and consumption statistics in making sales-tax neutrality tests of Hansen's type? The answer seems to be that most of Hansen's conclusions still hold. They may be a little less impressive as evidence of discrimination by sales taxes, however. On the basis of the synthetic constructions prescribed by Friedman's hypothesis, we derive the following conclusions:[17]

1. Large families pay more under most retail sales taxes than small families at the same level of permanent income.

2. Urbanites pay more sales taxes than rural families of the same permanent income level.

3. Discrimination between occupation groups is slight.

4. Negroes, not whites, are the disadvantaged race. But race is an insignificant determinant of sales-tax discrimination.

We cannot conclude on the note that according to the permanent-income hypothesis the sales tax is entitled to a high grade for its neutrality. Recall that under the hypothesis even units with the same permanent income and family size, who pay or receive the same rate of interest, may differ with respect to the factors which determine consumption. They differ with respect to w and u. That is, their ratios of assets to permanent income differ, and the families differ with respect to characteristics which shape time preferences. These characteristics include family size, age, family composition, and income variability.

To complete an analysis of neutrality, therefore, one would have to know how these factors influence consumption in order to see to what extent they create unneutralities between otherwise similarly circumstanced families. And, of course, this is not presently known. We do know, however, that according to the hypothesis families of the same size with the same permanent income can pay different amounts under consumption taxation (as, for example, retail sales taxation) because of differences in characteristics such as age composition and occupation of spouses, or even differences such as race and location. It is indeed hard for a tax on consumption to score high on neutrality tests in which income is the index of equality. But apparently this is the claim people are advancing nowadays on behalf of consumption taxation. The story is very different, of course, when consumption is argued for directly as the proper index of equality, as Fisher and Kaldor argue.

A Negative Appraisal of the Empirical Validity of the Friedman Hypothesis[18]

We have assumed throughout this chapter that the Friedman hypothesis could be supported empirically. We assumed this in order to draw out its implications for sales-tax analysis. But before we can invoke the hypothesis we must confirm its validity, and it is unlikely that this can be done. I shall try now to show why I believe the tests negate rather than confirm the basic tenets of the theory.

I shall review first the tests of one of Friedman's propositions for which evidence is mixed. This is the postulate of a zero correlation between consumption and transitory income. Friedman says that a consumer unit which receives a windfall, or any income which it regards as transitory, will simply increase its assets, that it will not increase its consumption. Remember that Friedman considers consumption to be the using up of physical goods. Durables purchased in a period are consumed in that period only to the extent that they are used up. Therefore, both "not spending" and spending for durables are nonconsumption activities or saving.

The postulate of zero (or very low) correlation between consumption and transitory income was first challenged empirically by Lawrence Klein and Nathan Liviatan.[19] They looked at receipts in the United Kingdom which might be considered to be windfalls—life insurance benefits, gambling winnings, cash gifts, cash legacies, postwar credits, and other lump-sum transfers of money. They concluded that the marginal propensity to consume out of windfall income was about 0.65. For upper-income employees it was 0.74. For retired and unoccupied units it was 0.92. These findings sharply contradicted the postulate that the marginal propensity to consume from transitory income is zero or some very low fraction. But the Klein-Liviatan findings are not a satisfactory refutation because for receipts to constitute Friedman "transitory income" they must be viewed by the receiver as the result of chance or accidental factors. Life insurance benefits may not fall into this category. And, says Friedman, "an expert gambler probably considers his winnings as expected income." Further, heirs can discount expected gifts.

Ronald Bodkin tested a more genuine windfall, one which Friedman himself had suggested, the National Service Life Insurance dividend paid to veterans in early 1950.[20] Robert Jones then supplemented Bodkin's work.[21] The National Service Life dividend was announced in November, 1949, and paid early in 1950, so that little time elapsed. It was a complete surprise to veterans. Under Friedman's hypothesis the marginal propensity to consume from this windfall should have been zero. Friedman argues for an alternative interpretation, however. A windfall should affect consumption only insofar as it raises the permanent income of the receiver. Based on a belief in an empirical time horizon of about three years and a k of about 0.9, Friedman had predicted a measured marginal propensity to consume (mpc) from windfall of approximately .3.[22] Bodkin's correlations show that the mpc from the dividend is much higher than 0.3, that in fact it is higher than from other income. This is true even if durables purchases are classified as saving in the year of purchase.

Jones investigated individual expenditure items. He obtained the surprising result that a larger fraction of dividend windfall was spent for food, housing, and clothing than was spent on these items from other income. This contradicted the expectation of the Friedman hypothesis because, if there is no correlation between transitory income and consumption, the dividend payment would be expected to raise expenditures on any given budget item less at any income level than if a corresponding increase in permanent income should occur.

Evidence more favorable to Friedman was presented by Mordechai Kreinin, based on windfalls received by Israeli families.[23] His data came from the Israeli Survey of Family Savings of 1957–58. The survey included data on the behavior of recipients of restitution payments from Germany. The estimate was that 45 per cent of the payments were saved in the form of liquid assets, 20 per cent were invested in real estate. The marginal propensity to consume both durables and nondurables was 0.167. When durables were excluded, the mpc was 0.156. Kreinin concluded that the mpc under Friedman's definition of consumption would lie between 0.156 and 0.167. He interpreted this low percentage to be consistent with the Friedman hypothesis.

Margaret Reid presented further tests from the BLS–Wharton *1950 Study of Consumer Expenditures* which were consistent with Friedman and Kreinin and which contradicted the conclusions of Bodkin and Jones.[24] Like the data of Bodkin and Jones, Reid's data were for urban dwellers in 1950. Her windfall gains were represented by the "other money receipts" category of the BLS-Wharton Study. This category includes, in addition to the National Service Life dividend, inheritances, occasional large gifts, and settlements of fire and accident policies. Very little of the windfall income was spent on items which are not usually classified as saving or investment or as consumer durables. In short, the marginal propensity to consume (according to Friedman's definition of consumption) is very low. Apparently, the windfall receipts stimulated the purchase of homes and set off a long-run program of saving. Oddly, the year of home purchase was a year of high expenditure. But the expenditure was not for "consumption" items as usually defined, or for consumer durables, but for such items as title clearance and other expenses which surround home purchases.

The second important tenet of the Friedman hypothesis is that permanent consumption is a multiple k of permanent income; k does not depend on the level of income and, *ceteris paribus,* will be the same at all levels of permanent income. This second tenet has fared much worse than the first in the empirical tests.

Friedman's *A Theory of the Consumption Function* expounds the favorable empirical tests in detail. Here I shall concentrate attention on the unfavorable side, which seems to me by all odds the more impressive.[25]

Evidence Unfavorable to the Hypothesis

Many of the empirical tests of Friedman's proportionality assumption are based on the BLS–Wharton *1950 Study of Consumer Expenditures,* which was not yet available to Friedman for his own empirical tests.

Friend and Kravis have provided some of the best direct tests.[26]

The permanent-income hypothesis cries for continuous income and consumption data, which are not now available. But the 1950 BLS–Wharton Study does at least give some data which might, with considerable tolerance, be taken to constitute a three-year time span. Consumer units reported data for 1949 and 1950 and gave anticipations for 1951. Perhaps in some instances this can approximate Friedman's suggestion that the empirical permanent-income horizon may be three years.

Friend and Kravis present data for over 3,000 families with "relatively constant" income, in the sense that they had about the same income in 1950 as in 1949 and anticipated about the same income in 1951. In general, the figures show the same marked differences in consumption-income ratios of middle- and upper-income groups as is true for families with more unstable incomes. In fact, the data can be said to show some tendency for consumption-income ratios of the constant families in the upper brackets to be lower than the corresponding ratios of the nonconstant group, which contradicts the expectation under Friedman's hypothesis. Friedman's theory is supported for the lowest brackets, however, in which the constant families have lower consumption-income ratios than the nonconstant families.

Another test by Friend and Kravis casts doubt on Friedman's belief that his data on "entrepreneurial," "farm," and "other" occupation groups actually support his hypothesis. By breaking down occupation groups much more fully than Friedman, Friend and Kravis find that the measured consumption-income ratios of different occupational groups *are,* contra Friedman, closely correlated with the average incomes of the groups. This is true "even though apart from the entrepreneurial group there is little reason to suppose that the ratio of transient to permanent components of income and consumption differ substantially among occupations."[27] On the Friedman assumption that mean averages of consumption and income for entire similar groups give a good indication of permanent relationships for the groups, this appears to be highly damaging data.

Thomas Mayer also used occupation groups to test the proportionality assumption of Friedman's permanent-income hypothesis.[28] He compared the saving-income ratios of manual occupation groups in the 1880's and 1890's and concluded that both the relative-income hypothesis and the absolute-income hypothesis predict better than the Friedman hypothesis. His data were from the actual budgets of workers, obtained from reports of State Labor Commissioners. Although the data were old and in some respects unsatisfactory, they enabled a means for testing what purports to be a general theory, applicable to any era. According to the absolute-income theory, the occupations with higher income should have the lower measured average propensities to consume. The cross-section version of the relative-income hypothesis also implies this, as we saw in Chapter III. But the permanent-income hypothesis says that, *ceteris paribus,* there is no reason to expect higher-income occupation groups to have lower average propensities to consume. Mayer qualifies his results, but he concludes that they are decidedly unfavorable to the Friedman hypothesis.

Klein and Liviatan damage the hypothesis further.[29] Uncertainty resulting from income variability plays a critical role in Friedman's framework in determining the saving ratio. Friedman believes that self-employed persons and other entrepreneurs have greater income variability than other occupation groups. Malcolm Fisher believes the same. The self-employed, managers, and technical people have saving ratios among the highest, and the Friedman-Fisher group offers high-income variability as the major explanation. Klein and Liviatan, however, question the validity of the assumption of high variability for these groups. From the *Surveys of Consumer Finances* data, they show that owners of unincorporated businesses do have greater variability of income expectations than have other businessmen, but that the variability is not greater for actual past income change. Data from the BLS-Wharton Study show that self-employed units report that they have experienced no change of income (1949–50) and no expected change of income (1950–51) at a higher rate than other occupational groups. Additional evidence provided by the Oxford Savings Surveys puts further doubt on the Friedman-Fisher hypothesis: "By the criterion of the degree of correlation between successive years' incomes, we arrive at opposite conclusions from those commonly accepted about income variability among occupations."[30]

Klein and Liviatan also question Friedman's contention that as we lengthen the time period the saving-income relation approaches proportionality. American reinterview samples apparently confirmed his hypothesis. But the 1954 reinterview sample from the Oxford Savings Surveys reached a contradictory conclusion:

Correlation between gross income and ratio of savings to
gross income, reinterview survey 1954

24 months' correlation 0.55
12 months' correlation 0.50.[31]

Friend and Schor have given the most thorough, constructive review and appraisal to date of American survey data on consumer saving.[32] They evaluate the survey data, especially the BLS-Wharton Study and the Federal Reserve–Michigan *Survey of Consumer Finances* data, present fresh tabulations, adjust the data conceptually and statistically, and present corrected estimates of the distribution of saving by income class. Several of their findings bear in an important way on the Friedman hypothesis.

They find such a strong concentration of saving in the upper brackets that it is inconceivable that the distortion of one-year data can explain the concentration. They examine the idea that people in the survey year with higher than normal income may save more than is customary while people with lower than normal current income may save less than usual. But they reject the idea that this in fact distorts the data significantly, because there is not a significant difference in consumption-income ratios of constant and nonconstant families.

There is, on the contrary, some basis for believing that the survey data for the prosperity year 1950 underestimate the concentration of saving among upper-income groups. The proportion of total saving accounted for by the upper groups is probably higher in a recession than in a boom. On the other hand, there is evidence that the saving-income ratio of the lowest-income bracket is understated. That is, their normal dissaving ratio is lower than the 1950 data indicate.

It appears that families with fluctuating incomes save *less* in cash and deposits than families with nonfluctuating incomes at all income levels, which also cuts against the Friedman hypothesis. On theoretical grounds the families with greater income variation are expected to need the larger reserve, especially liquid reserve.

The saving-income ratios, particularly in the highest income brackets, are markedly raised when corporate saving is included and distributed to those who benefit from them. Thus, concentration is exaggerated by this inclusion. However, another modification, which adds capital gains and losses to 1950 saving, indicates a lower concentration of these "increments of wealth" than of saving, which may be a surprising result.

For the highest income class Friend and Schor find that net business investment and changes in cash and deposits are the most important form which saving takes. This is followed, in order, by increased equity in dwellings and insurance and by increased equity in other real property. For the middle-income brackets equity in dwellings and insurance are the only important forms of saving. Increased consumer debt is the major offset. The lowest income classes have no form of net saving, but have major dissaving in cash, deposits, dwelling equity, and even business investment.

The permanent-income hypothesis has important insights to be sure. But it seems that the Friedman version is altogether too heroic and too inflexible. The Modigliani-Brumberg and the Modigliani-Ando versions seem more useful, and other adaptations seem more fruitful. The evidence still seems to indicate that in the lowest-income classes there are permanently poor people who spend all of their incomes and perhaps slightly more. In the lowest-income classes it is only the people who are temporarily "down" who behave according to Friedman's theory. The highest-income classes do indeed save higher portions of their incomes: they are able to do so. Prestige factors are different for this group, and they come largely from family backgrounds in which saving is traditional.

We are not yet at the point of being able to use the Friedman hypothesis with confidence in analyzing retail sales taxes.

V

SALES TAXES AND THE GALBRAITH THESIS

Our urgent need today is to get more resources into the public sector of the economy. The source or method of finance is of secondary importance.

This statement is the nub of what we mean by the Galbraith thesis. John Kenneth Galbraith was not the first to espouse the doctrine; it was a commonplace before he wrote his best seller, *The Affluent Society*.[1] But Galbraith has been the most successful popularizer, and his particular rationale has been most widely debated. So when we talk about "the Galbraithians," we probably include many who would not march felicitously under Galbraith's banner. All "Galbraithians" do not accept Galbraith's rationale for his conclusions. But they share his ideas about the priority of social needs. And they agree with his insights on questions of strategy.

The Galbraith Thesis

The main ideas of *The Affluent Society* are as familiar as his morning eggs to that well-informed layman described in our book reviews. The American economy is characterized by a social imbalance: opulence in the private sector, penury in the public. The "conventional wisdom" fails to perceive the change which has come over America: it is no longer a nation of scarcity. Yet conventional economics assumes scarcity as its major premise. We are, in fact, so affluent that we must synthesize the wants for what we are technically able to produce.

Privately produced goods and services are so little needed that it takes a $10 billion industry—advertising—to convince us of their importance. Advertising not only redirects consumer demands, it

84

raises the level of total consumption. If wants are urgent, Galbraith argues, people need not be persuaded that they exist. And urgent wants cannot be altered easily by huckstering. So Galbraith resuscitates the doctrine of intertemporal diminishing marginal utility of income, at least as it relates to satisfaction derived from income spent on private goods. But he does not employ the diminishing-utility doctrine as others have done, to argue for income equalization or for progressive taxation. With Galbraith's special twist the doctrine becomes a rationale for more government service.

The private sector has Madison Avenue to contrive the desires for its output.[2] Many of our institutions—Duesenberry's emulation, for example—are at work in its behalf. The public sector has nothing comparable on its side. On the contrary, there are strong traditions—*laissez faire,* gospel of wealth, social Darwinism, frontier individualism—to persuade us of the unproductiveness of the public sector, or of the lesser desirability of its products. The result is the imbalance so eloquently depicted in a passage which is already classic:

The family which takes its mauve and cerise, air-conditioned, power-steered and power braked automobile out for a tour passes through cities that are badly paved, made hideous by litter, blighted buildings, billboards and posts for wires that should long since have been put underground. They pass on into a countryside that has been rendered largely invisible by commercial art. . . . They picnic on exquisitely packaged food from a portable icebox by a polluted stream and go on to spend the night at a park which is a menace to public health and morals. Just before dozing off on an air mattress, beneath a nylon tent, amid the stench of decaying refuse, they may reflect vaguely on the curious unevenness of their blessings. Is this, indeed, the American genius?[3]

In this curious unevenness it makes sense to help to even things up, says Galbraith, by taxing the private goods to provide the public services. Sales taxes are an acceptable device.

The relation of the sales tax to the problem of social balance is admirably direct. The community is affluent in privately produced goods. It is poor in public services. The obvious solution is to tax the former to provide the latter—by making private goods more expensive, public goods are made more abundant.[4]

Galbraith believes that sales taxes are efficient levies for state and municipal governments. Correction of social imbalance is the critical goal. Sales-tax yield, he thinks, is more flexible than yield from general property taxes. And the property tax, not the income tax, is the chief alternative to the sales tax at state and local levels of government, according to Galbraith. But the property tax is "income inelastic."[5]

The general property tax . . . is rigid and inflexible. Since its rates must ordinarily be raised for additional services, including those associated with increasing income and product, the burden of proving need is especially heavy. This tax is a poor servant of public balance.[6]

We shall evaluate the validity of this idea of property-tax inflexibility shortly. But first let us suppose that we accept the idea. And suppose further that we agree momentarily with Galbraith that among state and local governments enough people consider the income tax to be so effectively pre-empted by the federal government that it cannot serve as a major source of finance. In the face of these facts of political life—property-tax inefficiency and income-tax inaccessibility—"liberals" have refused to accept sales taxes, says Galbraith. Realistically viewed, then, liberals have been the enemies of social balance.

The American liberal has been, all things considered, the opponent of better schools, better communities, better urban communications, and indeed even of greater economic stability.[7]

But what about the way the sales tax is supposed to burden low-income groups and large families? Galbraith is right; this is indeed the conditioned reflex of the modern liberal.

Galbraith's answer is that generalized poverty no longer prevails. Poverty in the affluent society is "insular" and "case" poverty only. It is associated with limited groups and is largely immune to improvement through the normal processes of economic growth.

If we accept this assessment, the sales tax gains in equity rating relative to the income tax. Poverty is not a critical problem. And relative prestige, based on one's relative consumption, *à la* Duesenberry,[8] is of little social significance when wants for consumer goods are contrived. In this context the relative progressiveness of sales and income taxes is not very important.[9] The urgent need is to achieve social balance. Of course, the poverty which does remain in our affluent society is of pressing concern. But it can be alleviated or eradicated only by new public programs. Mere increases in per capita real income which arise from economic growth of the private sector cannot be relied on to do the job. Our remaining poverty is largely immune to the regular channels of economic growth.

Criticism of Galbraith's thesis has come from several directions. One group of critics denies that we have social imbalance which is unfavorable to the governmental sector. Some members of this group argue that in fact just the opposite is true: there is imbalance, but it is unfavorable to the private sector.[10] Other critics believe that Galbraith does not provide an adequate criterion for determining how much ought to be spent for each governmental program. His "theory of social balance"[11] has appeal, surely: it is in the tradition of the pragmatic philosophy of valuation, in the line of John Dewey, and the instrumentalists (philosophy) and the institutionalists (economics). But it does not take us far in determining either just how much *should* be spent or how much *will* be spent in the coming decade—for education, for housing, for social-assistance programs, or for the other social programs. Galbraith, surely, would grant this deficiency. He would probably say that his competence does not extend to such specific areas, that he has simply presented a theory which explains why we allocate too little to our public sector.

An evaluation of these particular criticisms of Galbraith is beyond the scope of this chapter. Admittedly, however, one cannot simply ignore these controversies. One's attitude toward them shapes his judgement as to the merit of Galbraith's rationale for the sales tax. Nevertheless, I should like to try to confine my attention to two other lines of criticism of Galbraith's case for the sales tax. One is advocated by men who may agree with Galbraith that the public sector should or will take an increasing percentage of income in the coming decade. But these men reject his idea that sales-tax finance is the proper vehicle for carrying the brunt of the load. The second line of criticism comes from people who reject Galbraith's theory about the nature and extent of poverty in the affluent society. If Galbraith is wrong about the characteristics, the causes, and/or the extent of today's poverty, it may be that his rationale for sales-tax advocacy is poorly grounded.

Let us examine these two lines of criticism. First, is the sales tax more flexible than other taxes, especially property taxes and income taxes? Next, if Galbraith's ideas about poverty are not correct, what difference will it make?

Sales Taxes Versus Property and Income Taxes Under the Galbraith Thesis

Suppose we agree that state and local governments, collectively, either should or will take an increasing percentage of income in the coming decade.[12] Is sales taxation called for as the major instrument of finance?

Many people will argue that Galbraith is wrong precisely in answering affirmatively. They will say that both income taxes and property taxes are superior for a future in which we forecast real "growth" with, perhaps, some inflation and an increasing governmental share of output. Galbraith wants taxes which will "serve social balance." Then he should want taxes which are income elastic, i.e., taxes with bases or yields that rise faster than income. With growth and inflation, an increasing percentage of income will flow automatically to the government under income-elastic taxes without government having to increase rates.

The graduated individual income tax generally has had high yield elasticity to income (both real and money income) as income rises. The average effective rate jumps as incomes rise: more income moves above the exemption levels and becomes subject to tax, and other incomes move into higher brackets.[13] Income elasticity of state personal income taxes has been estimated most frequently at between 1.4 and 2.0. This means that a 1 per cent increase in state income or in national GNP leads to an increase in tax base or tax yield of between 1.4 and 2.0 per cent. (Table 10 presents the principal studies. It compares income elasticities of sales, income, and property taxes.)

By contrast, retail sales taxes are usually thought to have an income elasticity ranging between 0.8 and 1.1 (Table 10). The figures of 0.9 and 1.0 are employed most frequently in revenue forecasts.

We conclude that if Galbraith is wrong in thinking that the federal government has for all practical purposes pre-empted income taxation, his own reasoning leads to the conclusion that income taxes are better than sales taxes. Income taxes will automatically jump the effective rate of taxation as incomes rise; sales taxes will not. If rate hikes are political poison for legislators and city councilmen, income taxes best "serve social balance." They enable a rising governmental share of output without rate changes. They have their rate changes built in, so to speak.

But suppose Galbraith is right: the facts of political life in most state and local governments prohibit the use of income taxation as a broad-base, mass tax. Is he then also right to think that retail sales taxes are more income elastic than general property taxes?

Until recently most authorities would have agreed with him. Now opinion is divided. In the past, scholars of the subject relied on the pioneer study by Groves and Kahn almost exclusively (Table 10). The Groves-Kahn study estimated the income elasticity of the Wisconsin property tax at a mere 0.2. Why so low? Most people explained that in the first place there is no reason for property values to fluctuate with output, as sales and income do. But even if they should, customary assessment practice results in property assessments that fluctuate far less than the market price of the property.[14]

The proper conclusion should have been that we therefore expect the property tax base to be more stable *over the business cycle* than income-tax and sales-tax bases. It does not follow that the bases of property taxes will grow less rapidly than the bases of income and sales taxes over a secular period. A secular income elasticity of 0.2 implies a five times more rapid rate of growth in income or product than in property values.[15] Could it not be that the period selected by Groves and Kahn (1929–1948) was unrepresentative? It was marked by a very low volume of construction and investment, and the Great Depression may have been the only recession in American history in which real property values fell.

Post World War II experience has been very different. Almost everywhere true market values have grown at a faster rate than income and output (Table 10). But can we expect such a trend to continue? Opinion is divided, but the consensus seems to be that market values of taxable property should continue to grow at least as fast as income during the next decade. A high rate of residential construction is expected because of the predictable high rate of family formation, and a high rate of automation is certain.

But what if assessments are insensitive to growth in wealth? For the property tax to "serve social balance" it is not enough that market value of taxable property grow as fast as income. If assessments appreciably lag changes in market value, actual yields from the property tax may not grow as fast as income. It is often argued that the

TABLE 10. Estimates of Income Elasticity for State Retail Sales, Income, and Property Taxes

Study	Period	Income-elasticity ratio or coefficient	Basis of study or comment
SALES TAXES			
Groves-Kahn[a]		1.00 over-all	Elasticity coefficients are with respect to state income payments, which are more stable than GNP, since they include trans-
Ohio	1937–48	0.99	fer payments, and exclude undistributed
N. Carolina	1940–49	1.00	corporate profits.
Iowa	1935–49	1.02	
Missouri	1938–49	1.03	
Michigan	1934–49	1.07	
Oklahoma	1937–39	1.11	
California	1934–49	1.11	
Illinois	1934–48	1.11	
Netzer[b]	1946–57	0.92	Estimate for U.S. with respect to GNP
Davies[c]	1933–59	1.00 approx.	Cyclical and secular coefficients for twenty-eight states, trend factors both included and removed.
INCOME TAXES			
Groves-Kahn[a]		1.50 over-all	
Indiana gross	1934–49	1.41	
Maryland indiv'l.	1942–49	1.54	
Wisconsin indiv'l.	1935–49	1.64	
N. Carolina indiv'l.	1938–49	1.81	
Netzer[b]			
Indiv'l. income tax	1946–57	1.53	
Soltow[d]	1933–51	2.00 approx.	Wisconsin income tax, with basic law fairly stable. Abstracts from surtax changes and changes in numbers of taxpayers.
Vickrey[e]		2.00 maximum	Range: 1.40 to 1.90. Nonempirical; deals with cyclical sensitivity (test of "built-in flexibility").

[a] Harold M. Groves and C. Harry Kahn, "The Stability of State and Local Tax Yields," *The American Economic Review*, XLII (March, 1952), 87–102.

[b] Dick Netzer, "Financial Needs and Resources Over the Next Decade: State and Local Governments" in *Public Finances, Needs, Sources and Utilization*, A Conference of the Universities–National Bureau Committee for Economic Research (Princeton, N.J.: Princeton University Press, 1961), 23–78.

[c] David George Davies, "The Sensitivity of Consumption Taxes to Fluctuations in Income," *National Tax Journal*, XV (September, 1962), 281–90.

[d] Lee Soltow, "The Historic Rise in the Number of Taxpayers in a State with Constant Tax Law," *National Tax Journal*, VIII (December, 1955), 371–81.

Study	Period	Income-elasticity ratio or coefficient	Basis of study or comment
		PROPERTY TAXES	
Groves-Kahn[a]	1929–48	0.22	Per cent increase over period in full value of property taxed in Wisconsin ÷ per cent increase in Wisconsin personal income (current dollars).
Netzer[b]	1946–57	1.00	Per cent change over period in tax base ÷ per cent change in GNP, weighted U.S. estimate. Deflated tax base is compared with constant-dollar GNP.
Lampman-Penniman[f]	1939–49	0.50	Per cent change over period in full value of property taxed in Wisconsin ÷ per cent change over period in GNP (current dollars).
	1945–55	1.80	
	1949–55	1.20	
	1955–60	1.30	
Mushkin-McLoone[g]			
Illinois	1928–55	0.60	Per cent change over period in full market value of real property ÷ per cent change in state personal income (current dollar basis).
Wisconsin	1929–55	0.60	
California	1937–55	1.00	
Illinois	1938–55	1.00	
Kentucky	1938–55	0.90	
Illinois	1941–55	1.40	
Kentucky	1941–55	1.00	
Wisconsin	1941–55	1.00	
Illinois	1948–55	1.70	
Kentucky	1948–55	2.00	
Wisconsin	1948–55	1.90	
California	1951–57	1.70	
New Jersey	1951–57	1.30	
Blank[h]	1929–48	0.75 to 1.00	Per cent increase in assessed value of private real property (U.S.) ÷ per cent increase in GPN (both in current prices).

[e] William Vickrey, "Some Limits to the Income Elasticity of Income Tax Yields," *Review of Economics and Statistics*, XXXI (May, 1949), 140–44.

[f] Robert J. Lampman, "How Much Government Spending in the 1960's?" *The Quarterly Review of Economics and Business*, I (February, 1961), 7–17; Lampman's estimates are based in part on Clara Penniman, "The Role of the Property Tax in Wisconsin Since 1929," *National Tax Journal*, IX (December, 1956), 333.

[g] Selma J. Mushkin and Eugene P. McLoone, Study in process. Preliminary report by Selma Mushkin in *Public Finances, Needs, Sources and Utilization, op. cit.*, 74–77.

[h] David M. Blank, "The Role of the Real Property Tax in Municipal Finance," *National Tax Journal*, VII (December, 1954), 319–26.

crises in local finance of recent—inflationary—years have sprung from the fact that assessments have not kept pace with market values of property. If this is correct, and if the problem persists, Galbraith is right: sales taxes will serve social balance better than property taxes.

But it is not at all clear that assessed property values will lag actual market values in the years immediately ahead. Dick Netzer argues that the fears on this score are unfounded:

There is no real evidence to indicate that assessments are in fact insensitive to secular changes in GNP. . . . The evidence that does exist is meager, but it suggests the contrary conclusion. . . .

Second, this criticism implies that with growth but no inflation, the ratio of assessed to market values of existing properties will continuously decline and/or new improvements and additions will be ignored on a wholesale scale by tax assessors. This seems wholly unreasonable.[16]

If Netzer is right, Galbraith is wrong to think that sales taxes are more responsive to growth and inflation than are property taxes. Doubtless Galbraith would be glad to be wrong on this point. If he is wrong, it means simply that one more tax serves social balance effectively. Income taxes serve well; sales taxes serve well; now, we may add, property taxes serve well. The job, then, in Galbraith's view, is simply to expand or to vote into existence *any* broad-base tax. We conclude that if our analysis is correct, sales taxes probably have no differential advantage over other broad-base taxes as servants of Galbraithian social balance.

Poverty in Our Affluent Society

If Galbraith underestimates the extent of generalized poverty or if he misinterprets its nature, his case for the sales tax may not be compelling. Suppose that our choice is between two taxes of equal yield, a retail sales tax and a graduated income tax. If the sales tax burdens large and low-income families more than the income tax, and if Galbraith underestimates existing poverty, the income tax might be clearly superior to the sales tax. If poverty is rare, on the other hand, differences in relative burdens may be of less social significance than economists have traditionally thought—and Galbraith is right.

To some extent, then, appraisal of Galbraith's thesis is an empirical question: what in fact is the extent of hard-core poverty today, and what are its characteristics and causes?

Poverty is a relationship between means and needs. To establish the amount of hard-core poverty, we need to define both means and needs and we need a distribution of their occurrence in the population. Decisions about what families of various composition need, and choices about what are to be considered to be their means for meeting the needs, are necessarily somewhat arbitrary. In recent years there has been a rash of studies attempting to assess the extent and nature of American poverty. Tables 11 and 12 enumerate the most important of them, and the reader can see at a glance that many approaches have been employed and many results obtained. Yet despite the method employed, most of the studies agree that more than one tenth and less than one third of the American population is in poverty status (Table 12). If this many people in America today are in poverty, it is hard to agree with Galbraith that our remaining poverty is merely "insular" and "case" poverty.

But do these leading studies actually isolate our "true," "permanent," or "hard-core" poverty? Most distributions of income by size brackets that have been employed exaggerate the true low-income problem. They are based on one year's statistics. Any one year's distribution has within it two groups which make interpretation difficult. One group has fluctuating income. The other has income which is not representative of its "true" economic status: its income will be higher in the future.

How should we isolate the chronic permanent poverty? Most approaches begin with a standard minimum budget as the yardstick of adequacy. Units falling below the budget standard constitute the low-economic-status group; those above constitute the adequacy group. Standards most frequently employed are the City Worker's Family Budget of the Bureau of Labor Statistics, the Budget Standard of the Community Council of Greater New York, the elderly couple's budget of the Social Security Administration,[17] and public-assistance budgets.

After selecting a standard budget as a cutoff point, one approach simply takes an income distribution and performs a series of adjustments to correct for biases, classification deficiencies, and perhaps for cyclical and secular factors. After the adjustments, any family or individual below the budget standard is in poverty status.

TABLE 11. Standards of Adequacy Commonly Employed in Studies of American Poverty

Name of study, or agency or persons responsible	Year for which study applies	Standard of adequacy	Equivalence ratios for families of varying size
Bureau of Labor Statistics "City Worker's Family Budget"[a]	1959	$6,000 in average urban city, for four-person family Range: $5,421 (Houston) to $6,629 (Chicago)	BLS equivalence scale (Dorothy Brady):[b] Number of family members / Living costs as per cent of four-person family 1 — 46.0 2 — 66.4 3 — 84.4 4 — 100.0 5 — 114.1 6 — 127.0 7 — 139.1 8 — 150.5
Community Council of Greater New York[c] (Short-cut formula by Martin David)[d]	1959	Standard of adequacy: depends on composition of family (see next column) Range: No provision for cost-of-living in different areas	Schedule of Estimated Annual Costs of Goods and Services I. Food, clothing, and other personal costs *Head* Employed or unemployed $1,144 — *Wife* Employed 1,092 Other (retired, disabled, housewife) 676 — Other 546 *Other adults* Employed, age 18–40 1,196 — *Children* Under 6 312 41 and older 988 — 6–11 416 Other 546 — 12–15 572 16–17 676 II. Rent, utilities, and other costs 1 person in unit — 1,040 2 — 1,248 3 — 1,404 4 — 1,508 5 — 1,664 6 — 1,924 7 — 2,080 8 and more — 2,184
Joint Economic Committee (Robert Lampman)[e]	1957	$2,500, 1957 dollars, four-person family, or equivalent income for other family sizes	BLS equivalence ratio (above) for other than four-person families
Subcommittee on Low Income Families of the Joint Committee on the Economic Report[f]	1949	$2,000 for urban families, $1,000 for rural families	
Social Security Administration, Elderly Couple's Budget	1947	$1,500, 1947 dollars, approx. Range: $1,365 (Houston) to $1,767 (Washington)	
Survey Research Center, *Income and Welfare in the United States.*[g]	1959	90% of the Community Council of Greater New York budget requirements (above)[h]	
Conference on Economic Progress, *Poverty and Deprivation in the United States*[i]	1960	$4,000, two thirds of City Worker's Family Budget (above)	
New York City Welfare Department[j]	1956	$2,650, 1956 dollars, for family of four with two children, father incapacitated	

A second approach starts with an income distribution and divides it into groups "above" and "below" the budget standard. Those below are further broken into two groups: 1) those with low current income, but with other assets or reasonable expectations of higher future income; (2) those with permanent substandard status. One variant of the second approach makes the segregation by means of consumption discriminants. Another variant segregates by taking account of assets possessed.

A third approach takes its cue from recent theories of consumer behavior, especially those of Milton Friedman and Franco Modigliani (see Chapters III and IV). This approach proceeds on the assumption that current consumption expenditure is a better gauge of true economic status than current income. Current consumption beneath a designated standard is regarded as the best indicator of permanent poverty.

With this introduction, let us review four important efforts that have been made to estimate and isolate the "permanent" low-income population. The best-known studies of poverty we have already enumerated in Tables 11 and 12. Here we are reporting on studies that have concentrated on methods of segregating permanent from temporary poverty. These are the inquiries of Daniel Creamer,[18] John Myers,[19] Eleanor M. Snyder,[20] and Martin David.[21]

[Notes to Table 11]

[a] *Monthly Labor Review*, LXXXIII (November, 1960), 1197–1200; *Monthly Labor Review*, LXXXIII (August, 1960), 785–808; see also Conference on Economic Progress, *Poverty and Deprivation in the United States: The Plight of Two-fifths of the Nation*, 1962, pp. 13–18.

[b] U.S. Bureau of Labor Statistics, *Workers' Budgets in the United States: City Families and Single Persons, 1946 and 1947*, Bulletin No. 927, pp. 49–51; *Monthly Labor Review*, LXVII (February, 1948), 179; and *Monthly Labor Review*, LXXXIII (November, 1960), 1197–1200, especially Table 2.

[c] Community Council of Greater New York, *Annual Price Survey and Family Budget Costs*, October, 1959 (New York: December, 1959).

[d] James Morgan, Martin David, Wilbur Cohen, Harvey Brazer, *Income and Welfare in the United States* (New York: McGraw-Hill, 1962), p. 189; see also Martin David, "Welfare, Income and Budget Needs," *The Review of Economics and Statistics*, XLI (November, 1959), 393–399.

[e] Robert J. Lampman, "The Low Income Population and Economic Growth," *Study Paper No. 12*, Study of Employment, Growth, and Price Levels for Consideration by the Joint Economic Committee, 86th Cong., 1st Sess., 1959, Appendix.

[f] U.S. Congress, Subcommittee on Low-Income Families of the Joint Committee on the Economic Report, *Low-Income Families*, 84th Cong., 1st Sess., 1955.

[g] James Morgan, *et al., op. cit.* (see note d, above).

[h] *Ibid.*, pp. 189–191.

[i] Conference on Economic Progress, *Poverty and Deprivation in the United States: The Plight of Two-fifths of the Nation* (Washington, D. C., 1962), chap. III and Technical Notes.

[j] Unpublished data, used by John G. Myers, "Income Distribution and Economic Welfare in New York State in 1956" (unpublished Ph.D. dissertation, Department of Economics, Columbia University, New York, 1960) chap. II.

TABLE 12

Percentage of Families and Persons Having Low-income Status According to Leading
Studies of American Poverty

Study	Per cent under $2,000 — Current dollars, 1950	Per cent under $2,000 — Current dollars, 1957	Per cent under $2,000 — Current dollars, 1960	Per cent under $3,000 — Current dollars, 1950	Per cent under $4,000 — Current dollars, 1960	Percentage below minimum income levels for four-person families or minimal "equivalent incomes" for other sizes of family (basis: BLS equivalence ratios) — Current dollars, 1957 — $2,000	$2,500	$4,000	90 per cent of Coummunity Council of Greater New York requirements for families of varying composition, 1959 (per cent of families under 90 per cent of requirement)	Distribution of equivalent income levels, New York State, 1956 (basis: BLS equivalence ratios and New York Community Council ratios) (per cent beneath equivalent-income levels:) — $2,000	$3,000	$4,000	Families under $4,000, single persons under $2,000, 1960 income and prices (per cent of units beneath designated levels)
Census Bureau													
Total: Families plus unattached individuals	23[a]					17[a]	21[a]						
Families		15[a]	13[b]		31.5[b]	12[a]	17[a]						
Unattached individuals		59[a]	54[b]		77.0[b]	37[a]	42[a]						
Persons	16[a]					15[a]	19[a]	36[a]					
Office of Business Economics													
Total: Families plus unattached individuals	14[c]					10[c]	14[c]						
Families		8[c]	7.3[d]		23.1[d]	8[c]	12[c]						
Unattached individuals		41[c]	36.6[d]		72.9[d]	17[c]	25[c]						
Persons	11[c]					9[c]	13[c]						
Survey of Consumer Finances													
Spending units		21[e]											
Bureau of Labor Statistics													
Families plus single consumers	18.6[f]			36.9[f]									
Joint Economic Committee (Robert Lampman)													
per cent of persons							19[c]						
Survey Research Center									20[g]				
State of New York (John G. Myers)													
Families and individuals, according to equivalent income										8[h]	16[h]	26[h]	
Conference on Economic Progress													
Total persons													20[i]
Families													27.5[i]
Individuals													36.5[i]

DANIEL CREAMER—

THE INCOME APPROACH

Creamer estimates the permanent poverty in New York state in 1949 by the income approach. He selects the Budget Standard of the Welfare and Health Council of New York City for a family of four (only). He employs Dorothy Brady's BLS method (see Table 11, note *b*) for approximating the equivalent standard of adequacy for families of different size. For units of two with head over 65, the standard used by Creamer is the special budget for elderly couples of New York Welfare and Health Council. His low-income yardstick for New York, 1949, is as follows:

Size of family	Income of family or unrelated individual	
	Under 65	65 and over
A. New York City and other urban communities		
1	$1,750	$1,500
2	2,500	2,000
3	3,000	3,000
4	3,500	3,500
5+	4,750	4,750
B. Rural, farm and nonfarm		
1	$1,500	$1,250
2	2,000	1,500
3	2,500	2,500
4	3,000	3,000
5+	4,000	4,000

[Notes to Table 12]

[a] Robert J. Lampman, "The Low Income Population and Economic Growth," *Study Paper No. 12*, Study of Employment, Growth, and Price Levels for Consideration by the Joint Economic Committee, 86th Cong., 1st Sess., 1959, Appendix (based on U.S. Congress, Subcommittee on Low-Income Families of the Joint Committee on the Economic Report, *Characteristics of the Low-Income Population and Related Federal Programs*, 84th Cong., 1st Sess., 1955, Sec. 1, "Characteristics of Low-Income Families, 1948–54").

[b] Bureau of the Census, *Current Population Report, Consumer Income*, Series P-60, No. 37, January, 1962.

[c] Robert Lampman, *loc. cit.*

[d] Office of Business Economics, *Survey of Current Business*, May, 1961.

[e] Robert Lampman, *op. cit.* (based on *Characteristics of the Low-Income Population, op. cit.*, Sec. 2, "Characteristics of Low-Income Families, 1948, 1953 and 1954").

[f] *Characteristics of the Low-Income Population, op. cit.*, Sec. 3, "Characteristics of Low-Income Urban Families, 1950."

[g] James Morgan, Martin David, Wilbur Cohen, and Harvey Brazer, *Income and Welfare in the United States* (New York: McGraw-Hill, 1962), pp. 190–91.

[h] John G. Myers, "Income Distribution and Economic Welfare in New York State in 1956" (unpublished Ph.D. dissertation, Department of Economics, Columbia University, New York, 1960), chap. II.

[i] Conference on Economic Progress, *Poverty and Deprivation in the United States: The Plight of Two-fifths of the Nation* (Washington, D. C., 1962), chap. IV.

Creamer's income distribution is based on the New York Census of Population, with adjustments. Aggregate income was underestimated in the Census distribution, and Creamer makes an upward adjustment. Also, students living away from home were incorrectly counted as unrelated individuals; so Creamer makes another correction.

On the basis of the adjusted distribution and his low-income criterion, Creamer estimates that 30 per cent of the combined total of families and unrelated individuals had low income in 1949 (26 per cent of all families, 42 per cent of unrelated individuals).

Using a lower standard, a New York public assistance budget, Creamer finds 13 per cent of all families and 30 per cent of unrelated individuals to be beneath the assistance level. (The public assistance budget is 70 per cent of the low-income budget for a family of four. Creamer takes this standard to be clearly beneath the poverty line.)

But this is an estimate for one year (1949) only. What part of the poverty group is in the class only temporarily? In order to isolate the hard-core poverty group, Creamer adjusts for cyclical and secular factors. Since the estimate is for 1949, a recession year, unemployment surely caused extra-normal numbers to have temporarily low incomes. Creamer estimates that 15 per cent of families had temporarily low incomes for cyclical reasons. Some young persons can reasonably be expected to rise above poverty status. Using amount of schooling as a discriminant for judging who among the young are in "poverty" only temporarily, a number of young individuals and family heads are eliminated.

The final estimate is that 26 per cent of New York's population (families and individuals combined) were in permanent poverty in 1949.

John G. Myers
The Consumption Approach

Myers applies and tests the theory of Friedman, Vickrey, and Modigliani and Brumberg that consumption is superior to income as a measure of the true economic position of individuals. He uses income and consumption data from the BLS-Wharton *1950 Study of Consumer Expenditures* for large northern United States cities. As the criterion of adequacy, he selects the BLS City Worker's Family

Budget (of $3,500 for four persons in 1950 prices), and he uses Brady's BLS equivalence scales for establishing budgets for other family sizes.

Those beneath the budget standard *in consumption,* says the theory, may be considered to be in permanent poverty. To test whether consumption, or income, or both, best isolate poverty classes, Myers gives a distribution by consumption and a distribution by income. Of his units, 32 per cent have "low income," 31 per cent of his units have "low consumption." (Medians, modes, and means of the two distributions are practically identical.) By analyzing the correlation of income determinants—education of head, occupation of head, age of head, number of earners in family, and size of family—with *both* consumption and income levels, Myers finds that the characteristics of low-income units and low-consumption units are very similar.

Under Myers' analysis, the group with both low consumption and low income sets it off "fairly distinctly" from the rest of the (sample) population. He concludes that the double criterion, low income and low consumption, gives the best means for obtaining a homogeneous low-economic status group, theoretical considerations notwithstanding.

Under his double criterion, Myers concludes that 24 per cent of northern, urban families were in the classification "low economic status."

ELEANOR SNYDER—THE CONSUMPTION
DISCRIMINANTS APPROACH

Snyder also draws the line between "adequacy" and "poverty" on the basis of the BLS City Worker's Family Budget and Brady's equivalence-income scales for family sizes other than four. For elderly couples she uses the Social Security Administration's "elderly couple's budget." Her income and expenditure data are taken from the BLS-Wharton *1950 Study of Consumer Expenditures.*

Since the income data are for only one year, units falling beneath the standard cannot all be said to be in permanent poverty. Snyder tries to segregate the "temporary" from the "permanent" on the basis of consumption discriminants. If any of the following expenditures was found for a consumer unit classified below the budget minimum, the unit was assumed to be only temporarily low in income:

1. Annual expenditure on food plus housing in excess of total reported income (1950).
2. Expenditures on home equipment and furnishings in excess of 10 per cent of current income.
3. Purchase of a home in 1950.
4. Purchase of a car in 1950.

The rationale for the first discriminant is that chronically substandard units cannot long exceed their income (by much) because they have poor access to credit. The second discriminant is thought plausible because it relates to budget items with high income elasticity. Over 10 per cent of income spent on equipment and furnishings would be more than the average level of spending for all urban families. The third and fourth discriminants involve "relatively large cash outlays" or increases in debts for items "whose purchase could be considered temporarily deferable."[22]

Snyder's approach leads her to conclude that, while 35 per cent of all units are below the income budget level, only 19 per cent are really hard-core poverty.

MARTIN DAVID—A BROAD INCOME-
ASSETS APPROACH

David suggests an "index of welfare" which he defines as the ratio of current resources of the household to the cost of its basic needs. He includes as "current resources" (1) disposable money income; (2) value of food grown for home consumption; (3) imputed rental value of self-owned homes. David estimates the "basic needs" from the schedules of the Welfare and Health Council of New York City.

An index of welfare is computed for each unit as the ratio between current resources and basic needs, and a distribution of levels of welfare is presented. The difficulty with this distribution, as we have seen, is that it will understate the "true" level of welfare of units which are temporarily low (and, of course, overstate for those which are temporarily high). To correct for this, David presents a second distribution which takes into account the amount of liquid assets held by a household. Liquid assets, he argues, give an indication of a household unit's ability to maintain its customary level of living in the face of negative transitory occurrences. David suggests that his two indexes of welfare, one with only current resources in relation to need, the other with both current resources and assets relative to need, may give upper and lower limits of the "true" levels of welfare.

His distributions indicate that between 28 per cent and 35 per cent (approximately) of the United States population (1956) is beneath the budget level. Presumably, the 28 per cent figure is somewhat nearer to being representative of permanent poverty.

If, instead, we should choose 70 per cent of the budget as the criterion of poverty, to conform with the public assistance budget, something like 15 to 20 per cent would be below the line.

On the basis of these four approaches, we conclude that hard-core poverty encompasses between 15 per cent and 30 per cent of the American population. These approaches give results that are not inconsistent with the leading studies which were cited in Tables 11 and 12.

Existing Poverty and Sales Taxes: An Evaluation of the Galbraith Thesis

The trouble with Galbraith's theory is that just about everything he says is wrong. But it has a lot of wisdom nevertheless!

What is wrong with it? First, he grossly understates the prevalence of poverty in America, as we have just shown. As one critic put it, he should take more thirty-minute walks around Boston. Second, Galbraith misinterprets the causes of the poverty that persists. Finally, he is incorrect in his view that existing poverty is not being reduced and is not amenable to the normal processes of economic growth.

With so much wrong, what can be right about his theory? He is right in his view that our remaining poverty is being reduced far too slowly. The recent rate of reduction of poverty may decline in the coming decades, though the explanation is different from Galbraith's. Also, he is right to think that strong public (tax-supported) programs are essential to eradicate the poverty that remains. He *may* be right in his view that differences in progressivity of the taxes which finance these public programs are not really significant. Effects of differences in progressivity among taxes may be swamped by the redistributional effects of the expenditure side of the budget process. Thus, Galbraith may have an important insight when he says in effect that the critical factor today is the level of expenditure and not the source of finance.

GALBRAITH'S FAULTY THEORY OF AMERICAN POVERTY

We have already shown that Galbraith understates the poverty problem. But he also misinterprets its causes and its composition. He asserts that the remaining poverty is caused by

some quality peculiar to the individual or family involved—mental deficiency, bad health, inability to adapt to the discipline of modern economic life, excessive procreation, alcohol, insufficient education, or perhaps a combination of several of these handicaps.[23]

Galbraith's list of causal variables is completely at odds with those of the leading studies on poverty.[24] They all emphasize that poverty is best correlated with old age, color, female headship of family, disability, and low-education status, each of which Galbraith ignores, except education deficiency.

Galbraith insists that the poverty which remains—island and case poverty—is declining very slowly. Economic growth affects it very little. Only positive programs outside the market economy will do the trick:

The most certain thing about modern poverty is that it is not efficiently remedied by a general and well-distributed advance in income. Case poverty is not remedied because the specific individual inadequacy precludes employment and participation in the general advance. Insular poverty is not directly alleviated because the advance does not necessarily remove the specific frustrations of the environment to which the people of these islands are subject.[25]

Actually, the hard core is declining and it is amenable to economic growth. The Joint Economic Committee study on low income[26] estimates that hard-core poverty declined from 26 per cent of the population to 19 per cent in the decade of the 1950's, which is the decade Galbraith is talking about. The same study shows that mobility was a leading factor in causing the reduction—both movement off farms and shifts to more productive occupations. The study concludes further that most of the causes of what Galbraith calls case poverty can be moderated over time.[27]

So we can expect poverty to decline further with future economic growth. A tax program which exempts poverty classes or which taxes them minimally can make an important contribution by protecting private amenities of life. These amenities are still of urgent importance. They are not trivial, contrived wants.

THE MERIT OF GALBRAITH'S THEORY

But a program that protects private amenities and leaves the rest to economic growth is not enough. Galbraith sees this clearly. At present, progress is too slow. The Joint Economic Committee estimates that if we continue to eradicate it at the present rate, 14 per cent will be in poverty status a decade from now and 10 per cent may still be in poverty in 1987.[28] Worse than this, there is reason to expect the rate of reduction to slacken. In making this dismal forecast, the Committee does not rely on such reasons as diminished rate of economic growth and rising levels of unemployment. Rather, it projects the incidence of old age, disability, and female headship of family, with their inevitable problems.

Most studies agree with Galbraith that a strong public program must be the foundation of the onslaught on poverty. The programs most frequently mentioned are education, retraining, social insurance (especially old age, disability, and unemployment), public assistance (especially old-age assistance and aid to dependent children), guidance, counseling, rehabilitation, the elimination of discrimination and occupational barriers, and programs to aid farm mobility. Notice how many of these are concerns of state and local governments, which is our interest in this book. In the United States the welfare state is found mainly at the state and local levels of government.

The monumental work of the Survey Research Center of the University of Michigan, *Income and Welfare in the United States,*[29] reaches some pertinent conclusions. It says that poverty is still a problem, but that it could be overcome simply with transfer payments if we should choose this route. That is, we can now readily afford to eradicate poverty by the simplest devices of income redistribution. But we want to eliminate its causes; we must eliminate dependency. The key is education. The Center's multivariate analysis indicates that education has the greatest effect on earnings; it has the most powerful effect on occupational advancement, job security, and income stability; and it has the most profound effect on attitudes:

Hence it is clear that formal education is the major dynamic mechanism by which economic level is passed on from one generation to the next, or by which intergenerational change takes place.[30]

TABLE 13. Four Estimates of Taxes Paid and Benefits Received, by Income Class

Income class	Taxes paid: per cent of income or absolute amount	Benefits received: per cent of income or absolute amount	

Musgrave-Daicoff[a]
Michigan, State and Local, 1956
(per cent of income)

Income class	Taxes paid	Case I	Case II
Under $2,000	19	70	42
$ 2,000–2,999	12	20	14
3,000–3,999	9	15	12
4,000–4,999	8	11	10
5,000–6,999	7	9	9
7,000–9,999	6	6	7
10,000 and over	6	3	6

Brownlee[b]
Minnesota, State and Local, 1954
(absolute amounts)

Income class	Taxes paid	Benefits received
Under $500	$ 66	$487
$ 500– 1,000	100	318
1,000– 2,000	151	358
2,000– 3,000	178	422
3,000– 4,000	196	483
4,000– 5,000	235	501
5,000– 6,000	310	565
6,000– 7,500	401	606
7,500–10,000	610	607
10,000 and over	1,622	686

Morgan, David, Cohen, Brazer,[c] 1959
(property tax and public expenditure benefits, absolute amounts)

Income class	Taxes paid	Benefits received
Under $1,000	$ 30	$ 54
$ 1,000–1,999	60	101
2,000–2,999	89	175
3,000–4,999	93	203
5,000–7,499	112	277
7,500–9,999	173	261
10,000 and over	253	220

Adler[d]
Federal, state, and local levels combined, 1946–47
(per cent of income)

Income class	Taxes paid	Benefits received
Under $1,000	19.6	80.5
$ 1,000–1,999	15.1	32.5
2,000–2,999	17.3	24.6
3,000–3,999	17.7	21.0
4,000–4,999	22.9	18.5
5,000–7,499	24.2	14.6
7,500 and above	36.3	12.9

The Michigan Study also demonstrates that disability is a more important cause of poverty than is generally recognized. Our programs are inadequate and wrongly directed: we should shift from concentration on levels of benefit payments to vocational and physical rehabilitation, guidance, counseling, more effective employment services, and sheltered workshops.[31]

What has all this to do with Galbraith and his advocacy of the sales tax? It all adds up to the conclusion that expensive government programs are essential if we are to defeat poverty and dependency quickly. Consider how many expensive governmental programs at the state and local levels of government are of greatest relative benefit to the lower-income classes. Perhaps it turns out that the essence of Galbraith is that he talks such good sense about the best strategy to use in the political arena. If we are concerned about eradication of poverty as well as about social balance, maybe what Galbraith is telling us is that what matters is not the kind of tax adopted—it is getting the rates hiked. The importance of differences in progressiveness between various sources of finance is easily less vital when compared to the effects of the benefits derived from the expenditure programs. Whatever tax we can get through the state legislature or the city council we should take. Perhaps we would prefer an income tax to a sales tax. But the choice is not vital; the expenditure program is.

It is not a new idea that the redistributive aspects of public expenditure can swamp any redistribution attributable to taxation. Many studies of national fiscal systems have presented this idea forcefully.[32] But now we also have estimates for state and local budget systems in America. Table 13 presents the results of four such studies. Even employing very different approaches in distributing the benefits of governmental programs to the various income classes, they

---

[Notes to Table 13]

ᵃ Richard A. Musgrave and Darwin W. Daicoff, "Who Pays the Michigan Taxes?" *Michigan Tax Staff Papers* (Lansing: October, 1958).

ᵇ O. H. Brownlee, *Estimated Distribution of Minnesota Taxes and Public Expenditure Benefits* (Minneapolis: The University of Minnesota Press, 1960).

ᶜ James Morgan, Martin David, Wilbur Cohen, and Harvey Brazer, *Income and Welfare in the United States* (New York: McGraw-Hill, 1962), chap. IX.

ᵈ John H. Adler, "The Fiscal System, the Distribution of Income, and Public Welfare," in Kenyon E. Poole, ed., *Fiscal Policies and the American Economy* (Englewood Cliffs, N.J.: Prentice-Hall, 1951), 359–409.

reach the same general conclusion: the net effect of high taxation and expenditure is to redistribute income to the lowest classes. Even though the taxes may be slightly regressive[33]—such as sales and property taxes—when only the taxing side of the budget process is viewed, the benefits of the expenditures are more regressive, which makes a redistributive impact toward the lowest classes (Table 13).

There is a persuasive objection to this line of reasoning. It is that it misconceives the nature of governmental programs. Benefits from practically all governmental services are corporate and inseparable, the argument runs. Of the many methods used to distribute benefit none makes sense. Perhaps this objection does not really damage the central point, however. We are not really concerned about redistribution per se. We are concerned about eliminating the causes of poverty. Education, retraining, and rehabilitation, for example, have been found to be key mechanisms. So even if benefits from these programs are not theoretically allocable to the income classes, they serve the desired purpose. And even if the lowest income classes do bear some tax burden, it may be worth the price. It is not that we want to put tax burden on these classes. But if the political facts of life make the choice either the sales tax (or its expansion) or no program, we should not hesitate to choose the sales tax.

In summary, it is the strategy issue which Galbraith argues persuasively, not the substantive issue. The wisdom of Galbraith's case for the sales tax rests on his insights into the workings of the American political processes and on his intuitions about what is of central importance in solving today's pressing problems.

VI

SALES TAXES AS LEVIES ON CONSUMERS: THE ROLPH HYPOTHESIS

Almost everyone thinks of retail sales taxes as consumer-burden levies. Harry Gunnison Brown challenged this popular notion in 1939,[1] and in recent years Earl Rolph has attacked it frequently.[2]

Brown argued that we cannot say that consumers pay a completely general sales tax. Under his assumptions, factors of production bear the burden. Brown's article was neglected, strangely, but Earl Rolph has revived Brown's theory and extended it.

Briefly, here is the gist of Rolph's hypothsis. Whereas Brown had argued that consumers do not pay a "general" sales tax, Rolph denies that consumers in general pay even a single excise tax or a partial system of excises. In practice, the typical retail sales tax is a partial system of excises with a uniform rate. So the hypothesis is relevant for analysis of retail sales taxes.

A single excise tax, per se, says Rolph, will raise the price of the taxed good and restrict its output, true enough. But it will also work to increase the output of nontaxed goods and lower their prices. The reason that consumers in general may be no worse off is that they will lose on the one hand but gain on the other.

For a partial system of excises, and for typical retail sales taxes, the analysis is similar. As the scope of the tax is broadened, the tax-induced shift of resources is channeled toward fewer industries. Reductions of prices in these nontaxed areas deepens. With a perfectly general sales tax there will be no resource shift because there is no place to go for higher returns. Then Brown's 1939 proposition would hold: a general sales tax leaves output and composition unchanged and need not raise a general price index.

107

Implications of Rolph's Hypothesis

What are the implications of Rolph's ideas? First, the typical retail sales tax may be relieved of its stigma as a regressive levy. Sales-tax burden should not be thought to be borne in accordance with the sales-taxable consumption expenditures of families. Rather, we should think of sales taxes as taxes on resource owners. Like all taxes, sales taxes reduce the money incomes of factors of production, the reduction being equal to the government's yield. Who are these "factors"? They can be owners of resources employed in the taxed industry. Or they can be owners of resources on which consumers economize as a result of spending more for the sales-taxed good. Or they can be owners of resources that are competitive with either of these groups. If the economy is competitive enough, resources alike enough, mobile enough, etc., we have a modern diffusion theory: sales and excise taxes may be like proportional factor-income taxes in their "income effects."[3] Suppose we are measuring the progressiveness of a retail sales tax. And suppose we measure it according to some size-bracket distribution of income. Perhaps the best first approximation under Rolph's hypothesis would be that the tax is proportional. But if we push the analysis beyond the first approximation, we probably conclude that under this hypothesis there is simply no way to say how progressive a sales tax is. There is no satisfactory basis for distributing the money burden to the income brackets.

A second implication is that an excise tax on motor fuel could conceivably be a burden on the producers of corn flakes. The brunt of an excise is apt to be diffused among producers of many items, items perhaps far removed from the taxed industry. An excise on gasoline can cause gasoline prices to be higher. But there is no reason to conclude that incidence is with motorists. On other things they buy motorists may get lower prices after the tax has been imposed. There is a tax-induced resource shift out of gasoline. Gasoline taxes should not be thought to be special benefit taxes that are borne by motorists and truckers. Therefore, why continue to earmark the use of receipts from them?

As a third implication, the case for a food exemption under the retail sales tax is damaged by the Rolph hypothesis. Most of us believe that the food exemption alleviates sales-tax regressiveness. But we believe it because we think that the sales-tax burden is borne "ultimately" according to consumption expenditure on taxed items. For Rolph, however, incidence rests with producers, and not necessarily with food producers either. Along the same line, the rationale for exempting from sales tax the purchases of governmental units and charitable and educational institutions is lost.

Finally, Rolph's hypothesis shatters the popular notion that sales taxes are better for investment and growth than income taxes. The conventional idea is that sales taxes as taxes on consumption do not affect investment adversely, except perhaps indirectly through their effects on consumer expenditure. Income taxes, by contrast, are thought to strike directly at saving (therefore at investment, according to some students) as well as at consumption. But in Rolph's view, sales taxes reduce money incomes of factors and thus strike at investment and saving in a manner very similar to income taxes. Thus there is little to choose between them so far as growth aspects are concerned.

Rolph's Concepts and Method

The factor-burden doctrine of sales-tax incidence is often called the Brown-Rolph hypothesis. This is misleading because Rolph's hypothesis is much the bolder and the more vulnerable theory. But it is true that the two have much in common. Brown's contention was that factors of production bear the incidence of a truly general sales tax; its incidence is much like that of a proportional income tax of comparable yield. When a general, uniform sales tax is applied, factors of production have no place to go for higher rewards. (We shall leave open for the moment what was meant by the term "general sales tax." Several interpretations are possible and the conclusions are affected by the interpretation we select.)

Brown assumes that the real level of government expenditure has been decided on. He reasons from a perfectly competitive model of the economy with all that that model implies. He assumes inelastic factor supply even in the long run. And he assumes a fixed stock of money with a constant income velocity. In other words, he fixes the level of aggregate demand (see note 7).

Brown then introduces the new general sales tax. It reduces the money earnings of firms. Operating under conditions of perfect competition, the firms are price-takers, which means that they will adjust output in response to the new situation but cannot charge a price different from the market-determined price. Therefore, the new tax lowers the net prices of products sold by the firms. Brown refers to this difference between actual and net price as the "wedge" which the new sales tax drives.

After the new tax is imposed, each firm has an incentive to cut its output. This means a fall in money demand for factors of production. Since long-run factor supply is assumed to be fixed, factors must take a lower money price for the resources they are offering. Brown goes on to demonstrate that under his assumption a completely general sales tax leaves the composition of output the same as would a factor income tax which has no announcement effects. Brown does recognize, however, that output composition can be altered—if government's demand is changed by the fiscal operation.

Rolph approves Brown's position. The merit of Brown's work and of his own, as Rolph sees it, is that each is able to show why excise and sales taxes are deflationary rather than inflationary. Rolph says:

Since in fact any tax which has a yield takes money out of private hands, a person unacquainted with accepted tax theories might conclude that such taxes, by reducing aggregate demand, should lower rather than raise prices. Yet we solemnly explain that excise taxes are deflationary because they raise prices, that is, because they are inflationary.[4]

Rolph's theory shows that sales taxes per se, like other taxes, reduce money incomes and are therefore deflationary. He first employs a set of assumptions similar to Brown's. Then he relaxes them by introducing market imperfections.

Unlike the general sales tax, the single excise changes the composition of output, or the product mix. Similarly, the typical retail sales tax would change the product mix because its scope also is limited rather than general. So the sales tax raises the prices of taxed items and reduces their output. But the prices of untaxed items are lowered. Notice that Rolph is assuming that both aggregate money expenditure and total real output are unchanged by the imposition of the tax. It follows that a general price index is not raised by the new tax. If we assume that composition of output is ideal under perfect competition, sales taxes do create a welfare burden because they move us away from this ideal composition. But if we are skeptical about this, or if we relax the initial assumptions, the result is different. Consumers in general may be no worse off because of the new tax. They get less of the taxed product, more of other products. They pay higher prices for the taxed products but lower prices for the exempt products. So if resource allocation is not ideal before the sales tax is introduced, there need be no "excess burden" of indirect taxation.[5]

Rolph distinguishes between "income effects" and "price and reallocation effects." Income effect is the difference in a man's money income which is occasioned by a tax. A tax should be thought to reduce people's private money incomes in order to increase the government's income. Rolph suggests that his income-effect concept might be substituted for the conventional concept of incidence. Price and reallocation effect means "the change in the allocation of resources and any changes in the prices of resources and of products required by the new allocation that results from the tax."[6]

In the initial version of the theory Rolph was obscure about what the government was assumed to do with the tax revenue.[7] Evidently we are to assume that the revenues are used somehow so that aggregate money demand remains unchanged as a consequence of taxation-expenditure policy. At some points in *Public Finance,* his recent book with George Break, Rolph assumes that the excise is to be substituted for another equal-yield tax, holding government expenditure in money terms constant. Let us review his older analysis, then his newer.

The basic idea is familiar. Assume first a two-commodity economy producing X and Y. Unitary demand elasticity for both X and Y is the simplest case. This is because with unit elasticity we need not redraw the demand schedule for one commodity when the price of the other is changed. In Diagram 5 we assume unitary elasticity for both X and Y. In Period 1 demand for X is D_{x1}; demand for Y is D_{y1}. Output of X is OQ_{x1}; price is OP_{x1}. Output of Y in Period 1 is OQ_{y1}; price is OP_{y1}. Now introduce a new excise on X only. As producers of X see it, a new net demand schedule will go into effect for X, a schedule of demand prices minus excise-tax liability. Call this new net demand schedule D_{x2}.

There is incentive for producers of X to reduce output. If owners want to reduce output, it means that they will now be willing to hire

X
,PRICE
RECTANGULAR
HYPERBOLA
P_{x2}
P_{x1}
D_{x1}
D_{x2}
O
Q_{x2} Q_{x1}
Quantity of X
Y
PRICE
RECTANGULAR
HYPERBOLA
P_{y1}
P_{y2}
D_{y1}
O
Q_{y1} Q_{y2}
Quantity of Y
112

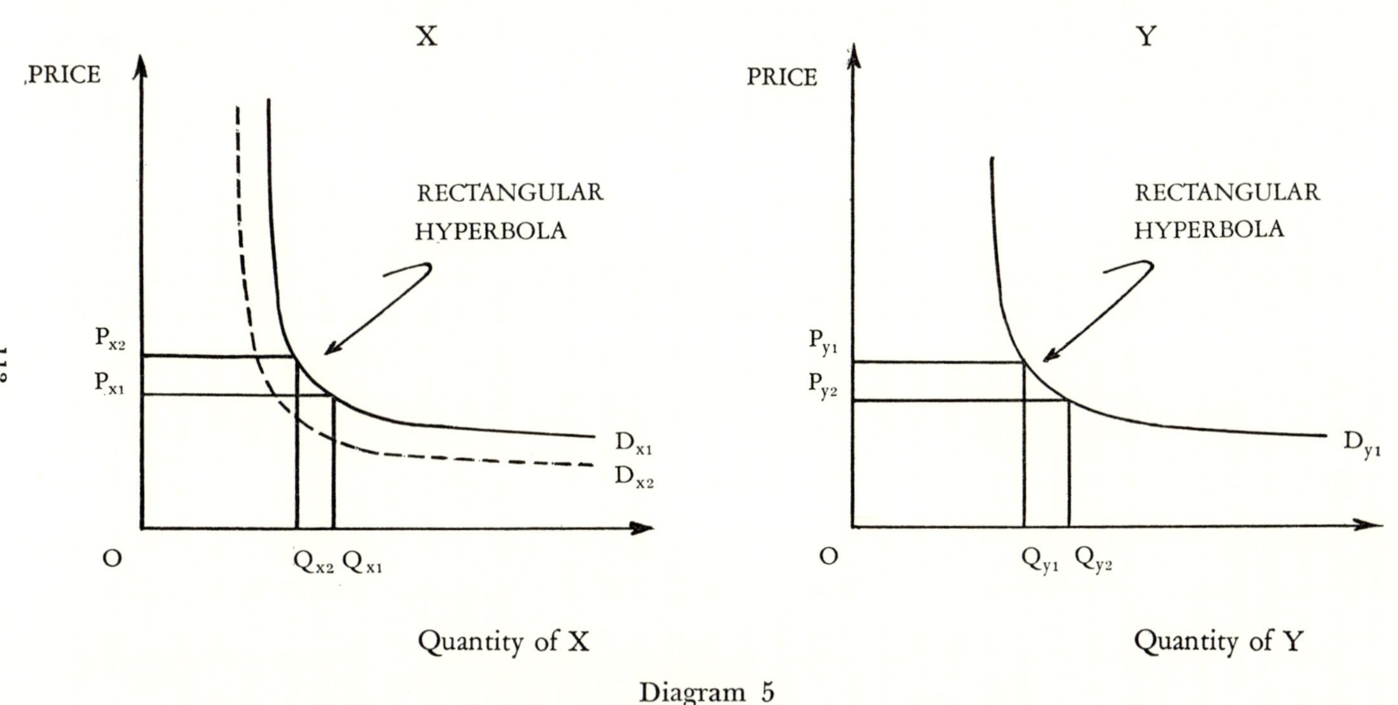

Diagram 5

a smaller quantity of factors at a given set of factor prices. So money demand for factor services falls. If factors—owners of both property and nonproperty resources—are able to produce Y, they will move to do so and partially avoid the lower returns from producing X. Equalization of earnings at the margin is achieved by selling more factor services to Y. Owners producing Y can buy factor services at a lower price per unit. Output of Y increases, its price declines. If factor resources are unable to produce Y, or if they are unwilling, they will simply have to take lower money earnings. If the resources do in fact shift from X to Y and equalize earnings at the margin, output of Y will be higher, as, for example, OQ_{y2} in the diagram. Price of Y will be lower, say OP_{y2}. Output of X will be lower, say OQ_{x2}; its price will be higher, as OP_{x2}.

In an economy that produces more than two commodities the idea is the same. The tax forces resources from the taxed field to the exempt fields. Output of the taxed item is reduced, its price rises; outputs of exempt items increase, their prices fall. As we extend the coverage of the tax, as with a typical retail sales tax, the price rise for any taxed item is ever smaller, and the price decline for each exempt item greater.

But what if demand elasticity is not unitary? Excise taxes are usually placed on commodities which are thought to have low demand elasticity over the relevant ranges of price. And many people think that demand elasticity is low for most items found in the typical retail sales tax. Suppose then that we assume that price elasticity of demand is less than unity, i.e., less than -1. Rolph facilitates this analysis by saying in effect: let us lump all of the taxed items and consider them to be one composite commodity with an elasticity of demand between 0 and -1. Call the composite commodity X. Similarly lump all exempt items. Call this composite commodity Y.

The demand schedules for X and Y are interdependent. This means that the demand schedule for Y can be prescribed only after the price of X is fixed. And the new tax will affect the price of X.

Before the sales tax on X is imposed, we have a set of outputs and prices for X and Y. Say we introduce the new sales tax on X. Pretend that it is a very significant tax, one that takes a big percentage of sales receipts. After the tax is imposed there will be a sharp decline in the *net* prices to producers of X until output of X can be changed.

But output will be changed. Any other event would be disastrous. As producers of X cut back output, its market-determined price rises.

Because demand is inelastic, there will now be a greater total gross money expenditure for X than there was before the tax was imposed. The result is that the entire demand schedule for Y falls. Therefore, once again less of X is produced at a higher price and more of Y is produced at a lower price because the tax has been imposed. But if demand for X is inelastic, its output may not fall much. So it is possible that the allocation of resources between X and Y is not much altered. If the tax were perfectly general in the sense of applying to the final value of all new production—all new investment goods as well as all new consumer goods—the product mix would not be altered.

Rolph's conclusion from this analysis is surprising: in their effects on resource allocation and in their effects on the size and distribution of money incomes, *selective* excise taxes (and typical retail sales taxes) are similar to *general* sales or *general* income taxes.[8]

(1) Resource allocation. General sales or income taxes may leave resource allocation unaffected, as compared with the pretax allocation. If, instead of general taxes, limited sales taxes are employed, and if the items which are taxed are quite inelastic in demand, again there will be little resource shift.

(2) Size and distribution of money income. After the selective sales tax is levied, the taxed industry will recoup earnings partially by cutting output and getting higher prices as a result. Since demand for the taxed items is inelastic, more money is spent on them after the tax than was spent on them before the tax. This lowers the demand schedules of exempt items. Therefore, says Rolph, producers of exempt items will get lower money earnings.

Critique of the Rolph Approach

In résumé, Rolph concludes that consumers in general may be no worse off because of the imposition of a new sales tax. They pay higher prices for sales-taxed products but they get lower prices for the other things they buy. Still, they have less income in money terms, and their diminished money income equals the government's yield. There is no telling whose money incomes will be lowered. It could be the owners of resources that produce the taxed item, but it could just as well be the owners of resources that produce other things.

There are two major lines which criticism of Rolph can take. One line is to quarrel with his assumptions. Are they not so unrealistic a picture of today's market structure and credit system as to yield faulty conclusions? There is much wisdom in this line of attack. But Rolph is prepared to meet it. He does so by introducing more realistic market structures.[9] He believes that he demonstrates that his conclusions are not affected significantly. So we accept his judgment until we can improve on his analysis. The second line of criticism may be more pertinent. It argues that Rolph's conceptual framework is faulty. The framework is alleged to produce misleading if not incorrect results. The criticism has several adherents, and they differ among themselves.

One group of critics of Rolph argues that he is wrong because he merely traces the effects of sales and excise taxes in isolation. All that happens in his framework is that the new sales tax is levied to add to the government's surplus or to reduce its deficit. Evidently we are to assume that the government does not increase its expenditures in real terms along with the tax increase. In other words, there is no withdrawal of resources at the expense of the private sector of the economy. This must be true because Rolph contends that while a sales tax decreases the output of taxed goods it increases the output of exempt goods; prices of taxed items rise, prices of exempt items fall; a general price index is unaffected. This incidence concept of raising a tax without an increase in the size of the public sector Richard Musgrave has popularized as specific or absolute incidence.[10]

The incidence concept which many conventional writers prefer, often without realizing it, is one in which the government is assumed to increase its real expenditure along with the tax increase. The government exerts a resource pull at the expense of the private sector. We yield private goods and services, and it is this real loss from the private sector which is the burden we are trying to distribute. Musgrave calls this "balanced-budget incidence." We raise (or lower) government expenditure and taxes by an equal amount. If the government does not step up its real expenditure, there is no real burden because there is no loss of private goods and services.[11]

We are saying in opposition to Rolph that it is the real burden rather than the money burden which is the important thing to examine. The mere imposition of a new sales tax produces no real aggregate burden if it leads to no reduction in goods and services available to the private sector of the economy.[12]

To repeat, many people will argue that balanced-budget incidence is more relevant for policy purposes than Rolph's specific incidence. This is argued because with a new tax resources do not simply flow from the sales-taxed industry to another industry also in the private sector of the economy.[13] Typically, the tax accompanies a higher level of government activity. Some resources flow from the private sector to the government sector. Consumers of the taxed items now face higher prices for them than they faced before the tax was imposed. Full-offset declines in prices of other private consumption items need not occur. Consumers can be worse off in real terms: their money incomes buy less in the way of private goods and services. Thus does the sales tax ration the lower output which is available as a result of the stepped-up governmental activity. When Rolph says that, while some prices are higher, other prices are lower, and that an aggregate price index is unaffected by a new sales tax, he obviously refers to a general price index and not to an index of prices of consumer goods, or even to an index of (private) consumer and investment goods.

Under balanced-budget incidence, as a result of the higher (lower) tax which accompanies a higher (lower) level of government activity, at least three results are possible: (1) resource transfer; (2) redistribution of income; (3) output or income effects.[14]

(1) Resource transfer: There is a resource transfer as government steps up its output. Presumably the output of the private sector is reduced.

(2) Redistribution of income: There is also a redistribution of real income available for private use. This happens because relative prices and earnings are changed by the new policy. In order to trace the direction of the redistribution we must analyze expenditure as well as taxation. We must take account of the direction of the government's demand for services and products.

(3) Output or income effects: Total output, government and private output combined, can change as the result of budget policy. If

we do not assume that there is automatic full employment of resources in each equilibrium, before and after the change in budget policy, real output in the economy can be altered. If we do assume automatic full employment, the level of output can change in money terms. Output effects are often neglected in incidence analysis. For one reason, they greatly complicate the analysis: the price of realism is high. Another reason for the traditional neglect is that until recently most students thought that the effect of a change in government spending on total output is neutral if there is an equal change in taxes. (Earl Rolph and many other analysts assume away output effects.)

It seems to be more meaningful to carry on incidence analysis in real terms rather than in money terms. Rolph's discussion of income effects, however, runs only in money terms. Presumably, if money returns are not lowered by the tax, there is no income effect. Surely it is conceivable outside of Rolph's initial rigid assumptions that money incomes may not decline in response to the imposition of a sales tax. Rolph in fact admits as much.[15] But the absence of a money burden does not indicate that there is no real burden, if by burden we mean loss of private goods. If the government steps up its spending and its share of real output as the sales tax is imposed, there is no reason for money incomes to fall. But we would not conclude that there is no burden accompanying the sales-tax–expenditure policy. There is a loss of goods available for private use, and this is just what many people mean by burden.

We are working toward Musgrave's point that Rolph should take account of the uses to which money earnings are put.[16] If money earnings are unaffected as real government expenditure rises, accompanied by a sales tax, yet prices for private goods and services are forced up, then households still bear a real burden.

It makes a great deal of difference if uses of income are brought into the analysis. The criticisms which Challis Hall and Richard Musgrave have leveled at Rolph's doctrine make this point clear.

Challis Hall challenges Rolph's conclusion that if selective sales taxes are placed on items with inelastic demand the distribution of burden will be much the same as it would be under a general income tax or under a general sales tax.[17] It is true that if demand for the sales-taxed items is inelastic, more will be spent for the taxed items and less for exempt items after the tax is imposed. Money income of owners of resources which produce exempt items will fall. But, Hall points out, we must go further in order to describe the after-tax long-run equilibrium. In the new equilibrium, prices of taxed items exceed factor-cost prices by the amount of the tax. The lower money expenditure for exempt items may depress incomes of factors producing the exempt items. But if resources are mobile, money costs will also be made lower in taxed areas as earnings at the margin are equalized. In the new equilibrium, which emerges as a result of the new sales tax, the relative price structure puts the "taxed-induced real income loss" on consumers of taxed items. Thus, Hall concludes, conventional analysis is correct and Rolph is in error. Notice that Hall reaches his conclusion by including in his analysis prices paid by households as well as money income earned by households. That is, he accounts for use of income as well as for source of income.

Richard Musgrave likes to approach the question through the framework of differential incidence. In effect, Musgrave asks this question: what would be the effect on the distribution of income if we were to substitute a sales tax for a proportional factor income tax of equal yield while holding constant the real level of government expenditure? Under Rolph's hypothesis we should expect the answer to be approximately "no change." Rolph himself has employed the differential-incidence approach in his most recent book.

Under Musgrave's analysis, if a nongeneral sales tax (such as the typical retail sales tax) is substituted for a general factor-income tax, the distribution of income will be affected. Prices of the sales-taxed items will rise relative to other prices. It is relative prices which count here.[18] If we take account of how people use their income, as Rolph does not do, the distribution will be adverse for those income classes which spend the highest percentages of income on the sales-taxed items. Thus, differential incidence would be progressive for sales taxes on luxuries and regressive for sales taxes on necessities.

Our approach indicates that the conventional view that sales taxes are levies on consumers is nearer right than is Earl Rolph's approach. If under the typical retail sales tax the lowest income brackets spend higher portions of their incomes than do higher income brackets, we conclude that incidence is regressive. It would take a proportional sales tax on all final investment and consumer goods to leave the distribution of income unaffected when such a tax is substituted for a proportional factor income tax on all factor incomes.

But, to Earl Rolph's credit, in reaching our conclusion we have come a very long way from the naïve view that the sales tax is a consumer-burden tax pure and simple.

VII

REFORM PROPOSALS

In considering policy guidelines for taxation, it is important to decide whether we wish the sales tax to be a levy on consumption or on social income. A good case can be made for either of these. But as we have seen, as things stand now the typical retail sales tax is neither a true income tax nor a true consumption tax. Today's sales tax reminds one of the song about Alexander—half swan, half goose, Alexander is a swoose! Perhaps our swoose simply cannot be made to be either a swan or a goose. If we were to decide to make it a consumption tax, and if to accomplish this purpose we were to tax consumer expenditure and exclude saving and expenditure for investment goods, we still might not wind up with a consumer-burden tax. Earl Rolph has impressed this idea on us. But this view seems unduly defeatist, and not altogether correct.

The retail sales tax is best rationalized as a tax on consumption. After all, if we prefer a tax on something like Haig-Simons income, an individual income tax is a superior instrument. If we prefer a tax on social income—the final value of both consumption and investment output—some form of factor-income taxation is better. If we want a business activity tax, rationalized according to collective benefit received from government serving as a fifth factor of production, a value-added tax is preferable. And if we want to reallocate resources, several taxes perform more efficiently.

Suppose we take the following guidelines. Any proposal to go outside these lines bears a burden of proof:

1. Tax *only* consumption-expenditure items.
2. Tax *all* consumption expenditure.
3. Tax only sales to *final* (nonbusiness) consumers.

The sales tax should be a genuine single-stage tax, not a multiple-stage one. Multiple-stage taxes discriminate against nonintegrated

120

firms, whether or not they induce pyramiding. It is only by taxing at the point of retail sale that we avoid double taxation and yet tax the final value of consumption output. This value is roughly equal to the value of all services performed along the production-distribution route until the product reaches its consumer. More important, the retail form of sales taxation facilitates the inclusion of services in its base, while a sales tax on manufacturers, wholesalers, or extractors is likely to perpetuate the error of omitting services. One of the major defects of retail sales taxation has been its nearly exclusive application to tangible commodities. Fortunately, the prejudice against service inclusion is breaking down, though not rapidly enough.

Sales Taxation of Services

The propensity to define "retail sale" along the lines of tangible personal property is not so strong today as it was just a decade ago. But the habit is hard to break. Even today we usually do not consider services to be retail sales if they are entirely divorced from the transfer of property. Services of doctors, dentists, lawyers, optometrists, and pharmacists have all been held by the court not to be "sales."[1] Even when the service is "mixed with property," decisions in some states have held for exclusion from the category of sales. This has happened with services of textile and fur cleaners, dyers and repairers, watch repairers, auto mechanics, painters, and launderers.

Such thinking is unfortunate. As John Due has observed,[2] it probably springs from the attachment of the tax to the articles subject to it rather than to the persons who bear it. A tax on services is thought to be a "tax on labor," and therefore bad. But, says Due properly, a tax on barber services is no more a tax on labor than is a tax on bread. Tangible goods are simply the result of a series of operations or services.

Services gratify "wants" no less than goods. If tangibles are taxed and services are excluded from the base, the sales tax discriminates against the individual whose tastes run to goods vis-à-vis the individual who prefers services. And we may infer that the allocation of resources is altered by the present policy of restricted scope. More tangibles and fewer services are produced than would be true in the absence of the tax.[3]

If the inclusion of "services" is plausible, which services have we in mind? Surely we do not mean that all services should be taxed. The value of all services approximates the value of genuine (final-value) retail sales.[4] To tax both final retail sales to households and factor services (incomes) is levying twice on the same value.

Which services then? Mainly the services sold to households, which together with tangible goods compose the final value of retail sales. We should like to include all services performed at retail for personal (household, nonbusiness) gratification. And we should like to exclude services performed for business: the service sold to business becomes a component of the cost of the business product and is included ultimately in the taxable retail-sales base. This approach is consistent with the rationale of the sales tax as a neutral, consumption-base tax. It may not appeal to the person who favors putting as much of a state's tax impact as possible on "business."

Many students of sales-tax administration believe that a policy of taxing services performed for households while excluding services performed for businesses runs the risk of administrative impracticality and evasion. We need not debate this issue. Suppose we accept the view. It is possible to approximate the goal we seek with a scheme which is administratively feasible. To decide whether a service should be taxed we can ask the question: is this service performed primarily for business or primarily for households? If the answer is households, we tax it. If selected for taxation, the service is taxed whether it is actually performed for personal use or for business use.

SERVICE TRADES, ETC.

The categories of the *Census of Business—Service Trades* suggest a solution along these lines. From the census classification a wide group of services is easily distinguished as being predominantly for personal gratification. Another group is provided for business in the main. Other groups of services are consumed by both businesses and households and cause some difficulty.

The census breakdown is reproduced in Table 14. According to it, personal services and amusement and recreation are mainly for personal enjoyment. They should be taxed. The business-services category should be excluded. Miscellaneous repair services are predominantly the kind that could be taxed. Automobile repair serv-

TABLE 14

Suggested Taxable Status of Services, Based on Classification
of Census of Business, *Selected Service Trades*

Kind of business	Suggested tax status
Personal services	Tax
Barber, beauty shops	
Barber shops	
Beauty shops	
Barber and beauty shops combined	
Funeral service, crematories	
Photographic studios (including commercial photography)	
Shoe repair shops, shoeshine parlors, hat cleaning shops	
Shoe repair shops	
Shoeshine parlors	
Hat cleaning shops	
Cleaning, pressing, dyeing, garment repair	
Pressing, alteration, garment repair (except fur)	
Cleaning, pressing shops, and independent plant outlets	
Garment repair, alteration (except fur)	
Fur repair, storage	
Cleaning, dyeing plants	
Cleaning, dyeing plants (except rug cleaning)	
Rug cleaning, repairing plants	
Laundries, laundry services	
Power laundries, self-service laundries	
Power laundries*	
Self-service laundries	
Industrial laundries*	
Linen supply	
Diaper service	
Laundries (except power)	
Miscellaneous personal services	
Costume, dress suit rental	
Turkish bath, massage parlors	
Rug, furniture cleaning on location	
Coin-operated service machine establishments	
Miscellaneous personal services, n.e.c.	
Business services	Exclude
Advertising	
Advertising agencies	
Outdoor advertising	
Miscellaneous advertising	
Consumer, mercantile credit; adjustment, collection agencies	

*=probable exemption.

[TABLE 14—continued]

Kind of business	Suggested tax status

Private employment agencies
News syndicates
Duplicating, addressing, mailing, stenographic services
Blueprinting, photocopying services
Services to dwellings, other buildings
   Disinfecting, exterminating services*
   Window cleaning*
   Miscellaneous services to dwellings, other buildings*
Business services, n.e.c.
   Auctioneers' establishments (service only)
   Coin-operated machine rental, repair services
   Detective agencies
   Interior decorating service
   Photofinishing laboratories
   Sign painting shops
   Telephone answering service
   Window display service
   Other business services, n.e.c.

Automobile repair services, garages   Tax or give
                                                                mixed treatment

Automobile repair
   General automobile repair shops
   Battery, ignition repair and service
   Glass replacement, repair
   Paint shops
   Radiator repair shops
   Tire repair shops
   Top and body repair shops
   Automobile repair shops
     Brake repair shops
     Wheel, axle, spring repair shops
     Other automobile repair shops, n.e.c.
Automobile storage, parking
   Parking structures, storage garages
   Parking lots
Automobile, truck rentals (without drivers)
Automobile services (except repair)
   Automobile laundries
   Automobile services, n.e.c.

Miscellaneous repair services   Tax

Watch, clock, jewelry repair
Upholstery, furniture repair

   *=probable exemption.

[TABLE 14—continued]

Kind of business	Suggested tax status
Electrical repair shops	
Radio, television repair shops	
Refrigerator service, repair shops	
Other electrical repair shops	
Blacksmith shops	
Miscellaneous repair shops	
Armature rewinding, electric motor repair and rebuilding	
Bicycle repair shops	
Leather goods repair shops	
Locksmith, gunsmith shops	
Musical instrument repair	
Repair shops	
Lawnmower, saw, knife, tool sharpening and repair shops	
Typewriter repair shops	
Welding repair shops	
Other repair shops	
Amusement, recreation services (including motion pictures)	Tax
Motion picture theaters	
Motion picture theaters (except drive-in)	
Drive-in motion picture theaters	
Motion picture production, distribution, services*	
Billiard and pool parlors, bowling alleys	
Billiard, pool parlors	
Bowling alleys	
Race track operation (including racing stables)	
Automobile	
Dog	
Horse (including racing stables)	
Sports promoters, commercial operators	
Baseball, football, athletic fields, sports promoters	
Baseball clubs	
Football clubs	
Other sports clubs, promoters	
Bathing beaches	
Golf courses	
Riding academies	
Skating rinks	
Swimming pools	
Commercial sports operators	
Boat, canoe rentals	
Other commercial sports operators	
Theatrical presentations and services	
Bands, orchestras, entertainers	
Dance halls, studios, schools (exc. children's, professional)	

*=probable exemption.

ices and garages and hotels, motels, tourist courts, and camps pose problems since they provide for both personal and business use. Automobile repair services could be segregated by type of user. If the car or truck were proved to be business-owned, the service would not be taxed. If experience indicates that this policy is expensive to comply with, or if it opens an escape hatch, perhaps all such services should be taxed. Services of hotels, motels, resorts, and camps would cause too many problems if our criterion were followed. Expediency dictates that receipts from both business and individual clients be taxed. The legislator's intuition here is probably sound. The states are moving wisely and rapidly in the direction of taxing these services.

This scheme for sales taxation of services has much to recommend it. Administration is facilitated by the publication each four years of the Census of Business. It gives the number of establishments of each kind together with their sales receipts for the state and for the metropolitan areas. With these figures there is a basis for revenue-yield estimation and for curbing evasion on initiation of the program. There will, of course, be some problems. Our list is only meant to be suggestive. There is room for debate, for example, about the tax status of professional services, which we have omitted from the list in Table 14.

There is precedent for including services under a retail sales-tax base. Today, seven states tax services broadly, though not in the way we have proposed. These states are Arizona, Hawaii, Indiana, Mississippi, New Mexico, Washington, and West Virginia. Every retail sales-tax state today includes in its base at least some kinds of services, and the scope is expanding rapidly. The favorite services to tax are those of hotels and motels, amusements and recreation, utilities, and a few personal services. In Appendix Table IV we present the most extensive survey to date of service taxation under American sales-tax bases. Here we shall simply summarize a few of the major conclusions.

Personal Services. Hotel, motel, and lodging service is the most frequently taxed personal service. Twenty-five states now sales tax this service and many others tax it under special taxes. Seven states tax the services of tailors, six tax dyers, and seven tax the services of dressmakers and seamstresses.

Repair and Improvement Services. Six states tax automobile painting;

eight tax the repair of air conditioning, heating, and refrigeration equipment; seven tax radio and television repair; eight tax the repair of musical instruments; six tax jewelers' services; four or five states tax the services of each of the following: blacksmiths, bookbinders, cabinet-makers, roofers, and fumigators.

Public Utilities. Electricity is sales taxed in twenty-one states, natural gas in twenty, telephone and telegraph service in seventeen, and water in twelve.

Amusements. Amusements, admissions, and recreation are subject to sales tax in nineteen states today.

Professional and Technical Service. Professional service is very seldom taxed, except in gross-income states. However, twenty-six states sales tax photographers' services, thirty-two tax custom printing, and twenty-one tax the entire bill charged by engravers of plates used in printing.

Most advisory groups and most scholars who have examined the desirability of including services in the sales-tax base have been in favor of doing so.[5] The reasons most frequently cited are (1) service inclusion alleviates regressivity and improves neutrality;[6] (2) inclusion makes the sales tax more income elastic;[7] (3) service inclusion can raise much revenue;[8] and (4) inclusion is administratively feasible.[9]

PUBLIC UTILITIES

Public utility services are now sales taxed more often than not. The question of inclusion or exclusion is a complex one because it involves the rationale of public utility pricing. Court and commission decisions make it probable that utility companies, where regulation exists, will try to reimburse themselves for higher taxes by charging higher prices. I shall not try to debate the merits of exclusion versus inclusion here but nevertheless shall give my conclusion.

The conclusion is that utility services for residential consumers should be included in the sales-tax base and that such services should be excluded from the base for sales to industrial and commercial buyers. Exemption for the latter is consistent with the approach of excluding business expense items. It is true, as Clinton Oster has observed, that the exclusion of utility and fuel sales to business can create administrative and compliance difficulties if such services are used jointly for business and domestic purposes. But, as Oster also observes, these problems may be no greater than those which we have now when we try to exempt commodities "used directly in production"[10] in contrast to commodities employed for other business uses.

We can say, though Earl Rolph would disagree, that residential utility consumers will bear the burden of the sales tax on utility service. But these consumers are not identical with the general public. According to our rationale for choosing a consumption tax, consumers should be taxed on the basis of their capacities to pay taxes. And the consumption-tax advocate should argue that in part people manifest capacity to pay by their purchases of utility services.

Our position on sales taxation of utilities is one which Harold Groves depicts as a "midway house" between the extremes of no taxation of utilities and extra-high tax rates (because of monopoly position). It is consistent with our policy guideline that all consumption sales should be taxed.

RENT

Rent is a necessary exception to our guide rule that services be taxed. If home rentals are not exempt, preferential treatment is given to home owners over tenants. It seems fair to impute a rental value for home owners for tax purposes; yet this is still over the horizon for most states. Unless such an imputation is made, the tax burden on home owners will be lighter than that on tenants (or on the owners of rental houses, depending on incidence assumptions). The income tax already provides serious discrimination against tenants; there is no reason for a sales tax to further aggravate the problem.

"Housing" expenditure declines slightly as a percentage of measured income as income rises. So its exclusion is expected to make the sales tax less regressive than if it were taxed. The permanent-income hypothesis alters this conclusion somewhat, however. Under it, "permanent housing" is roughly proportional to permanent income.

We should be consistent in our decision to exclude housing by excluding the sale of construction materials. If shifting is forward, the sales taxation of construction materials places considerable burden on home owners and/or tenants. It is a disguised tax on housing. If incidence is borne by owners of businesses or their workers, the sales tax on construction materials is unwarranted and capricious. If we are moving in the direction of exempting sales of other materials, lubricants, and capital items sold to businesses, it makes sense to exempt these also.

The Problem of Double Taxation of Excised-Taxed Items

Double taxation is said to arise when a general sales tax is added to existing special excise taxes. There is, of course, no proscription against double taxation. There is not necessarily a proscription even if it implies a doubly high rate. But the double rate must be justified. What, then, is sensible policy in this matter for sales taxation?

Many states give an exemption from the general retail sales tax to prevent discrimination against goods already hit by the excise (see Appendix Table II). The following are often so treated: alcoholic beverages, cigarettes and tobacco products, amusements, motor fuel, and luxury excises. Several states have given blanket exemption to such items. The buyer is excused from paying the tax if it is less than the retail sales tax. But if the sales tax is less, the buyer pays the difference.

If the sumptuary rationale for many of the excises were genuine, exemption from the general sales tax would make little sense. If the sales tax is not applied to the excise-taxed good, the relative tax burden on its use is reduced. Actually, of course, much of the sumptuary justification is flimsy. Therefore, an exemption for alcoholic beverages, tobacco, etc., can be justified. For form's sake, since we want to tax all items uniformly, it might be wise to levy the general sales tax and reduce excise rates where desired.

The case for motor-fuel exemption is weaker. It is still common, though no longer universal, to earmark motor-fuel taxes for highway construction and maintenance. The idea is that motor-fuel consumption is a fair gauge of miles traveled and of benefit derived from roads and highways. Retail sales taxes, on the other hand, are not usually for the particular benefit of any class of taxpayers. Thus, a revenue-reducing exemption may work to prevent motor fuel from bearing its proper portion of the general tax burden. Here, however, the financing and earmarking provisions of the individual state would have to be analyzed carefully before a decision is reached. In practice, motor fuel gains exemption from sales tax far more frequently than cigarettes and tobacco (see Appendix Table II). This is contrary to our suggestion.

Casual and Isolated Sales

Casual and isolated sales are exempted in many states in an attempt to lessen administrative and compliance costs and to avoid confusion. Like most exemptions, these raise perplexing problems.[11] Many of the casual and isolated sales are of used items, especially automobiles, furniture, and machinery. Under our guidelines there are no reasons, except administrative ones, to exempt these sales. We are taking consumption expenditure as the manifestation of ability to pay. It does not matter that the item may have been taxed once before, or even many times before. The practice of taxing the net difference between sales price and trade-in allowance, followed by many states, seems most sensible.

Most states give too much to administrative expediency in their exemption of casual and isolated sales. A broad exemption may reflect an unwillingness to set a high level of enforcement. Or the view may be that the revenues lost may not cover the enforcement costs of collection, so why bother. Some states, however, are turning to a very narrow interpretation of casual, occasional, and isolated sales, so that two, three, or a very few sales constitute taxable status. California sets a good example for other states in this regard.

The exemption of casual and isolated sales raises about as many administrative headaches as it relieves. Surely there is no reason to exempt any item that requires a transfer of title, such as motor vehicles and trailers.

Sales to Business Units

As we saw in Chapter II, a complex structure of rules, regulations, and legal logic has emerged concerning the sales of items by one business unit to another. Under the guise of defining retail sale in a logical way and in a way that will prevent evasion, a capricious business turnover tax has been constructed.

The existing structure is not really so difficult to reform. The question to decide is whether we really want a single-stage tax at the retail level instead of a levy which to a large extent is based on the principle that Professor Groves refers to as "the most feathers for the least squawking." If we want a consumption-base tax, the policy should be straightforward: tangible property sold by one business to another should be classified "sales for resale" and therefore immune from tax. If we want to tax social income, which includes the value of investment goods as well as consumption goods, we should simply tax new capital items sold to businesses and nothing else.

To the critic who charges that this policy opens the way for evasion, the answer is simple. It opens the way to evasion slightly more than present policy. At present, sales to wholesalers and retailers of food, alcohol, tobacco, drugs, clothing, furniture, home furnishings, appliances, hardware, etc., are made without sales taxes applying. These are statutory "sales for resale." So if compliance is poor, the door to evasion is already wide open. It is hard to see how the exemption of items such as industrial and agricultural machinery, business and industrial fuel, construction materials, display cases, calculating machines, and like items can open it any wider. It is no trick not to collect taxes on such items. The trick is to collect them.

Exemptions, Credits, and Rate Graduation

We have seen that the deficiencies of sales taxes which most critics stress are the following:
1. They are hard on low-income families.
2. They are regressive (this need not be the same as 1).
3. They do not take account of relative family circumstance and need (family size is stressed most frequently here).
4. They tax economically similar families unequally.

Some observers are convinced that these deficiencies are inherent in the nature of the tax and are virtually impossible to eliminate.[12] This may be overly severe and pessimistic. Much improvement in the way of reform through tax credit or exemption policy is possible.

Should a minimum be excluded before the tax applies? The answer probably is that there should be a minimum exemption. The theories of Duesenberry, Galbraith, and Friedman have dented the venerable doctrine of subsistence minimum exemption, but they have not destroyed it. There are many "objective" reasons for exempting a minimum: the significance of income and consumption (or their utility) surely does not derive purely from consideration of relative status. Friedman may contend that lowest-income groups spend about the same fraction of their permanent incomes as the highest groups. But this implies nothing about their objective needs, as he would be the first to say. So it seems to make sense to stay with the tradition generally subscribed to by economists of the left, right, and middle way—the tradition of making a subsistence minimum immune from taxation.

Proposals for Exemption Policy

Everybody does not agree, however, on the lines along which exemption policy should be formulated. Let us enumerate some preferences and then see what form their application would take.

First, exemption policy should be formulated on the idea that the family is the proper unit of taxation. We should reject the notion that taxation should be related to welfare conceived in terms of "sacrifice" and regarded as an individual or per capita matter. The family is an economic as well as a social unit. Its status, power, and needs are shared in common. (Of course, this view encounters constitutional and statutory difficulties in many states.)

The best rationale for the minimum exemption is the fact of social interest in preserving basic private amenities from taxation. The essential amenities increase with family size. (But it is not only with family size that they vary.) After an allowance is made for safeguarding amenities, children may be regarded as a choice of consumption. That is, as we reach into the higher consumption and income brackets, children are due no supplemental state subsidy beyond the minimum allowance for basic amenities. So far as society is concerned, at these higher levels children are a personal consumption preference.

If we follow this line, the allowance for children should be based on their minimum objective needs, or the costs which their guardians incur and in which society has an interest. It cannot seriously be argued that these are "constant costs." All studies indicate that the cost of each additional child in a family is a "declining" cost. It is not proper to give the same exemption or credit for each family member regardless of how many members the family may have. This follows from an acceptance of the family rather than the individual as the proper taxable unit.

Further, needs and costs do not vary simply with family size. Other items in a family's composition are relevant, such as the employment status of the head (employed, unemployed, or retired), the employment status of the wife (employed or housewife), the ages of the members, and the location of the family (rural or urban, etc.).

The relative minimal needs of families of differing compositions should be as nearly "objectively" determined as possible: the purchases necessary for adequate nutrition, housing, medical care, clothing, and transportation necessary to achieve some specified standard of life. Several extensive studies of relative objective needs have been made, of which the BLS City Worker's Family Budget, the Social Security Administration "elderly couple's budget," and the budgets of the Community Council of Greater New York City are perhaps best known (see Chapter V). The studies are concerned with the very problems which are most pertinent for tax exemption or credit policy and can be put to effective use. The Community Council schedules are illustrative. They enable us to distinguish between the cost of basic needs of children, and they show the marginal cost of increasing the size of the household. Table 15 presents a short-cut formula devised from the Council schedules by Martin David to compute the annual budget costs for families of different composition.[13] These are thought to be the "necessary minimum costs" for achieving prevailing standards for health, efficiency, and social participation.

David's schedule not only provides a basis for exempting a subsistence minimum, it also facilitates taking into account several factors which determine relative family need. Such factors have usually been thought to be too difficult to ascertain for tax-exemption or tax-credit policy. Surely a family with a working wife has greater requirements than one in which the wife remains at home. Surely a retired person (or couple) has smaller needs than one who is still actively employed. Surely age of children as well as number of children determine relative needs. These factors have all been carefully weighed in establishing the equivalence for attaining the budget standard.

The credits or exemptions allowed could be proportional to the equivalences of Table 15 (or perhaps Part I of Table 15). This is done, roughly, in Table 16, which suggests the nucleus of a sales-tax credit form.[14] Such a form could be either integrated with an income tax or reported separately. The legislature would have discretion as

TABLE 15

Schedule of Annual Budget Costs Necessary to Achieve
New York Health and Welfare Budget Standard, 1954

I. Food, clothing and personal expenses	
A. Single persons	
Employed	$1053.00
Retired:	
Men	677.30
Women	625.72
B. Amount per person for units containing	
1. Head	
Employed	1024.40
Retired	648.70
2. Dependents	505.70
3. Income earners (full time)	975.83
4. Children	
1	208.00
1– 5	275.60
6–11	388.70
12–14	526.50
15–20	625.30
II. Household overhead: rent, utilities and other costs, etc.	
Number of persons	
1	897.00
2	1047.80
3	1183.00
4	1250.60
5	1346.80
6	1593.80
7	1684.80
8	1770.00
9	1850.00
10	1930.00

Source Martin David, "Welfare, Income and Budget Needs," *Review of Economics and Statistics*, XLI (November, 1959), 395.

to what percentage of the population is to be immune from tax: Martin David has computed a cumulative frequency distribution of welfare for the nation based on this budget standard.[15] Alternatively, a legislature can decide what percentage of the budget standard it wants to exempt.

To illustrate, suppose that a legislature should decide to exempt 60 per cent of the welfare budget standard. About 15 per cent of the families and individuals have a welfare level below this standard.

TABLE 16

Suggested Form for Sales-tax Credit

From the list of credits below, select those applicable to your family status. Enter in the right-hand column the amounts indicated. When credit is not applicable, enter the figure "0."

	Amount of credit	Column for computing total credit
I. Food, clothing and personal expense credit		
A. Single and unattached individuals		
1. Employed	$12.50	
2. Retired	8.00	(a) ______
B. Multi-person household units		
1. Head		
a. Employed	12.00	
b. Retired	7.50	(b) ______
2. Spouse		
a. Full-time earner	11.50	
b. Non full-time earner	6.00	(c) ______
3. Children:		

Age	Number children of each age		Subtotals	
a. 1	______	$2.50	______	
b. 1– 5	______	3.00	______	
c. 6–11	______	4.50	______	(d) ______
d. 12–14	______	6.00	______	
e. 15–20	______	7.50	______	

II. Credit for household overhead
(rent, utilities, etc.)
Number of persons

	Amount of credit	Column for computing total credit
One	$11.00	
Two	12.50	
Three	14.00	
Four	15.00	(e) ______
Five	16.00	
Six	18.00	
Seven	19.00	
Eight and over	20.00	

Total Credit: Sum of (a) through (e)	______

Table 16 is based, roughly, on this 60 per cent standard. It assumes a two per cent sales-tax rate and a tax of the very broadest scope. For example, the $8 tax credit for food, clothing, and personal expense for a retired, single individual represents an exemption of $400 from tax, at the 2 per cent rate. This is about 60 per cent of his minimum budget requirement for this purpose.[16]

The amount of exemption can be increased or decreased, keeping the relative credit the same for the various compositions of family. Or the relative credit might be varied. Perhaps the credit for some particular status of family might be dropped or another added.

This proposed credit-refund approach is expedient from an administrative point of view. It would be much simpler to administer than the food exemption. It requires only a conceptually simple check on taxpayer honesty.

With the standard and minimum budgets that have been developed there is no longer any necessity for confining credits or exemptions to a constant amount per person. If one accepts the family as the taxable unit, the constant-per-person credit causes appreciable horizontal inequity between families of various composition.[17]

Suppose that a legislature should consider a bit radical or unnecessary this idea of varying the credit on the basis of several factors. It is still feasible to vary the size of credit on the basis of family size alone. If this is desired, it can be done without giving equal credit per person. For this purpose something like the City Worker's Family Budget, with its equivalence scale for families of various size, may serve.

To illustrate the idea, suppose that a basic credit is adopted for a representative family of four. Say that it is $30, which under a 2.0 per cent sales tax exempts $1500, or about one fourth of the City Worker's Family Budget standard, according to the most recent revision. (This would constitute a meager exemption and it is used only for illustrative purposes.) The Bureau of Labor Statistics estimates that a family of two needs only 66 per cent of the income of the family of four in order to attain the same level of welfare. A family of three needs 87 per cent as much; a family of five 120 per cent as much. Other (older) estimates are: one needs 46 per cent; six need 128 per cent; seven or more need 149 per cent.

Adhering roughly to these equivalence estimates, we might set up the following sales-tax credits:[18]

Family size	Credit
One	$15
Two	20
Three	25
Four	30
Five	35
Six	38
Seven and over	40

This type of approach has many advantages over the food-exemption approach. This is because it has greater inherent flexibility. The food-exemption plan is more or less either an "in" or an "out" proposition. We either have a food exemption, or we have none. The credit refund, however, can be increased or reduced fractionally. It can give just about any burden distribution pattern we desire.

The pattern of needs of a family is a complex matter. The family's expenditure on food is not a perfect indicator of it. It makes better sense to utilize the extensive studies that have been compiled for the very purpose of gauging relative needs than it does to trust that food expenditure reflects them.

Contrary to what many think, the food exemption encounters more administrative difficulties than would a credit refund.[19] The principal difficulty under the food exemption is the determination of what is and what is not food. The statutes can never spell this out sufficiently. Let us cite a few examples. In Alabama it was necessary to go to court to prove that self-rising flour was indeed flour and therefore food; in Arkansas, to determine that "butterfats" (statutory "food") included whole milk. A Hershey bar has been found to be a candy and not a food, but a chocolate peppermint has been ruled a food. The sale of a dairy cow—ultimately to be slaughtered for human consumption—has been ruled a food.[20] Coffee and tea have been declared food, but Coca-Cola and Kool Aid have not in Ohio. Ice cream bars are food, but popsicles are not in Ohio.[21] Vitamin preparations and health foods have caused an endless stream of questions. "Metrecal" is food in Texas, but similar competing products are not.

Even so, it must be granted that the food exemption has strong merit. It does effectively eliminate most of the regressivity from the sales tax and it simultaneously reduces or eliminates most of its horizontal inequities. For example, the food exemption virtually eliminates the discrimination against large families. It effectively eliminates the advantages which farmers enjoy over urban dwellers under a sales tax. And food expenditures by family size follow reasonably well the welfare budgets' computed patterns of "need" according to family size.

There are other approaches to improving the equity and administrative feasibility of sales taxes.

One proposal which merits consideration is a combination of the tax-credit refund and the old Ohio-type prepaid-tax-receipts plan. Such a combination can improve distributive equity and administration. Instead of following the schemes just outlined, the tax credit might be based on a refund schedule for each family size according to the actual value of taxable consumption for the tax year. At the same level of consumption the larger family would gain a larger refund than the smaller family. The larger family would therefore pay a lower effective rate of tax.

To get the refund, the family would have to turn in stamps representing consumption purchases. Sellers could be required, as they were in Ohio, to purchase such stamps (or "prepaid tax receipts") from the Department of Taxation or its agents. Then, as sellers make taxable sales, they would reimburse themselves by collecting from buyers, surrendering stamps to the buyers equal to purchase value.

The buyers would have an incentive to demand the stamps because their refunds would be based on the amount of stamps they presented at year's end. If buyers do in fact demand the stamps, it is hard for sellers to evade the tax. The method is not evasion-proof, but if supplemented by a good audit and enforcement program the chances of complete and equitable collection would be excellent. This plan can be integrated with the income tax in states which have both taxes,[22] or it can be implemented alone.

The stamp plan ties the rationale of the tax to consumption: refunds are based on actual consumption purchases. The rationale of the refund not tied to stamps is more flexible. Thus it could be said either that the tax credit is a refund for consumption expenditure or that it is a credit for lowered factor earnings caused by the sales tax.

Although the stamp plan promises fairly efficient compliance, apparently it is expensive.[23]

A sales tax can be transformed into a much more flexible instrument. The devices that we have suggested introduce progressive features. The protection of a minimum is the rationale. If this protection is granted, the rate of progression will be degressive. If we should wish it to be constant or even to accelerate, this too is conceivable under a sales tax.[24]

These proposals should make actual sales taxes into genuine, one-stage retail taxes which will eliminate discrimination against non-integrated firms and against types of enterprise which are now relatively hurt by sales taxes. Collectively, these proposals constitute a radical departure from existing sales-tax practice. But reform is overdue. Most changes in sales-tax laws today are in the right direction, but the pace is unconscionably slow. With the adoption of these suggestions we can surely improve on what has been called the "meat-cleaver approach" to taxation—an approach which has seemingly been all too characteristic of contemporary sales-tax practice.

REFERENCE MATTER

APPENDIX TABLE I. Selected Aspects of Retail-sales and Use-tax Structure and Yield

State	Type of tax	Rate in per cent, July 1, 1963	Year first adopted	Total yield ($ millions), 1962	Per capita yield fiscal 1960	Sales tax as per cent of total taxes fiscal 1960	Legal basis	Per cent distributed to general fund, fiscal 1960 or 1961	Vendors' discount (per cent)	Administration costs as per cent of tax collections, 1960, '61, or '62	Number of auditors and examiners, 1960, '61 or '62
Alabama	Retail sales	3	1937	98.4	$27	32.6	Seller	0.75	Varies	1.85	120
Arizona	General sales	3	1933	78.0	49	38.9	Seller	26.4	None	?	30
Arkansas	Retail sales	3	1935	64.0	31	34.5	Buyer	100	2	Approx. 1.30	29
California	Retail sales	3	1933	777.3	45	33.7	Seller	100	None	1.59	796
Colorado	Retail sales	2	1935	56.2	28	26.1	Buyer	27.9	5	1.64	Approx. 20
Connecticut	Retail sales	3.5	1947	100.0	30	32.5	Seller	0	None	?	50
Florida	Retail sales	3	1935	187.5	34	32.8	Seller	89.4	3	Approx. 1.00	59
Georgia	Retail sales	3	1929	166.3	37	39.6	Seller	100	3	1.16	168
Hawaii	Gross income	3.5	1935	67.4	97	50.0	Seller	72.9	None	0.98	Approx. 20
Illinois	Retail sales	3.5	1933	524.5	37	44.8	Seller	83.3	2	Approx. 1.00	213
Indiana	Retail sales	2	1963	—a	—a	—a	Seller	?	None	—a	—a
	Gross Income	0.5	1933	204.5	40	47.3	Seller	?	None	?	?
Iowa	Retail sales	2	1934	86.9	29	30.4	Buyer	83.5	None	1.27	65
Kansas	Retail sales	2.5	1937	82.2	34	35.5	Buyer	20.0	None	1.05	98
Kentucky	Retail sales	3	1934	99.7	31*	31.0*	Seller	86.3	2	Approx. 1.30	Approx. 90
Louisiana	Retail sales	2	1936	93.7	27	19.5	Buyer	0	2	0.76	32
Maine	Retail sales	3	1951	30.0	28	31.4	Buyer	100	None	1.46	35
Maryland	Retail sales	3	1935	94.0	24	21.6	Seller	100	2	1.14	77
Michigan	Ret. & adj. gross	4	1933	481.7	46	39.7	Seller	37.5	$50/mo.	Approx. 1.00	250
Mississippi	Gross receipts	3	1930	78.9	33	36.9	Seller	78.4	None	1.08	50
Missouri	Retail sales	3b	1934	129.4	27	38.0	Buyer	100.0	3	?	60
Nevada	Retail sales	2	1955	18.2	45	28.8	Seller	100.0	2	1.60	10
New Mexico	Gross receipts	3	1935	37.4	43	33.2	Seller	0c	None	1.90	12
North Carolina	General sales	3	1933	141.7	19	19.2	Seller	100	3	1.34	68
North Dakota	Retail sales	2.25	1935	15.8	25	26.1	Buyer	0c	None	0.90	8
Ohio	Retail sales	3	1935	267.1	27	30.4	Buyer	90.9	2	4.91	435
Oklahoma	Retail sales	2	1933	61.6	24	20.4	Buyer	0	3	1.30	18
Pennsylvania	Ret. (selective)	5	1932	389.6	29	32.0	Buyer	0	2	1.50	485
Rhode Island	Retail sales	3	1947	28.3	29	28.6	Seller	100	None	?	20
South Carolina	Retail sales	3	1951	78.3	28	28.8	Seller	0	Varies	1.54	104
South Dakota	Retail sales	2	1933	17.7	23	29.7	Seller	100	None	0.92	16
Tennessee	Retail sales	3	1947	117.8	29	34.4	seller	0.7	2	0.67	54
Texas	Ret. (limited)	2	1961	148.0	16*	16.0*	Seller	100	None	Approx. 1.30	Approx. 171
Utah	Retail sales	3	1933	40.3	32	28.5	Buyer	86.7	None	0.89	32
Washington	Retail & gross	4	1933	232.8	91	56.8	Buyer	96.0	None	Approx. 0.70	83
West Virginia	Retail & gross	2	1921	44.4	46	47.2	Buyer	0	None	Approx. 1.00	9
Wisconsin	Selective sales	3	1962	57.0	14*	7.0*	Seller	100	None	Approx. 3.33	Approx. 130
Wyoming	Retail sales	2	1935	12.4	37	29.6	Buyer	100	None	1.06	4

* 1962.

For columns 2 and 3 ("Type of tax" and "Rate in per cent, July 1, 1963"): Commerce Clearing House, *All-State Tax Reporter* and *Sales and Use Tax Statutes*, Rules and Regulations of the Various States.

For Column 5: Federation of Tax Administrators, *Administrators News*, March, 1963.

For Columns 6, 7, 9, 10, 11, and 12: Tax Foundation, Inc., *Retail Sales and Individual Income Taxes in State Tax Structures*, Project Note No. 48, January, 1962; and miscellaneous, including estimates from the states.

a Tax is too new for an estimate or record of experience.

b Effective October 13, 1963.

c However, use tax collections are placed 100 per cent in general fund.

APPENDIX TABLE II. Taxable Status of Commodities and Selected Services, July 1963

Category	Alabama	Arizona	Arkansas	California	Colorado	Connecticut	Florida	Georgia	Hawaii	Illinois	Indiana Retail Sales	Indiana Gross Income	Iowa
Food and medicine													
Food consumed off premises	T	T	T	E	T	E	E	T	T	T	T	T	T
Restaurant meals	T	T	T	T	T	Ta	T	T	T	T	T	T	T
School lunches	E	E	E	E	E	E	E	E	E	E	E	E	E
Employee's free meals	E	E	E	E	E	E	E	?	?	E	E	E	E
Medicine and drugs	T	T	T	E	T	E	E	T	T	T	T	T	T
Excise-taxed goods													
Alcoholic beverages	T	T	T	T	E	T	T	T	E	T	?	Te	E
Cigarettes	T	T	E	T	E	E	T	T	E	T	?	Te	E
Motor fuel	E	E	E	E	E	E	E	T	E	T	E	Te	E
*Utility services**													
Gas and electricity*	E	Tj	T	E	T	E	E	T	E	E	T	T	T
Water*	E	Tj	T	E	E	E	E	Ek	E	E	T	T	T
Telephone and telegraph*	E	Tj	T	E	T	E	E	Tg	E	E	T	T	T
Transportation*	E	Tj	E	E	E	E	E	T	E	E	E	T	E
Other selected services													
Hotels, motels, lodging*	E	T	T	E	T	T	T	T	T	E	T	T	E
Admissions and amusements*	T	T	T	E	E	E	T	T	T	E	?	T	T
Repair and installation*	E	E	E	Er	E	E	E	E	T	E	E	T	E
Sales to governments, etc.													
State and local governments	E	T	T	T	E	E	E	E	E	E	E	E	E
Federal government	E	E	E	E	E	E	E	E	E	Es	E	E	E
Educational, charitable, religious organizations	T	E	E	T	E	E	E	T	E	E	E	E	E
Other items													
Newspapers	E	E	E	E	E	E	E	T	T	E	E	E	E
Containers, returnable	T	?	T	T	T	T	T	E	?	?	E	T	T
Containers, nonreturnable	E	E	E	E	E	E	E	E	E	E	E	T	E
Direct sale, farm produce	E	E	E	E	T	E	E	E	E	T	T	T	T

* The taxability status of these services is merely a general summary statement. See Appendix Table IV for specific, precise enumeration.

Sources

Commerce Clearing House, *Sales and Use Tax Statutes*, Rules and Regulations of the Various States; *CCH, All-State Tax Reporter;* Nevada Legislative Tax Study Group, *Financing State and Local Government in Nevada,* January, 1960, pp. 401–404; Tax Foundation, Inc. *Retail Sales and Individual Income Taxes in State Tax Structures,* Project Note No. 48, p. 25; Federation of Tax Administrators, *Administrators News,* January through June; information from tax departments of several states.

Kansas	Kentucky	Louisiana	Maine	Maryland	Michigan	Mississippi	Missouri	Nevada	New Mexico	N. Carolina	N. Dakota	Ohio	Oklahoma	Pennsylvania	Rhode Island	S. Carolina	S. Dakota	Tennessee	Texas	Utah	Washington	W. Virginia	Wisconsin	Wyoming
T	T	T	E	E	T	T	T	T	T	T	T	E	T	E	E	T	T	T	E	T	T	T	E	T
T	T	T	T	T[a]	T	T	T	T	T	T	T	T	T	T[b]	T	T	T	T	T	T	T	T	T	T
E	?	E	E	E	E	E	E	E	?	E	E	E	E	E	E	E	E	E	E	E	E	E	E	E
E	?	E	E	E	T[c]	?	E	?	E	?	?	E	E	E	E	E	?	E	E	E	E	E	E	?
T	T	T	E	E	E[d]	T	T	T	T	E	E	E	T	E	E	T	T	T	E	T	T	T	E	T
E	T	T	E[f]	T	T[g]	T	T	T	T	T[h]	E	E	T[g]	T[g]	T	T	E	T	E	T[g]	T	T	T	E
T[i]	T	T	E	T	T	T[e]	T	T	T	T	E	E	E	E	E	E	E	E	E	T	T	T	T	E
E	E	E	E	E	T[e]	T[e]	E	E	E	E	E	E	E	E	E	E	E	E	E	E	E	E	E	E
T	T	E	T	T	T	T[e]	T	E	T	E	T	E	T	T	T	T[g]	T	E	T	T	E	E	E	T
T	T	E	T	E	E	T[l]	T	E	T	E	T	E	T	T	E	T	E	E	E	E	E	E	E	E
T	T	E	E	T	T	T	E	T	E	T	E	T	T	T	T	T	T	E	T	E	E	E	E[m]	T
E	E	T	E	E	E	T[n]	T	E	E	E	E	E	T	E	E	E	E	T	E	T[g]	E	E	E	T
T	T	T	T	T	T	T	T	E	T	T	T	T	T	T	T	T	T	T	E	T	T	T	T	E
T	T	T	E	E[o]	E	E[o]	T	E	T	T	T	E	T	E	E	E[o]	T	T[p]	E	T	T	E	T[q]	T
E	E	T	E	E	E	T[g]	E	E	E	T	T	E	T	E	E	E	E	E	E	T	T	T	E	T
E	E	T	E	E	E	E	E	E	E	E	E	E	E	E	E	E	E	E	E	E	E	E	E	E
E	E	E	E	E	E	E	E	E	E	E	E	E	E	E	E	E	E	E	E	E	E	E	E	E
E	T[g]	E	E	E	E[t]	E	E	E	E	E	E	E	E	E	E	E	E	E	E	E	E	E	E	E
E	E	E	E	E	E	E	E	E	E	E	E	E	E	E	E	E	E	E	E	E	E	E	E	E
T	E	T	E	T	?	?	T	E	?	E	T	T	T	E	T	T	?	E	T	T	T	T	?	T
E	E	E	E	E	T[u]	E	E	E	T[u]	T[u]	E	E	E	E	E	?	E	E	E	E	E	E	E	E
T	?	E	T	E	T[g]	E	T[g]	E	E	E	T[g]	E[g]	E	E[g]	E	E	E	E	E	E	E	E	E	T

Notes

[a] Meals under $1.00 are exempt.

[b] Meals under $0.50 are exempt.

[c] Taxable at $0.15 per meal.

[d] Only 50 per cent of prescription drugs is exempt.

[e] Special excise tax deductible from gross receipts.

[f] Sold by state liquor store in Maine.

[g] With exceptions.

[h] Beer and some wines are taxed; other liquor is exempt.

[i] Effective June 1, 1961.

[j] At rate of 1.5 per cent.

[k] Only when sold by municipalities.

[l] Except municipally owned.

[m] However, telegraph service to business, industrial, professional, and commercial users is taxed.

[n] Income from transportation of school children under contract with school district is exempt. Intrastate transport of some agricultural products is exempt.

[o] Has an admissions tax.

[p] The theater tax is 1 per cent of gross receipts.

[q] Admissions to motion picture theaters costing $0.75 or less are not taxed.

[r] See Code Amendment of September, 1959.

[s] Sales to federal government were taxable until passage of new laws in 1963.

[t] Sales to charitable organizations are taxable, however.

[u] At reduced rate or wholesale rate.

APPENDIX TABLE III

Taxable Status of Items Employed by Business Enterprises in the Production-Distribution Process, by States, July 1963

	Raw materials, components, etc.	Industrial machines, tools, equipment	Fuel for industrial processing	Office equipment and supplies, display equipment, etc.	Construction materials, supplies, etc.	Feed, seed, fertilizer	Livestock, trees, etc.	Agricultural machines, tools, etc.
Alabama	E	T[a]	E[b]	T	T	E	E	T
Arizona	E	T	T	T	T	E	E	T
Arkansas	E	T[c]	T	T	T	E	E	T
California	E	T	T	T	T	E	E	T
Colorado	E	T	E[b]	T	T	E	E	T
Connecticut	E	E[b]	E[b]	T	T	E	E	T
Florida	E	T	E	T	T	E	E	T
Georgia	E	E[d]	T	T	T	E	E	T
Hawaii	E	T	E	T	T	E	E	T
Illinois	E	T	T	T	T[e]	E	E	T
Indiana								
retail sale	T	E	E	T	T	E	?	E
gross income	T[f]	T[f]	T[f]	T[f]	T[f]	T[f]	T[f]	T[f]
Iowa	E	T[g]	E[b]	T	T	E	E	T
Kansas	E	T	E	T	T	E	E	T
Kentucky	E	E[h]	T[i]	T	T	E	E	T
Louisiana	E	T	E	T	T	E	E	T
Maine	E	T[j]	T	T	T	E	E	T
Maryland	E	T	E[b]	T	T	E	E	T
Michigan	E	E[b]	E[b]	T[k]	T[l]	E	E	E
Mississippi	T[f]	E[m]	T[n]	T	T	E	E	T[o]
Missouri	E	T	T	T	T	E	E	T
Nevada	E	T	T	T	T	E	E	T
New Mexico	T[f]	T[p]	T[f]	T	T	T	E	T
North Carolina	T[f]	T[q]	T[f]	T	T	E	E	T[r]
North Dakota	E	T[g]	T	T	T	E	E	T
Ohio	E	E[b]	E[b]	E[s]	T	E	E	E
Oklahoma	E	E[b]	E[b]	T	T	T[t]	E	T[u]
Pennsylvania	E	E[b]	E[b]	T	T	E	T	E
Rhode Island	E	T	E[b]	T	T	E	E	T
South Carolina	E	E	E[b]	T	T	E	E	E
South Dakota	E	T	T[v]	T	T	E[w]	E	T
Tennessee	E	T[x]	E[b]	T	T	E	E	T
Texas	E	T	E	T	T	E	E	E
Utah	E	T	E	T	T	E[y]	E	T
Washington	E	T	T	T	T	E	E	T
West Virginia	E	E[b]	T	T	T	E	E	E
Wisconsin	E	T	E	T[z]	E	E	E	E
Wyoming	E	T[g]	E[b]	T	T	E	E	T

Key: T = Taxable, E = Exempt.

Sources

Commerce Clearing House, *Sales and Use Tax Statutes*, Rules and Regulations of the Various States; CCH, *All-State Tax Reporter;* and Commerce Clearing House, *State Tax Review;* Clinton Oster, *State Retail Sales Taxation*, p. 85; Ohio Department of Taxation, *Retail Sales Tax Comparative Tables;* Tax Foundation, Inc., *Retail Sales and Individual Income Taxes in State Tax Structures*, Project Note No. 48, p. 25; Federation of Tax Administrators, *Administrators News*, January through June, 1963.

Notes

[a] Rate of 1.5 per cent for most items.

[b] If used "directly" in manufacturing, processing, etc.

[c] Exempt from use tax if used for replacement or expansion of existing facilities.

[d] Machinery used directly for "new and expanded industry" (only) is exempt effective April 1, 1963.

[e] Act of Illinois legislature, 1961, should end long doubt about exemption of construction, building, etc., supplies, equipment, fixtures, and the like. These items were most often not taxed before this action.

[f] Taxed at wholesale or reduced rate.

[g] Exempt when "not readily available" in taxing state.

[h] Machinery used directly for "new and expanded industry" (only) is exempt.

[i] All fuel used in manufacturing, processing, mining, or refining is exempt to the extent that it exceeds 3 per cent of cost of production.

[j] Except expendable items expected life of less than a year.

[k] Offices, etc., related to production and processing are exceptional.

[l] Construction materials for real estate improvement are taxed at a 1 per cent lower rate, effective May 10, 1961.

[m] Gas, petroleum, electricity, and fuels for industrial, commercial, and agricultural purposes are taxed at 1 per cent. Sales in excess of $500 of industrial machinery to be used in the state are exempt.

[n] Gas, petroleum, electricity, and fuels for industrial commercial, and agricultural purposes are taxed at 1 per cent.

[o] Farm tractors taxed at 1 per cent in Mississippi.

[p] Some agricultural machinery and equipment is exempt, however,

[q] Mill machinery, parts, and accessories sold to manufacturers are exempt; agricultural machines, parts, and accessories are exempt; sales of machinery to laundries, dry cleaners, and freezer locker plants are exempt; switchboard equipment is exempt; boats and supplies sold to commercial fishermen are exempt; medical and dental supplies and instruments are exempt; manufactured products sold to other manufacturers, producers, wholesalers, or retailers for resale are exempt. Other items may be taxed.

[r] Taxed at only 1 per cent.

[s] Exemption applies only to property "used directly" in making retail sales (display merchandise, show cases, refrigeration merchandise, shelves, store furniture fixtures, etc.).

[t] Only feed is exempt in Oklahoma.

[u] Trade-in allowance on machinery excluded from sale price.

[v] Exempt from use tax.

[w] Seed for commercial agriculture is taxable in South Dakota.

[x] Machinery for "new and expanded industry" taxed at 1 per cent only.

[y] Seed is taxed if used to grow feedstuffs in Utah.

[z] Office supplies such as forms, paper, other expendables are not taxed.

Retail Sales Taxation of Services in the United States
(as of July, 1963)

	Alabama	Arizona	Arkansas	California	Colorado	Connecticut	Florida	Georgia Hawaii*	Illinois	Indiana* Iowa	Kansas	Kentucky	Louisiana
1. *Personal services*													
Babysitters	Em	Em	Em	Em	Em	Em	Em	Em	Em	Em	Em	Em	Em
Barbers, hairdressers, cosmetologists, and bootblacks	E	E	E	E	Em	E	E[1a]	E	E[1b]	E	E	E[1a]	E[1a]
Chauffeurs	Em	Em	Em	Em	Em	Em	Em	Em	Em	Em	Em	Em	Em
Dressmakers, seamstresses	T	Em	Em	E	Em	Em	Em	Em	Em	Em	Em	Em	T[1e]
Dyers	Em	Em	Em	Em	Em	Em	Em	Em	Em	Em	Em	Em	T
Gardeners	Em	Em	Em	Em	Em	Em	Em	Em	Em	Em	Em	Em	Em
Hospital facilities	E	Em	Em	E	Em	Em	E	Em	Em	E	Em	Em	E
Hospital meals and rooms	E	Em	Em	E	Em	Em	E	Em	Em	E	Em	Em	Em
Hotels, motels	E[1h]	T	T[1i]	Em	T	T[1i]	T	T[1i]	E	E	T	T	T
Housekeepers, butlers, maids, etc.	Em	Em	Em	Em	Em	Em	Em	Em	Em	Em	Em	Em	Em
Laundry and dry cleaning	Em	Em	Em	E	Em	E	E	Em	Em	E[1b,1a]	E	E	T
Resorts	E[1h]	T	T[1i]	Em	T	T[1i]	T	T[1i]	E	E	Tm	T	Tm
Rooming and boarding houses	E[1j]	T	T[1i]	Em	T	T[1i]	T	Em	E	E	Em	Em	E
Shoemakers, repairers (except factory)	E[1b]	E[1b]	Em	E[1k]	Em	E[1b]	Em	Em	Em	E[1a]	E[1b]	E[1a]	T
Summer camps	Em	Tm	Tm	E[1m]	T	E	Tm	T[1i]	E	Em	Em	Em	Tm
Trailers	T	Em	Em	Em	Em	T[1f]	Em	Em	E[1b]	Em	Em	Em	T[1n]
Trailer camps	Em	T	Em	Em	T	Em	T	Tm	E	Em	Em	Em	E
2. *Repair, improvement and kindred workers' services*													
Automobile painting	E	E[2a]	Em	E	Em	Em	E[2b]	Em	Em	E	E[2a]	Em	T
Blacksmiths	Em	Em	Em	Em	Em	Em	Em	Em	E[2a]	E	Em	Em	Tm
Bookbinders	Em	Em	Tm	E[2a]	Em	Em	Em	Em	Em	E	Em	Em	Em
Brickmasons, stonemasons, tilesetters	E[2a]	Em	Em	Em	Em	Em	E[2a,2b]	Em	Em	Em	E[2b]	E[2b]	Em
Cabinetmakers	E[2a]	Em	Em	Em	T[2c]	Em	E[2a,2b]	Em	Em	Em	T	Em	Em
Carpenters	E[2a]	Em	Em	Em	Em	Em	E[2a,2b]	Em	Em	Em	E[2b]	E[2b]	Em
Cement and concrete finishers	E[2a]	Em	Em	Em	Em	Em	E[2a,2b]	Em	Em	Em	E[2b]	E[2b]	Em
Electricians	E[2a]	Em	Em	Em	Em	Em	E[2a,2b]	Em	Em	Em	E[2b]	E[2b]	Em
Fumigators	Em	Tm	Em	Em	Em	Em	E[2b]	Em	Em	E	Em	Em	Em
House movers	Em	Em	Em	Em	Em	Em	Em	Em	Em	Em	Em	Em	Em
Installation	E[2d]	E[2d]	E[2d]	E[2d]	E[2d]	E[2d]	E[2d]	E[2d]	E[2d]	E[2d]	E[2a]	E[2d]	T
Jewelers, watchmakers, goldsmiths, and silversmiths	E[2a]	E[2a]	Em	E[2a]	Em	E[2a]	E[2a,2b]	Em	E[2a]	E[2a]	E[2a]	Em	T
Land clearing	Em	T	Em	Em	Em	Em	Em	E	Em	Em	Em	Em	Em
Mattress renovators	Em	Em	Em	Em	Em	Em	E[2a,2b]	Em	Em	E[2b]	E[2a]	E[2b]	Tm
Mechanics and repairmen: air conditioning, heating and refrigeration	E[2a]	E[2a]	Em	E[2a]	Em	Em	E[2a,2b]	Em	E[2a]	Em	Em	Em	T
Mechanics and repairmen: automobile	E[2a]	E[2a]	Em	E[2a]	Em	E[2a]	E[2a,2b]	Em	E[2a]	E[2a]	E[2a]	Em	T
Painters	E[2a]	Em	Em	E[2a]	Em	E[2a]	E[2a,2b]	Em	Em	E	E[2b]	E[2b]	Em
Paperhangers	E[2a]	Em	Em	Em	Em	Em	E[2a,2b]	Em	Em	E	E[2b]	E[2b]	Em
Piano and organ tuners and repairmen	E[2a]	Em	Em	Em	Em	E[2a]	E[2a,2b]	Em	Em	Em	Em	Em	Tm
Plasterers	E[2a]	Em	Em	Em	Em	Em	E[2a,2b]	Em	Em	Em	E[2b]	E[2b]	Em
Plumbers and pipefitters	E[2a]	Em	Em	Em	Em	Em	E[2a,2b]	Em	Em	Em	E[2b]	E[2b]	Em
Radio and television technicians	E[2a]	E[2a]	Em	E[2a]	Em	E[2a]	E[2a,2b]	Em	E[2a]	Em	Em	Em	T
Roofers and slaters	E[2a]	Em	Em	Em	Em	Em	E[2a,2b]	Em	Em	Em	E[2b]	E[2b]	Em
Tire and tube repairs	T[2g]	E[2a]	Em	E	Em	E	E	E[2a]	E[2a]	Em	E[2a]	E[2b]	T
Upholsterers	T[2a]	E[2a]	Em	Em	Em	Em	E[2a,2b]	Em	E[2a]	E[2b]	Em	Em	T

* No research for this particular table.

T = Taxable Em = Not mentioned explicitly in the tax law or regulation, but implicitly exempt.
E = Exempt Tm = Not mentioned explicitly in the tax law or regulation, but implicitly taxable.

Maine	Maryland	Michigan	Mississippi	Missouri	Nevada	North Carolina	North Dakota	Ohio	Oklahoma	Pennsylvania	Rhode Island	South Carolina	South Dakota	Tennessee	Texas	Utah	Washington	West Virginia	Wisconsin	Wyoming
Em	Em	Em	Em	Em	Em	Em	Em	Em	Em	Em	Em	Em	Em	Em	Em	Em	Em	Em	Em	Em
E	E	E[1a]	Tm	E[1a]	E[1a]	E[1a]	E	Em	E[1a]	E[1a]	E	E	E	E[1a]	Em	E[1a]	E[1c]	E[1d]	Em	E[1a]
Em	Em	Em	Em	Em	Em	Em	Em	Em	Em	Em	Em	Em	Em	Em	Em	Em	Em	Em	Em	Em
Em	Em	Em	Tm	E[1a]	Em	Em	Em	Em	T[1f]	Tm	E[1a]	Em	Em	Em	Em	Em	Tm	Tm	Em	Em
Em	Em	Em	T[1g]	E[1a]	E[1a]	Em	Em	Em	Em	T	E[1a]	T	E	Em	Em	Em	Tm	Tm	Em	Em
Em	Em	Em	Em	Em	Em	Em	Em	Em	Em	Em	Em	Em	Em	Em	Em	Em	T	Em	Em	Em
Em	Em	Em	E	Em	E	E	E	Em	Em	Em	Em	E[1a]	E	Em	Em	Em	E	Em	Em	E
Em	Em	Em	E	Em	E	E	E	Em	Em	Em	Em	E	E	Em	Em	Em	E	Em	Em	E
T	T	T	T	T	Em	T	T	T	T	Em	E	T	T	T	Em	T[1i]	T	T	T	Em
Em	Em	Em	Em	Em	Em	Em	Em	Em	Em	Em	Em	Em	Em	Em	Em	Em	Em	Em	Em	Em
Em	E[1a]	E	T	T	E[1a]	E	T	Em	E[1a]	T	E	T	E	T[1a]	Em	T	T	T	Em	E
T	Tm	Tm	T	T	Em	T	E	T	T	Em	E	T	E	T	Em	T	T	T	T	Em
T	Em	T[1i]	Em	Em	Em	T[1i]	E	E[1i]	T	Em	E	T[1i]	T	T[1i]	Em	T[1i]	T[1i]	T	T[1i]	Em
E[1b,1a]	Em	E[1l]	T[1g]	E[1a]	E[1a]	E[1b]	E	Em	E[1a]	T	E[1a]	E[1a]	E	E[1a]	Em	Em	T	Tm	Em	E
T	Tm	Tm	Tm	Tm	Em	Tm	Em	Em	T	Em	Em	Tm	Em	Tm	Em	Em	Tm	Tm	Em	Em
Em	Em	E	T	Em	Em	Em	Em	Em	T[1f]	E[1b]	Em	Em	Em	Em	Em	Em	Tm	Tm	Em	Em
T	Em	Tm	Em	E[1i]	Em	Em	Em	Em	Em	Em	Em	Em	Em	E	Em	T[1i]	Em	E	Em	Em
E	Em	Em	Tm	E[2b]	E	E[2b]	E	Em	E[2b]	T	Em	E[2b]	Em	E[2b]	Em	T	T	T	Em	Em
Em	Em	E[2a]	Tm	E[2b]	Em	Em	E	Em	E[2b]	Tm	Em	Em	E	Em	Em	Em	Tm	Tm	Em	Em
E	Em	E[2b]	Em	E[2b]	Em	E	E	Em	Em	E	Em	E	Em	Em	T	Em	Tm	Tm	Em	Em
Em	Em	E[2b]	E[2a]	Em	Em	Em	Em	Em	Em	Em	Em	Em	Em	Em	Em	Em	Em	Tm	Em	Em
Em	Em	Em	E[2a]	T	Em	Em	Em	Em	Em	Em	Em	Em	Em	Em	Em	Em	Em	Tm	Em	Em
E[2a,2b]	Em	E[2b]	E[2a]	Em	Em	Em	Em	Em	E[2b]	Em	Em	Em	Em	Em	Em	Em	Em	Tm	Em	Em
Em	Em	Em	Em	Em	Em	Em	Em	Em	Em	Em	Em	Em	Em	Em	Em	Em	Em	Tm	Em	Em
E[2a,2b]	Em	E[2b]	T	Em	Em	Em	Em	Em	Em	Em	Em	Em	E[2a]	Em	Em	Em	Em	Tm	Em	Em
Em	E[2b]	Em	T	Em	Em	Em	Em	Em	E[2b]	Em	Em	Em	Em	Em	Em	Em	T	T	Em	Em
Em	Em	Em	Em	Em	Em	Em	Em	Em	Em	Em	Em	Em	Em	Em	Em	Em	T	Tm	Em	Em
E[2a]	E	Em	E[2d]	E[2d]	Em	E[2d]	Em	E	E[2d]	T	E	E[2d]	Em	E[2d]	E	E[2d]	Tm	Tm	E	Em
E[2a,2b]	E[2a,2b]	Em	T[2e]	E[2a]	E[2b]	E[2a]	T	Em	E[2b]	T	E[2b]	E[2b]	E	E[2a]	Em	Em	T	Tm	Em	E[2b]
Em	Em	E	Em	Em	Em	Em	Em	Em	Em	Em	Em	Em	Em	Em	Em	Em	T	T	Em	Em
Em	Em	Em	T[2e]	Em	Em	Em	T	Em	Em	Tm	Em	Em	T[2f]	Em	Em	T	Tm	Tm	Em	Em
Em	Em	E[2a]	T	Em	E[2a]	Em	T	Em	Em	T	E[2a]	Em	Em	E[2a]	Em	T	T	Tm	Em	T
E[2a]	E[2a,2b]	E[2a]	Tm	E[2a]	E[2a]	E[2a]	T	Em	Em	T	E[2a]	E[2a]	Em	E[2a]	Em	T	T	Tm	Em	T
Em	Em	Em	T	Em	Em	Em	T	Em	E[2b]	Em	E	E	E	Em	Em	Em	T	T	Em	Em
Em	Em	Em	Em	E[2a]	Em	Em	T	Em	E[2b]	Em	Em	Em	E	Em	Em	Em	T	T	Em	Em
Em	Em	E[2a]	Tm	Em	Em	E[2a]	Em	T	Em	Em	T	Em	Em	Em	T	Tm	Tm	Em	Em	T
Em	Em	Em	Em	Em	Em	Em	T	Em	Em	Em	Em	Em	Em	Em	Em	Em	T	Em	Em	Em
E[2a,2b]	Em	E[2b]	T	Em	Em	Em	T	Em	E[2b]	Em	Em	Em	E	Em	Em	Em	Tm	Em	Em	Em
E[2a]	Em	E[2a]	T[2e]	Em	E[2a]	Em	Em	Em	Em	T	E[2a]	E[2a]	Em	Em	Em	T	Tm	Tm	Em	T
Em	Em	Em	E	Em	Em	Em	T	Em	Em	Em	Em	Em	Em	Em	Em	Em	Tm	Em	Em	Em
E[2a]	E	Em	T[2e]	E[2b]	E[2b]	E	T	Em	Em	T	E[2b]	Em	T[2h]	E	Em	T	Tm	Tm	Em	T
Em	Em	E[2b]	T[2e]	E[2a]	Em	Em	T	Em	Em	T	E[2a]	Em	Em	Em	Em	T	Tm	Tm	Em	Em

APPENDIX TABLE IV · (*Continued*)

	Alabama	Arizona	Arkansas	California	Colorado	Connecticut	Florida	Georgia / Hawaii*	Illinois	Indiana* / Iowa	Kansas	Kentucky	Louisiana
3. *Communication, transportation and other public services*													
Air transportation	E3a	T	Em	Em	Em	Em	E	T	Em	Em	Em	Em	Em
Electric light and power	E	T	T	E	T	E	E	T	Em	T	T	T	Em
Natural gas	E	T	T	E	T	E	E	T	Em	T	T	T	Em
Pipelines	E	T	Em	E	Em	Em	Em	T3d	E3e	E3e	E3f	E	E3e
Railroad express service	E3e	T	E3e	E3e	E3e	E3e	E	T3d	E3e	E3e	E3f	E3e	E3e
Sewage disposal	Em	Em	Em	Em	Em	Em	Em	Em	Em	Em	Em	T	Em
Street railways and bus lines	E	T	E	Em	Em	Em	Em	T	Em	Em	Em	E3e	E
Taxi cabs	E	T	Em	Em	Em	Em	E	T	Em	Em	Em	Em	E
Telegraph	Em	T	T	E	T	E	E	T3g	Em	T	T	T	Em
Telephone	Em	T	T	E	T	E	E	Tm	Em	T	T	T	Em
Trucking service	E3e	T	E3e	E3e	E3e	E3e	E	T3g	E3f	E3f	E3f	E3e	E3e
Warehousing and storage	E	Em	Em	Em	Em	Em	E	Em	E	Em	Em	Em	T
Water	E	T	T	E	Em	Em	E	Em	Em	T	T	T	Em
Water transportation	E3e	Tm	E3e	E3e	E3e	E3e	Em	T3g	E3e	E3c	E3f	E3e	E3e
4. *Amusement and recreation services*													
Amusement parks	T	T	Tm	Em	Em	Em	T	T	E	Tm	T	T	Tm
Athletic contests	T	T	T	Em	Em	Em	T	T	Em	T	T	T	T4b
Bowling alleys	T	T	Tm	Em	Em	Em	Tm	T	E	E	Tm	T	T
Carnivals, circuses	Tm	T	Tm	Em	Em	Em	Tm	Tm	E	Tm	Tm	Tm	Tm
Golf courses	T	Tm	Tm	Em	Em	Em	E	Tm	E	Tm	Tm	E	T
Jukeboxes	T	T	Em	Em	Em	Em	T	T	Em	T	T	Tm	Tm
Opera houses	T	T	Tm	Em	Em	Em	T	T	E	Tm	T	T	Tm
Pool, billiards	T	T	Tm	Em	Em	Em	E	T	E	Tm	T	Tm	Tm
Private clubs	Tm	Tm	Tm	Em	Em	Em	Tm	T	Em	Tm	Tm	Em	Tm
Public dance halls	T	T	Tm	Em	Em	Em	Tm	T	E	Tm	T	E4c	Tm
Race tracks	T	T	Tm	Em	Em	Em	T	T	Em	Tm	T	E4d	Tm
Skating rinks	T	Tm	Tm	Em	Em	Em	T	T	Em	T	T	E4c	Tm
Ski lifts	Em	Tm	Em	Em	Em	Em	Em	Em	Em	Em	Tm	Tm	Tm
Slot machines, mechanical horses, etc.	T	T	Em	Em	Em	Em	T	T	Em	T	T	T	Tm
Swimming pools	T	Tm	Tm	Em	Em	Em	E	T	E	T	T	T	Tm
Theaters, motion picture houses	T4e	T	Tm	Em	Em	Em	T	T	E	Tm	Tm	T	T
5. *Professional, technical, and related services*													
Accountants, auditors, bookkeepers	E	E	Em	Em	Em	Em	Em	Em	Em	Em	Em	Em	Em
Architects	Em	Em	Em	Em	Em	Em	Em	Em	Em	Em	E	E5a	Em
Chiropractors	E5d	Em	Em	E	Em	Em	Em	Em	E5d	Em	Em	Em	Em
Cremators	Em	Em	Em	Em	Em	E	Em	Em	Em	Em	Em	Em	Tm
Dentists	E5d	E	Em	E5d	Em	Em	E5d	Em	E5d	E5a	E	E5d	E5d
Engravers	T5e	T	Tm	Tm	Em	T	Em	Em	Em	Em	Em	Em	Tm
Florists	T	T	T	T	T	T	T	Tm	T	T	T	T	T
Florists' telegraphic	T5f	T	T	T	T	T	T	Tm	T	T	T	T	T
Interior decorators	Em	Em	Em	Em	Em	Em	E5g	Em	Em	E	Em	Em	Em
Lawyers	E	Em	Em	Em	Em	Em	Em	Em	Em	Em	Em	Em	Em
Morticians, embalmers, et al.	E5d	E5d	Em	E5d	E5d	E5d	T5h	Em	E	E5d	T	E5a	T
Ophthalmologists, oculists, optometrists	E5d	Em	Em	E5d	E	E5d	E5d	E5a	E5d	E5a	E5d	E5a,5d	E5d
Osteopaths	E5d	Em	Em	Em	Em	Em	Em	Em	E5d	Em	Em	Em	Em
Photographers	T5k	T5l	T	T5k	T	T	T5k	E5m	T5k	T	T	E5a	T5k
Printing	T5g	T5g	T	T	T	T	T	T	T5g	T	T	T	T
Physicians, surgeons	E5d	E5d	Em	E	Em	Em	E5d	Em	E5d	E5a	E	E5d	E5d
Real estate agents and brokers	Em	Em	Em	Em	Em	Em	Em	Em	Em	Em	Em	Em	Em
Registered nurses, practical nurses and mid-wives	E5d	Em	Em	Em	Em	Em	Em	Em	Em	Em	Em	Em	Em
Stock and bond brokers	Em	Em	Em	Em	Em	Em	Em	Em	Em	Em	Em	Em	E
Taxidermists	Em	Em	Em	E5m	Em	Em	E5a	Em	Em	Em	Em	E5a	Tm
Therapists and healers	E5d	Em	Em	Em	Em	Em	Em	Em	Em	Em	Em	Em	Em
Veterinarians	E	Em	Em	Em	Em	Em	E	Em	E5a	E5d	E	E	Em

T = Taxable   Em = Not mentioned explicitly in the tax law or **regulation,** but implicitly exempt.
E = Exempt   Tm = Not mentioned explicitly in the tax law or **regulation,** but implicitly taxable.

Maine	Maryland	Michigan	Mississippi	Missouri	Nevada	North Carolina	North Dakota	Ohio	Oklahoma	Pennsylvania	Rhode Island	South Carolina	South Dakota	Tennessee	Texas	Utah	Washington	West Virginia	Wisconsin	Wyoming
Em	Em	Em	T	T	Em	Em	Em	Em	T	E	Em	Em	Em	Em	Em	Tm	E[3b]	E[3c]	Em	T
Tm	T	T	T	T	E	E	T	E	T	Tm	T	T	T	Em	T	Tm	E[3b]	E[3c]	Em	T
Tm	T	T	T	T	E	Em	T	E	T	Tm	T	Em	T	Em	T	Tm	E[3b]	E[3a]	Em	T
E[3e]	E[3f]	E[3e]	T	Tm	Em	Em	Em	Em	Em	Em	Em	Em	Em	Em	Em	E	Em	E[3c]	Em	Em
E[3e]	E[3f]	E[3e]	T	T[3e]	Em	Em	Em	Em	Tm	Em	Em	E[3e]	E[3e]	E[3e]	E[3e]	Em	E[3e]	E[3c]	Em	T
Em	Em	Em	Em	Em	Em	Em	Em	Em	Em	Em	Em	Em	Em	Em	Em	Em	Em	E[3c]	Em	Em
Em	Em	Em	E	Em	Em	Em	Em	Em	T	Em	Em	Em	Em	Em	Tm	E[3b]	E[3c]	Em	T
Em	Em	Em	T	Em	Em	Em	Em	Em	T	Em	Em	Em	Em	E	Em	Em	E[3b]	E[3c]	Em	T
Em	E	Em	T	T	Em	Em	T	E	T	T[3h]	T	T	T	T	E	Em	E[3b]	E[3c]	T	T
Em	E	Em	T	T	Em	Em	T	E	T	T[3h]	T	T	T	T	E	Em	E[3b]	E[3c]	T	T
E[3e]	E[3f]	E[3e]	T	Tm	Em	Em	Em	Em	Tm	Em	Em	E[3e]	E[3e]	E[3e]	E[3e]	E[3e]	E[3e]	E[3c]	E[3e]	Em
Em	Em	Em	T	E	Em	Em	Em	Em	Em	Em	Em	Em	Em	Em	Em	Em	E[3i]	E[3c]	Em	Em
Tm	E	E	T	T	E	Em	T	E	E	T[3h]	T	E	T	Em	E	Em	E[3b]	E[3c]	Em	Em
E[3e]	E[3f]	E[3e]	Tm	T[3e]	Em	Em	Em	Em	T	Em	Em	Em	Em	Em	Em	Tm	E[3b]	E[3c]	Em	Tm
Em	Em	Em	Tm	T	Em	Em	Tm	Em	T	Em	Em	Em	Tm	Em	Em	Tm	E[4a]	T	Tm	Tm
Em	Em	Em	Tm	T	Em	Em	Tm	Em	T	Em	Em	Em	T	Em	Em	Tm	E[4a]	T	Tm	T
Em	E	Em	T	E	Em	Em	Tm	Em	T	Em	Em	Em	T	Em	Em	Tm	E[4a]	T	Tm	Tm
Em	Em	Em	Tm	T	T	Em	T	Em	Tm	Em	Em	Em	T	Em	Em	Tm	E[4a]	T	Tm	Tm
Em	E	Em	Tm	E	Em	Em	Tm	Em	T	Em	Em	Em	T	Em	Em	Tm	E[4a]	T	Tm	Tm
Em	Em	Em	E	E	Em	Em	Em	Em	T	Em	Em	E	T	Em	Em	Tm	E[4a]	T	E	Tm
Em	Em	Em	Tm	Tm	Em	Em	Tm	Em	Tm	Em	Em	Em	T	Em	Em	Tm	E[4a]	T	Tm	Tm
Em	E	Em	T	E	Em	Em	Tm	Em	T	Em	Em	Em	T	Em	Em	Tm	E[4a]	T	Tm	Tm
Em	E	Em	Tm	Tm	Em	Em	Tm	Em	Tm	Em	Em	Em	Tm	Em	Em	Tm	E[4a]	Tm	Tm	Tm
Em	E	Em	Tm	Tm	Em	Em	Tm	Em	T	Em	Em	Em	T	Em	Em	Tm	E[4a]	T	Tm	Tm
Em	Em	Em	Tm	Tm	Em	Em	Tm	Em	Tm	Em	Em	Em	T	Em	Em	Tm	E[4a]	T	Tm	Tm
Em	Em	Em	Tm	Tm	Em	Em	T	Em	Tm	Em	Em	Em	T	Em	Em	Tm	E[4a]	T	Tm	Tm
Em	Em	Em	Em	Em	Em	Em	Tm	Em	Tm	Em	Em	Em	Tm	Em	Em	Tm	E[4a]	Tm	Tm	Tm
Em	Em	Em	E	E	Em	Em	Em	Em	T	Em	Em	Em	T	Em	Em	Tm	E[4a]	T	E	T
Em	E	Em	Tm	E	Em	Em	Tm	Em	T	Em	Em	Em	T	Em	Em	Tm	E[4a]	T	Tm	Tm
Em	Em	Em	Tm	Tm	Em	Tm	Tm	Em	Tm	Em	Em	Em	T	Em	Em	Tm	E[4a]	T	T	Tm
Em	Em	Em	Em	Em	Em	Em	Em	Em	E[5a]	Em	Em	E	Em	Em	Em	Em	E[5b]	E[5c]	Em	Em
Em	Em	Em	Em	Em	Em	Em	Em	Em	E[5a]	Em	E	E	Em	Em	Em	Em	E[5b]	E[5c]	Em	Em
Em	Em	Em	Em	E[5a]	Em	Em	Em	Em	Em	Em	Em	E	Em	Em	Em	Em	E[5b]	E[5c]	Em	Em
Em	Em	Em	Em	Em	Em	Em	Em	Em	Em	Em	Em	Em	Em	Em	Em	Em	E[5b]	E[5c]	Em	Em
Em	Em	E	E[5d]	E[5a]	E[5a]	Em	Em	Em	E[5a]	Em	E[5a]	E	E	E	Em	E[5a]	E[5b]	E[5c]	Em	E
T	Em	Em	Tm	Tm	Tm	Tm	Em	Em	Tm	Tm	T	Tm	T	Tm	Tm	T	Tm	Tm	Em	Em
T	T	T	T	T	T	T	T	T	T	T	T	T	T	T	T	T	T	T	Em	T
T	T	T	T	T	T	T	T	T	T	T	T	T	T	T	T	T	T	T	Em	T
Em	Em	Em	Tm	E[5a]	Em	Em	Em	Em	Em	Em	Em	Em	E	Em	Em	Em	E[5b]	Tm	Em	Em
Em	Em	Em	Em	Em	Em	Em	Em	Em	E[5a]	E	E	E	Em	Em	Em	Em	E[5b]	E[5c]	Em	Em
E[5a]	E[5a]	E	Em	E[5d]	E[5d]	T[5i]	E[5d]	E[5d]	E[5d]	E[5d]	Em	E[5d]	E[5d]	T[5h]	Em	E[5d]	T[5j]	E[5c]	Em	T[5j]
E[5a]	E	E[5a]	E[5a]	E[5a]	E[5a]	E	E	Em	E[5a]	E	E[5a]	E	E	E	Em	E	E[5b]	E[5c]	Em	E
Em	Em	Em	Em	E[5a]	Em	Em	Em	Em	Em	Em	Em	Em	Em	Em	Em	Em	E[5b]	E[5c]	Em	Em
E	E[5m]	E[5m]	T	T[5k]	T[5k]	T	T[5k]	T	T	T	T[5k]	Tm	T[5k]	T[5k]	T[5k]	E[5a]	E[5b]	Tm	Em	T[5k]
T	T	E[5g]	T	T	T	T	T	T	T	T	T	E	T	Tm	T	Tm	T	T	Em	T
Em	E[5d]	E[5a]	E	E	E[5a]	Em	E	Em	E[5a]	E	E	E[5a]	E	E[5a]	Em	E[5a]	E[5b]	E[5c]	Em	E[5a]
Em	Em	Em	Em	Em	Em	Em	Em	Em	Em	Em	Em	Em	Em	Em	Em	Em	E[5b]	E[5c]	Em	Em
Em	Em	Em	Em	Em	Em	Em	Em	Em	Em	Em	Em	Em	Em	Em	Em	Em	E[5b]	E[5c]	Em	Em
Em	Em	Em	Em	Em	Em	Em	Em	Em	Em	Em	Em	Em	Em	Em	Em	Em	E[5b]	E[5c]	Em	Em
Em	Em	Em	Tm	Em	E[5a]	Em	Em	Em	Em	T	Em	Em	Em	Em	Em	Em	E[5b]	E[5c]	Em	Em
Em	Em	Em	Em	Em	Em	Em	Em	Em	Em	Em	Em	Em	Em	Em	Em	Em	Em	E[5c]	Em	Em
Em	Em	Em	Em	E[5a]	Em	Em	E	E	E[5a]	E	E	E	Em	Em	Em	Em	E[5b]	E[5c]	Em	Em

APPENDIX TABLE IV · *(Continued)*

	Alabama	Arizona	Arkansas	California	Colorado	Connecticut	Florida	Georgia Hawaii*	Illinois	Indiana* Iowa	Kansas	Kentucky	Louisiana
6. *Miscellaneous business services*													
Advertising, radio, and television	Em	T	Em	E	Em	Em	E	Em	Em	Em	Em	Em	Tm
Advertising space, newspaper	Em	T	E	E	Em	Em	E	Em	T	E	Em	Em	Tm
Armored car service	Em	Tm	Em	Em	Em	Em	Em	Em	Em	Em	Em	Em	Em
Auctioneers	E[6b]	Em	Em	Em	Em	Em	Em	Em	Em	Em	Em	Em	Em
Advertising agencies	E	T	E	E[6d]	Em	Em	Em	Em	Em	E	Em	Em	T
Automobile rentals	Em	T	T	T	T	T	T	T	T	E	T	T	T
Automobile towing	Em	Em	Em	Em	Em	Em	Em	Em	Em	Em	Em	Em	Em
Diaper service	Em	Tm	Tm	Tm	Em	Em	Tm	T	Em	Em	Tm	Em	Tm
Linen service	Em	Tm	Tm	Tm	Em	Em	T	T	Em	Em	Tm	E	Tm
Motion picture film rentals	E	Tm	Em	Tm	Em	Em	T	E	Em	Em	T	E	T
Parking and garage rental	T[6f]	T	Em	Em	Em	Em	E	Em	Em	Em	Em	Em	T
Photostating, blueprinting	Em	Em	Em	T	Em	Tm	T	E[6d]	T[6e]	T	T	T	T
Piped music service	T	Em	Em	Em	Em	Em	E	Em	Em	Em	Em	Em	Em
Rent: office buildings	Em	Tm	Tm	Em	Em	Em	Em	Em	E	Em	Em	Em	Em
Rent: residential, and apartment houses	Em	Em	Em	Em	Em	Em	Em	Em	E	Em	Em	Em	Em
Renting and leasing of tools	Em	Tm	T	T	T	T	Tm	T	T	E[6h]	T	E	T
Sign painting	Em	T	Em	T	Em	E	T	Em	Em	E	E	T	T[6i]
Stud fees	Em	Em	Em	Em	Em	Em	Em	Em	Em	Em	Em	Em	Em

T = Taxable   Em = Not mentioned explicitly in the tax law or regulation, but implicitly exempt.
E = Exempt   Tm = Not mentioned explicitly in the tax law or regulation, but implicitly taxable.

Source

Compiled from Commerce Clearing House, *All-State Sales Tax Reporter*. Compare with Dean Zehor and Edward Failor, *State Sales Taxes on Services* (Ames, Iowa: Institute of Public Affairs, State University of Iowa, December, 1954), pp. 20, 21.

Notes

1. Personal Services

[1a] Individuals performing this service are consumers of the materials and the supplies they use in their work and are subject to the tax thereon.

[1b] Labor and parts must be billed separately. Only parts or sales of tangible personal property are subject to the sales tax.

[1c] Taxed under the Business and Occupation Tax. Rates vary from $\frac{1}{8}$ per cent to 1 per cent. Professional and technical services are taxed at a rate of 1 per cent.

[1d] Exempt from the sales tax but subject to the Occupation Gross Income Tax. Rates vary from a fraction of a per cent to 7.85 per cent.

[1e] Tax applies to the renovators of old clothing.

[1f] Such receipts are subject to sales taxation if the item is made to order.

[1g] Tax applies to the gross income of the business unless services are rendered by a natural person who employs no assistant.

[1h] Such receipts are not subject to sales taxation. However, Alabama has a special lodgings tax.

[1i] Tax applies only to "transient guests," i.e. those who rent for less than a month.

[1j] If billed separately, only the meals are subject to the sales tax.

[1k] If a single charge is made, the tax applies to 25 per cent of the selling price.

[1l] Subject to tax is 35 per cent of the charge.

[1m] If billed separately, tax applies only to meals and other tangible personal property.

[1n] Tax applies to 50 per cent of the entire amount charged.

Maine	Maryland	Michigan	Mississippi	Missouri	Nevada	North Carolina	North Dakota	Ohio	Oklahoma	Pennsylvania	Rhode Island	South Carolina	South Dakota	Tennessee	Texas	Utah	Washington	West Virginia	Wisconsin	Wyoming
Em	E	Em	Em	Em	Em	E	Em	Em	Tm	Em	Em	Em	Em	Em	Em	Em	Em	T	Em	Em
Em	E	Em	Em	Em	Em	E	E	Em	E	Em	Em	Em	E	E	Em	E	Em	T	Em	Em
Em	Em	Em	Em	Em	Em	Em	Em	Em	Em	Em	Em	Em	Em	Em	Em	Em	E[6a]	Em	Em	Em
Em	Em	Em	Em	Em	Em	Em	Em	Em	Em	Em	Em	E	Em	Em	E	Em	E[6a]	E[6c]	Em	E
Em	Em	E	Tm	Em	E	Em	Em	Em	T	E[6e]	E[6e]	Em	Em	E	E	Em	E[6a]	T	Em	E
T	T	T	T	T	Em	Tm	Em	Em	Tm	T	Em	Em	Em	Em	E	Em	E[6a]	Tm	Em	Em
Em	Em	Em	Em	Em	Em	Em	Em	Em	Em	E	Em	Em	Em	Em	Em	Em	E[6a]	E[6c]	Em	Em
Em	Em	Em	Tm	T	Em	Tm	Em	E	Tm	E	Em	Em	Em	Em	Em	Em	Em	T	Em	Em
Em	E	E[6e]	T	T	Em	T	Em	E	Tm	T	Em	Em	Em	Em	Tm	Em	Em	T	Em	Em
Tm	T	E	Tm	E	Em	E	E	E	Tm	Tm	E	Em	E	E	T	Em	Em	Tm	Em	Em
Em	Em	Em	T	Em	Em	Em	Em	Em	T	Tm	Em	E	Em	T	E	Em	T	Tm	Em	Em
T[6e]	E[6d]	E[6d]	T[6g]	T	T[6g]	T	Tm	T	T	T	T	Tm	Em	Em	T	Em	T	Tm	Em	Tm
Em	Em	Em	Em	Em	Em	Em	Em	Em	Em	T	Em	Em	Em	Em	Em	Em	Em	Tm	Em	Em
Em	Em	Em	Em	Em	Em	Em	Em	Em	Em	Em	Em	Em	Em	Em	E	Em	E[6a]	E	Em	Em
Em	Em	Em	Em	Em	Em	Em	Em	Em	Em	Em	Em	Em	Em	Em	E	Em	E[6a]	E	Em	Em
T	T	T	T	T	Em	Tm	Em	Em	Tm	Tm	Em	Em	Em	Em	Em	Em	Em	Tm	Em	Em
Em	Em	E	Tm	E[6e]	T	T	E	T	Tm	Tm	E	Em	E	T	E	T	T	Tm	Em	Em
Em	Em	Em	Em	Em	Em	Em	Em	Em	Em	T	Em	E	Em	Em	Em	Em	Em	Em	Em	Em

2. Repair, Improvement, and Kindred
Workers' Services

2[a] Labor and parts must be billed separately. Only parts or sales of tangible personal property are subject to the sales tax.

2[b] Individuals performing this service are consumers of the materials and the supplies they use in their work and are subject to the tax thereon.

2[c] The full selling price of custom made items is subject to the tax.

2[d] Tax does not apply to installation charges if billed separately.

2[e] Tax applies to the gross income of the business unless services are rendered by a natural person who employs no assistant. In this case the amount of the services is deductible.

2[f] Tax applies to 50 per cent of the entire amount charged.

2[g] Tax does not apply to minor parts.

2[h] Tax applies to 50 per cent of total charges made for tire re-treading.

2[i] Such receipts are subject to sales taxation if the item is made to order.

3. Communication, Transportation, and
Other Public Services

3[a] Tax does not apply if rates are fixed by a public service commission.

3[b] The Public Utility Tax applies. Rates vary from $\frac{1}{2}$ per cent to 1 per cent on urban transportation to 3 per cent on communications, power, and most common carriers.

3[c] Exempt from the sales tax but subject to the Occupation Gross Income Tax. Rates vary from a fraction of a per cent to 7.85 per cent.

3[d] Taxable is 40 per cent of the repair charge.

3[e] Exempt if the buyer pays the freight charge directly to the carrier or if title passes at the point of origin.

3[f] Intrastate freight charges are deductible if billed separately.

3[g] Tax applies to intrastate service only.

3[h] Taxed at a special rate.

3[i] Taxed under the Business and Occupation Tax. Rates vary from $\frac{1}{8}$ per cent to 1 per cent. Professional and technical services are taxed at a rate of 1 per cent.

(Notes and Sources for Table IV, continued)

4. Amusement and Recreation Services

[4a] Taxed under the Business and Occupation Tax. Rates vary from ⅛ per cent to 1 per cent. Professional and technical services are taxed at a rate of 1 per cent.

[4b] Tax does not apply to events of schools, colleges, and universities.

[4c] The tax applies to spectator admission charges.

[4d] Taxable under another statute.

[4e] Tax applies to the net admission price if federal and state taxes are collected as separate items

5. Professional, Technical, and Related Services

[5a] Individuals performing this service are consumers of the materials and supplies they use in their work, and are subject to the tax thereon.

[5b] Taxed under the Business and Occupation Tax. Rates vary from ⅛ per cent to 1 per cent. Professional and technical people are taxed at a rate of 1 per cent.

[5c] Exempt from the sales tax but subject to the Occupation Gross Income Tax. Rates vary from a fraction of a per cent to 7.85 per cent.

[5d] Sales of tangible personal property are taxable. Professional services are not.

[5e] The reduced rate of 1½ per cent (which is applied to machines) is applied to these sales.

[5f] If the sale constitutes part of gross receipts, the tax applies.

[5g] No tax is paid if there is no transfer of tangible personal property.

[5h] The amount of the charge in excess of $500 is taxable.

[5i] Tax does not apply to the first $150 of the total.

[5j] Tax applies to 50 per cent of the entire amount charged.

[5k] Charges made for developing negatives belonging to a customer are not subject to sales taxation.

[5l] If the sale is to a final customer it is taxable.

[5m] Labor and parts must be billed separately. Only parts or sales of tangible personal property are subject to the sales tax.

6. Miscellaneous Business Services

[6a] Taxed under the Business and Occupation Tax. Rates vary from ⅛ per cent to 1 per cent. Professional and technical people are taxed at a rate of 1 per cent.

[6b] An auctioneer is not liable for the tax if he has been commissioned to act in the name of the owner. The service rendered by the auctioneer is not subject to the tax.

[6c] Exempt from the sales tax but subject to the Occupation Gross Income Tax. Rates vary from a fraction of a per cent to 7.85 per cent.

[6d] Labor and parts must be billed separately. Only parts or sales of tangible personal property are subject to the sales tax.

[6e] Individuals performing this service are consumers of the materials and the supplies they use in their work, and are subject to the tax thereon.

[6f] Tax applies to gross reciepts accruing from parking facilities at places of amusement.

[6g] If the sale is to a final customer, it is taxable.

[6h] Renters and lessors are considered the consumers or users of the property to be rented: therefore rent receipts are not subject to the tax.

[6i] If the painter furnishes the materials for the sign, then the entire selling price is subject to the tax. If the customer furnishes the materials, the tax does not apply.

APPENDIX TABLE V. Comparison of Sales, Property, and Income Taxes as Devices
for Exporting Burden to Nonresidents: Wisconsin, 1956

PART A: HYPOTHETICAL RETAIL SALES TAXES

Taxpayer category	Total tax collections (before offsets or "exports")	Federal tax offsets		Taxes "exported"		Total: offsets + "exports"	
		Amount	Per cent of total collections	Amount	Per cent of total collections	Amount	Per cent of total collections
*Plan I**							
Households	$ 77,639,942	$7,089,474	9.13	—	—	$ 7,089,474	9.13
Tourists, *et al.*	2,166,000	—	—	$ 2,166,000	100.00	2,166,000	100.00
Business	22,035,296	847,189	3.84	7,361,411	33.41	8,208,600	37.25
Total	$101,841,238	$7,936,663	7.82	$ 9,527,411	9.40	17,464,074	17.15
*Plan II***							
Households	$ 78,634,520	$7,018,873	8.91	—	—	$ 7,018,873	8.91
Tourists, *et al.*	1,749,000	—	—	$ 1,749,000	100.00	1,749,000	100.00
Business	33,052,943	1,270,780	3.88	11,042,124	33.33	12,312,904	37.33
Total	$113,436,463	$8,289,653		$12,791,124		$21,080,777	18.59
*Plan III****							
Households	$ 85,635,436	$7,393,790	8.63	—	—	$ 7,393,790	8.63
Tourists, *et al.*	2,166,000	—	—	$ 2,166,000	100.00	2,166,000	100.00
Business	6,215,681	33,150	5.36	3,042,197	48.95	3,375,347	54.31
Total	$ 94,017,117	$7,726,940		$ 5,208,197		$12,935,137	13.76

PART B: REAL AND PERSONAL PROPERTY TAXES, PERSONAL AND CORPORATE INCOME TAXES

Type of tax	Total collections	Burden borne outside Wisconsin			Estimated per cent of total tax collections borne by non-Wisconsin residents
		Offset against federal taxes	Amount shifted to out-of-state consumers	Amount borne by out-of-state dividend recipients	
Property					
Real					
Case A	$287,146,770	$20,741,489	$35,247,218	$ 745,195	19.76
Case B	287,146,770	22,431,031	32,283,105	1,410,341	19.55
Personal					
Case A	62,209,881	2,503,000	26,300,421	253,354	46.71
Case B	62,209,881	3,921,240	23,812,278	811,694	45.89
Income					
Personal	110,257,481	15,101,120	None	None	13.70
Corporate					
Case A	55,645,628	21,108,967	None	8,310,268	52.87
Case B	55,645,628	15,145,685	10,461,900	5,962,617	56.73

Source and Notes for Part A

University of Wisconsin Tax Study Committee, *Wisconsin's State and Local Tax Burden* (Madison, September, 1959), p. 46.

   * Plan I: 2 per cent tax, broadly taxing tangibles, applying component-part rule to business.

   ** Plan II: 3 per cent tax, taxing tangibles, exempting food, applying component-part rule to business.

   *** Plan III: 2 per cent tax, taxing tangibles, including food, extending tax to services, applying "direct-use" rule to business.

Source for Part B

Author's worksheets for *Wisconsin's State and Local Tax Burden.* For shifting assumptions and other details, see Chapter II, above.

NOTES

Chapter I

1 See John F. Due, *Sales Taxation* (Urbana: University of Illinois Press, 1957).

2 National Planning Association, *Long-Range Projections for Economic Growth: The American Economy in 1970,* Planning Pamphlet No. 107, 1959.

3 Committee for Economic Development, *Trends in Public Expenditures in the Next Decade,* 1959.

4 Dick Netzer, "Financial Needs and Resources Over the Next Decade: State and Local Governments," in *Public Finances, Needs, Sources and Utilization,* National Bureau of Economic Research (Princeton: Princeton University Press, 1961), pp. 23–65.

5 *Ibid.,* "Comments" by Allen Manvel, I. M. Labovity, C. Harry Kahn, and Selma Mushkin, pp. 65–77.

6 Robert J. Lampman, "How Much Government Spending in the 1960's?" *The Quarterly Review of Economics and Business* (February, 1961), pp. 7–17.

7 Robert Lampman, "Paying the Price for Higher Fertility," in *Problems of U.S. Economic Development,* Committee for Economic Development Essay Contest, vol. 2.

8 See Bureau of the Census, *Current Population Reports,* series P–25, No. 187.

Chapter II

1 The leading discussions of the scope of retail sales taxation in the United States relating to business transactions are: Clinton V. Oster, *State Retail Sales Taxation* (Columbus: Ohio State University Bureau of Business Research, 1957), chaps. V, VI; Felix S. Wahraftig, "Meaning of Retail Sales and Storage, Use or Other Consumption Taxes," *Law and Contemporary Problems,* VIII, No. 3 (Duke University School of Law, 1941), 542–60; George D. Brabson, "Analysis of Sales and Use Tax Exemptions with Comment as to More Uniform Applications," *Symposium on Sales Taxation, Vanderbilt Law Review,* IX (February, 1956), 294–315; John F. Due, *Sales Taxation,* chaps. XIV, XVII, XVIII; Denzel C. Cline, "Sales Tax Exemption of Producer Goods," *Proceedings of the National Tax Association* (1952), pp. 618–31; and Milton C. Taylor, "Toward Rationality in a Retail Sales Tax," *National Tax Journal,* III (March, 1952), 79–85.

2 Land and buildings are excluded from tax, however.

3 Wahraftig, in *Law and Contemporary Problems*, VIII, No, 3, 542.

4 *Ibid.*, p. 544.

5 *National Ice and Cold Storage Co.* v. *Pacific Fruit Express Co.* 11 Cal. (2d)283, 79p. (2d)380 (1938); *People* v. *Monterey County Ice and Development Co.*, 29 Cal. App. (2d)421, 84p. (2d)1069 (1938); *Warren* v. *Fink*, 146 Kan. 716, 72p. (2d)968 (1937).

6 *Kirk* v. *Johnson*, 37 Cal. App. (2d)224, 99p. (2d)279 (1940), is typical.

7 *Calbert Mill and Feed Co.* v. *Okla. Tax Comm.*, 109p. (2d)504 (Okla. 1941); *Salt Lake Union Stock Yards* v. *State Tax Comm.*, 93 Utah 166, 71p. (2d) 538 (1937); *Union Stock Yards* v. *State Tax Comm.*, 93 Utah 174, 71p. (2d)542 (1937).

8 *Moore* v. *Arizona Box Co.*, 59 Ariz. 262, 126p. (2d)305 (1942), dealing with vegetable crates; *McCarroll* v. *Scott Paper Box Co.*, 195 Ark. 1105, 115 S.W. (2d)839 (1938), dealing with pasteboard cartons; *Lee* v. *Hector Supply Co.*, 133 Fla. 849, 182 So. 489 (1938), dealing with crates; *American Molasses Co.* v. *McGoldrick*, 256 App. Div. 649, 11 N.Y.S. (2d)289 (1st Dep't. 1939), dealing with barrels, drums, pails; *Sterling Bag Co.* v. *City of New York*, 256 App. Div. 649, (2d)297 (1st Dep't. 1939), dealing with sugar bags. These cases are cited in Arthur S. Northrup, "The Measure of Sales Taxes," *Symposium on Sales Taxation, Vanderbilt Law Review*, IX (February, 1956), 252. The logic is that the price of the container will be reflected in the price of the product when it is sold at retail.

9 *Gay* v. *Supreme Distributors, Inc.*, 54 So. (2d)805 (Fla. 1951); *Department of Treasury* v. *Fairmont Glass*, 113 Ind. App. 684, 49 N.E. (2d)1 (1943); *Coca-Cola Bottling Plants* v. *Johnson*, 147 N.E. 327, 87A (2d)667 (1952). The reasoning behind the taxation of bottles is this. The distributor or bottler is said to buy the bottle. But the bottle is returnable, and the tax is only on the beverage, not on the bottle. The bottle's cost is in the price paid by the customer. But he only pays it as a deposit, since he can return it and get his money back. The resale of the container is not generally taxed.

10 Iowa, *Code of Iowa*, Sec. 422.42.

11 Court decisions and rulings kept the status of building materials in doubt much of the time in Illinois. But two recent cases and the sentiment of the Illinois legislature now leave little room for doubt. In the case of *Materials Service* v. *Isaacs*, decided June 6, 1962, the Supreme Court held that sales of building material to contractors are sales "at retail" and are subject to the occupation (sales) tax. The court, relying on a 1961 decision, *G. S. Lyon & Sons Lumber and Manufacturing* v. *Department of Revenue*, held that the contractors were users of the materials and therefore taxable. Before these two cases it had often appeared that sales of construction items were immune from tax. Construction contractors, at any rate, were generally avoiding liability when they incorporated materials and fixtures into a structure. Immunity seemed to accompany both the sale and the installation of brick, lumber, sheet metal, roofing materials, windows, storm doors and windows, weather stripping, insulation materials, venetian blinds, window shades, awnings, bath tubs, lavatories, sinks, faucets, water pumps, furnaces, boilers, heat-

ing pipes; ventilation, heating, refrigeration or electrical systems; and similar items. See Illinois, *Illinois Code,* Rule 6, cited in Commerce Clearing House *State Tax Reporter,* Illinois, I, p. 6109.

Perhaps a tenable interpretation of Illinois decisions over the years before the Lyons and the Materials Service cases would have been that they were pointing toward the following: a contractor was not "consuming" material when he used it in fabricating or repairing a structure for the property owner. But if he were building a house for resale, the materials sold to him were "consumed" by him and were therefore taxed.

12 Under the new Texas statute, for example, who remits the tax depends on the nature of the contract. The law defines a "contractor" or a "repairman" as the person who performs services upon tangible personal property or real estate. When the performer enters into a lump sum contract, i.e., one in which only one charge is made for both labor and materials, he is considered to be the consumer of the materials used. He must pay the tax. If, however, he makes a separate charge for materials and labor—that is, segregates them—he is considered to be the retailer who is selling the materials to the purchasing party. In the latter case he may give the suppliers resale certificates. But he must add and collect the tax when he bills the customer for the materials.

13 Cline, in *Proceedings of the National Tax Association* (1952), discusses this well.

14 Brabson, in *Symposium on Sales Taxation, Vanderbilt Law Review,* IX (February, 1956), presents extensive case citations and discussion.

15 Ohio, *Ohio Sales and Use Rules,* Rule 43, cited by Oster, *op. cit.,* p. 106.

16 University of Wisconsin Tax Study Committee, *Wisconsin's State and Local Tax Burden: Impact, Incidence and Tax Revision Alternatives* (Madison: September, 1959), pp. 80–109.

17 For definitions of the categories, see the *Wisconsin's State and Local Tax Burden* study, and the Appendixes and study papers.

18 This means that Tax Z excludes construction materials. This is not commonly done, however, in states with direct-use rule.

19 The estimates are now for 1956, and Construction is segregated from Industry, leaving the latter to be composed of manufacturing and mining concerns. The same relationships are assumed to prevail in 1956 as those which prevailed in 1954.

20 Our estimates seem to be in line with others. The estimates for the new "limited sales and use tax" in Texas is 28 per cent. See Texas Research League, "The Sales Tax and Business," *Analyzes,* June, 1961, p. 8. John Due's opinion is that from 20 to 25 per cent of sales-tax revenue comes from taxes on producer goods. See his *Sales Taxation,* p. 299. In Michigan, Musgrave, Daicoff and associates estimated that business paid $50 million. In 1956 this meant that they paid approximately 20 per cent of total yield. See Richard A. Musgrave and Darwin W. Daicoff, "Who Pays the Michigan Taxes?" Michigan Tax Study *Staff Papers* (Lansing: October, 1958), pp. 142 and 177. But Michigan Research Analyst O. T. Wharton thought that the Musgrave-Daicoff figure was an overestimate (letter to John A. Gronouski, Wisconsin Depart-

ment of Taxation, July 15, 1959). Wharton believed that the bulk of the business portion in Michigan came from the sale of vehicles and parts and from the building, lumber, and hardware category. H. C. Stansbury, Director, Department of Revenue, State of North Carolina, estimates that business pays only 8 per cent of total yield in that direct-use state (letter to John Gronouski, May 5, 1959).

21 For reservations on this score, see Chapters III, IV, and VI.

22 Nicholas Kaldor, *An Expenditure Tax* (London: George Allen & Unwin, Ltd., 1955).

23 But it usually exempts livestock, trees, houses, and buildings.

24 For a discussion of this intriguing subject, see Chapter VI, which discusses the Brown-Rolph hypothesis and its related literature.

25 See Robert M. Haig, "The Concept of Income: Economic and Legal Aspects," *The Federal Income Tax* (New York: Columbia University Press, 1921), reprinted in Richard A. Musgrave and Carl S. Shoup, eds., *American Economic Association Readings in the Economics of Taxation* (Homewood, Illinois: Richard D. Irwin, Inc., 1959), pp. 54–76; see also Henry C. Simons, *Personal Income Taxation* (Chicago: University of Chicago Press, 1938).

26 Another defect in taxing social income under an ability-to-pay rationale is said to be that the tax is not personalized. It takes no account of the family status of income recipients. But we are assuming that this can be done under the sales-tax approach (see Chapter VII).

Chapter III

1 Dorothy S. Brady and Rose D. Friedman, "Savings and the Income Distribution," in *Studies in Income and Wealth* (New York: National Bureau of Economic Research, 1947), X, 247–65.

2 James S. Duesenberry, *Income, Saving and the Theory of Consumer Behavior* (Cambridge: Harvard University Press, 1952).

3 For example: Arthur Smithies and J. Mosak, "Forecasting Postwar Demand," *Econometrica*, XIII (January, 1945), 1–14; James Tobin, "Relative Income, Absolute Income and Savings," *Money, Trade and Economic Growth: In Honor of John Henry Williams* (New York: The Macmillan Company, 1951), pp. 135–56.

4 For example: Tobin, *op. cit.;* William Hamburger, "The Relation of Consumption to Wealth and the Wage Rate," *Econometrica*, XXIII (January, 1955), 1–17; Lawrence R. Klein, "Estimating Patterns of Savings Behavior from Sample Survey Data," *Econometrica*, XIX (October, 1951), 438–54; James N. Morgan, "The Motivation of Savers," *Savings in the Modern Economy*, eds. Walter H. Heller, Francis M. Boddy, and Carl L. Nelson (Minneapolis: Minnesota Press, 1953), pp. 213–17; George Katona, Lawrence Klein, John Lansing, and James Morgan, "Statistical Elimination of Economic Relations from Survey Data," *Contribution of Survey Methods to Economics* (New York: Columbia University Press, 1954), pp. 189–240.

5 Franco Modigliani and Richard Brumberg, "Utility Analysis and the Consumption Function: An Interpretation of Cross Section Data," in *Post Keyne-*

sian Economics, ed. Kenneth Kurihara (New Brunswick, New Jersey: Rutgers University Press, 1954), pp. 383–436.

6 Milton Friedman, *A Theory of the Consumption Function* (Princeton: Princeton University Press, for the National Bureau of Economic Research, 1957).

7 This section reviews Friedman, *ibid.,* especially pp. 7–19.

8 *Ibid.,* p. 13.

9 For a similar point along this line utilizing indifference curves (which are not necessarily indifferent!), see Arnold Zellner, "Tests of Some Basic Propositions in the Theory of Consumption," *Proceedings of the American Economic Association* (1959), *American Economic Review,* L (May, 1960), 565–73.

10 Irving Fisher, *The Theory of Interest* (New York: The Macmillan Company, 1930), p. 62.

11 Irwin Friend and Irving B. Kravis, "Consumption Patterns and Permanent Income," *Proceedings of the American Economic Association* (1956), *American Economic Review,* XLVII (May, 1957), 539.

12 This point is suggested by Friend and Kravis, *ibid.,* p. 541.

13 For an extensive critique of the Friedman assumptions and those of the orthodox theory of the consumer, see David P. Lewis, "The Permanent Income Hypothesis: Its Assumptions and Theoretical Basis—A Critical Inquiry" (unpublished Master's thesis, Department of Economics, University of Tennessee, Knoxville, 1959), chaps. II, IV.

14 Duesenberry, *Income, Saving and the Theory of Consumer Behavior;* this section follows Duesenberry's exposition, especially pp. 17–37.

15 *Ibid.,* p. 3.

16 This formulation is that of Harry G. Johnson. See "A Note on the Effect of Income Redistribution on Aggregate Consumption with Interdependent Consumer Preferences," *Econometrica,* XVIII (August, 1951), 295–97.

17 In a letter to the author Friedman writes: "People may in fact be short-sighted and have a brief horizon, yet your or my ethics may still call for taxing them in terms of their long-run wealth position" (letter from Milton Friedman, Chicago, Illinois, November 29, 1960).

18 What is here called the "utilitarian" case for progressivity is more often referred to as the justification based on "sacrifice" theory. It is "utilitarian" in the sense that its roots lie in the Bentham-Mill stream of philosophy. More specifically, in economics it traces from the work of Menger and Jevons and their applications of the felicific calculus.

The basic ideas are not difficult. Government benefits are ignored, but the tax payments which they "require" are assumed to be painful, a "sacrifice." The sacrifice should be distributed equitably. What constitutes equity depends on people's reactions to income. Persons are assumed to be basically alike in their reactions, so that individual differences may be ignored. The assumption is that the only critical variable in the utility derived from income is the amount of income possessed. It seems plausible that the more income one has the less will be his utility from an additional unit of it, say an additional dollar. And the less will be the sacrifice in parting with any marginal dollar. The idea is usually expressed in the short-hand notation that "the marginal utility function for income (money) slopes downward" (assuming marginal utility of income to be plotted on the vertical axis of the graph and the quantity of income on the horizontal axis).

If equity should require inflicting an equal quantity of sacrifice on all tax-payers (equal sacrifice), if the marginal utility of income curve is steeper than a rectangular hyperbola, progressive taxes are required; if less steep than a rectangular hyperbola, regressive taxes are required; if the curve is a rectangular hyperbola, proportional taxes are called for.

If equity should require that all taxpayers should sacrifice the same percentage of total utility (proportional sacrifice), most declining marginal utility of income curves require progressive taxes. A few, however—"Cohen-Stuart curves," after their discoverer—might even require regressive taxes.

If equity should require a minimum of sacrifice on all taxpayers taken collectively (minimum aggregate sacrifice), any decline in the marginal utility curve requires that the taxes be taken from the highest-income taxpayers before any be taken from the less wealthy. In other words, "leveling" is called for.

No elaboration or assessment of these doctrines will be presented at present. Some discussion of their demise is given in the subsequent discussion of welfare economics. For discussions of sacrifice theory the reader untrained in mathematics will find especially helpful Walter Blum and Harry Kalven, *The Uneasy Case for Progressive Taxation* (Chicago: University of Chicago Press, 1953), pp. 39–63; Elmer D. Fagan, "Recent and Contemporary Theories of Progressive Taxation," *Journal of Political Economy,* XLVI (August, 1938), 457–97, reprinted in R. A. Musgrave and Carl S. Shoup, eds., *American Economic Association Readings in the Economics of Taxation* (Homewood, Illinois: Richard D. Irwin, Inc., 1959), pp. 19–53; and Harold M. Groves, *Financing Government* (New York: Henry Holt and Company, 1958), pp. 19–24. For the mathematically initiate, Richard A. Musgrave, *The Theory of Public Finance* (New York: McGraw-Hill Book Company, Inc., 1959), chap. V; and Paul A. Samuelson, *Foundations of Economic Analysis* (Cambridge: Harvard University Press, 1958), pp. 226–28, especially, and chap. VIII are helpful.

19 The case for an exemption of a minimum from tax helps to establish the case for at least some progressivity in the tax system, because unless tax rates are regressive above the minimum, the effective rate of taxation is progressive against total income if a minimum is first exempted.

20 A. C. Pigou, *A Study in Public Finance,* 3rd ed., revised (New York: The Macmillan Company, 1960).

21 This philosophical notion is mainly credited (originally) to Ludwig Wittgenstein, who published his monumental *Tractatus Logico-Philosophicus* in England in 1922, with an introduction by his celebrated mentor, Bertrand Russell. Wittgenstein was concerned with the relation of language to the world. He held that the propositions of speech must reduce to ultimate, atomic "facts." Expressions which are not so reducible are incapable of being either true or false and are therefore meaningless. To understand a proposition is to know what is true if it is the case. If this cannot be accomplished

by observation (scientific test, etc.), it is nonsense, meaningless, or a matter of emotive taste. Bertrand Russell for some while sadly accepted this view that "logic consists simply of tautologies." A. J. Ayer further entrenched the iconoclasm in his influential *Language, Truth and Logic*. In economics its most influential initial spokesman (and misinterpreter) was Lionel Robbins (*An Essay on the Nature and Significance of Economic Science*).

In recent years Wittgenstein, Russell, and Ayer have recanted somewhat. Ayer's new publication *Philosophy and Language* takes the view that the cleavage between ethical and (natural) scientific propositions is not nearly so sharp as he had earlier thought. The propositions of natural science are considerably less reducible to precise, bodily behavior. "What is the case" depends in an important way on the conceptual scheme we utilize. "Objectivity" may be elusive. This view drives Ayer closer to synthesis with the English school of philosophy which is closely akin to American pragmatism (in the line of Peirce, James, and Dewey). This school is perhaps best represented in England by J. Bronowski (see, e.g., his *Science and Human Values*).

22 In the rarefied world of welfare economics the conditions for maximizing the "welfare function" are: (1) prices of goods must be the same for all consumers and must be equal to marginal costs of production; (2) the price of each factor of production must be the same in each of its uses, and equal to the value of its marginal product.

The price of the factor "labor service" is, of course, the wage or salary paid to the person performing the service. The condition specified requires, therefore, that the wage of every individual equal the value of his marginal product. This wage "must" be his return net of taxes because (it is assumed) it is net wages which the laborer considers to be relevant in making his choice between goods (income) and leisure.

A policy aimed at reducing inequality requires that tax rates be higher for "factors" of high productivity than for factors of low productivity. But at the same time taxes must not interfere with the choice between goods and leisure. That is, they must not affect the amount of work done. A progressive tax on labor service, it is assumed, would interfere. Thus the conclusion before Duesenberry was that income equalization could be attained only at the expense of "allocation efficiency" (that is, at the expense of optimum production and exchange conditions).

23 For the demonstration, see Duesenberry, *op. cit.*, pp. 92–104.

24 Duesenberry suggests the kind of operational test which might be performed to gauge a person's "marginal rate of substitution" between income (consumption) for himself and income for others: "We could ask him . . . whether he would rather have his own income increased by 50 per cent while everyone else's increased tenfold, or have his income increased by 10 per cent while others had theirs increased by 10 per cent. It does not seem certain that everyone would prefer the first alternative." *Ibid.*, p. 103.

25 Duesenberry himself suggests this approvingly. He says (p. 104): "We can . . . define . . . utility in either of two ways: (1) in terms of preferences defined by choices between combinations of income for the subject and for

other people, or (2) we can define a measure of welfare independent of avowed preferences. Such a measure can be any objective behavior on the part of people with whose welfare we are concerned."

26 See especially I. M. D. Little, *A Critique of Welfare Economics* (London: Clarendon Press, 1950), chaps. III–VI.

27 See Robert J. Lampman, "Making Utility Predictions Verifiable," *The Southern Economic Journal*, XXII (January, 1956), 360–66.

28 Much of this chapter has proceeded as if the way people spend income is the best gauge of utility from the income. This is the assumption of two of the important relatively recent attempts to measure marginal utility: Irving Fisher, "A Statistical Method for Measuring 'Marginal Utility' and Testing the Justice of a Progressive Income Tax," in *Economic Essays: Contributed in Honor of John Bates Clark,* ed. Jacob H. Hollander (New York: The Macmillan Company, 1927); and Ragnar Frisch, *New Methods of Measuring Marginal Utility* (Tubingen, Germany: J. C. B. Mohr, 1932).

29 This verse *and* its context is borrowed from the brilliant article of Franklin Fisher and Jerome Rothenberg, "How Income Ought to be Distributed: Paradox Lost," *Journal of Political Economy*, LXIX (April, 1961), 162–80.

30 Among the leading articles which set forth objective criteria of social utility are: Elmer D. Fagan, in *Journal of Political Economy*, XLVI (August, 1938), 457–97; Harold M. Groves, "Toward a Social Theory of Progressive Taxation," *National Tax Journal*, IX (March, 1956), 27–34; Robert J. Lampman, in *The Southern Economic Journal*, XXII (January, 1956), 360–66. This approach will be recognized readily as the application of Dewey's instrumental philosophic position, which in its economic application has often been "institutional economics." The most ardent and incisive of the members of this school in defending the social utility approach against the more conventional hedonistic approaches has surely been Clarence E. Ayres.

Chapter IV

1 Franco Modigliani and Richard Brumberg, "Utility Analysis and the Consumption Function: An Interpretation of Cross Section Data," *Post Keynesian Economics,* ed. Kenneth Kurihara, pp. 383–436.

2 See Friedman, *A Theory of the Consumption Function,* pp. 18, 19.

3 David G. Davies, "An Empirical Test of Sales Tax Regressivity," *Journal of Political Economy*, LXVII (February, 1959), 72–78; and "Progressiveness of Sales Taxes in Relation to Various Income Bases," *American Economic Review*, L (December, 1960), 987–95.

We expect sales taxes to look less regressive or to be progressive according to permanent income (as compared with their appearance when "gross" or "net" income is employed as the income base). Saving and tax payments are both increasing functions of "measured" (yearly) gross income. If we omit taxes from the base, and if we posit that saving is a constant rather than an increasing function of disposable income, by hypothesis we eliminate the source of sales-tax regressivity. (Taxes are probably excluded from permanent income because it is the income total with respect to which individuals determine their consumption. Families probably plan their expenditures in terms of the income they expect on the average to have left over after paying personal taxes.) An income tax is often based largely on income before taxes, whereas a retail sales tax excludes the item of taxes in the consumer's budget. Thus, quite aside from the regressivity of the sales tax relative to the income tax caused by the exemption of saving—given the pattern of distribution of saving according to income class—regressivity arises from the fact that taxes (on the whole a progressive factor in budgets) are exempt from sales-tax bases.

By hypothesis, then, the Friedman theory makes sales taxes more progressive than they appear when one-year data are accepted as the bases for the progressivity tests. The critical question, however, is the empirical one: can we substantiate the thesis that permanent consumption is an invariant proportion of permanent income at the various levels of permanent income?

One neglected point should be noted here. It is that we cannot vindicate the Friedman hypothesis solely on the basis of data on disposable income. Important items are ignored under such income data, items which properly are to be counted as "income." Most important of these are: (1) increasing equity in social insurance funds, and (2) unrealized capital gains. Highest income brackets invest heavily in stock. Corporations reinvest earnings, and capital increments remain unrealized. Therefore, if our data *should* indicate that all "permanent" income classes appear to have the same ratio of saving to disposable income, it may indicate nothing more than the fact that the highest brackets take relatively large percentages of their accretion (income) in the form of unrealized capital gain. Because they do so, it might appear with respect to realized disposable income that they have the same saving ratios as lower-income classes.

4 For thorough reviews of studies of sales-tax regressivity and especially of the effect of a food exemption, see Daniel C. Morgan, Jr., "Toward Rationality in Retail Sales Taxation" (unpublished seminar paper, Department of Economics, The University of Wisconsin, Madison), pp. 13–26 (available on loan request). See also, Reed R. Hansen, "The Tax Treatment of Family Income" (unpublished Ph.D. dissertation, Department of Economics, The University of Wisconsin, Madison, 1960), chaps. III–VIII. See also Donald C. Miller, "Sales-Tax Progressivity Attributable to a Food Exemption," *National Tax Journal*, IV (June, 1951), 148–59.

5 The procedure is:
   (1) Classify families according to current "measured" income.
   (2) Compute mean total consumption for each income class or category.
   (3) Compute mean *taxable* consumption (total).

Then k [(3) ÷ (2)] will yield the relationship between permanent taxable consumption and permanent income (k is the permanent-consumption to permanent-income ratio). Friedman posits that there is no correlation between transitory consumption and permanent consumption. So we have for each income class estimates of permanent (total) consumption and permanent sales-taxable consumption, provided that "permanent income" means the same for taxed items as for total consumption. Since $C_p = kY_p$ (permanent consumption is a function k of permanent income),

$$(\overline{C}_{Tx}/\overline{C}_{pt}) \cdot k = \overline{C}_{Tx}/\overline{Y}_{p},$$

where $C_{Tx} =$ permanent taxable consumption, $C_{pt} =$ permanent (total) consumption, and $Y_p =$ permanent income. Mean (total) consumption $\div$ mean income is a measure of k on Friedman assumptions. See Milton Friedman, *A Theory of the Consumption Function*, pp. 207–208.

6 Helen Lamale and Margaret Stotz, "The Interim City Worker's Budget," *Monthly Labor Review*, LXXXIII (August, 1960), 785–808.

7 Interest in progressivity springs from a desire to know how taxes affect the distribution of income or welfare. Welfare, or ability to pay taxes, is a relationship between needs and the resources available to meet those needs. We are increasingly cognizant of the inadequacy of one-year's gross money income as a measure of resources. And we are increasingly alert to the importance of establishing relative needs for families of different composition.

One recent study of the incidence of the property tax showed the importance of the more sophisticated approach to progressivity measurement as contrasted with the more conventional approach. The study concluded that for residential nonfarm home owners the mean effective tax rate decreased with mean money income. In other words, the conventional approach reached the conventional conclusion: the urban property tax is regressive with respect to a money-income base. But then the study established a relationship between family resources and family needs—a family welfare ratio—and presented a distribution of family welfare ratios. Income imputations were added to money income. According to the resulting distribution of welfare, the property tax was roughly proportional.

It would be interesting to know what the same approach would yield for a typical retail sales tax. Our approach in the text is but a crude attempt, motivated by the same reasoning as that which underlies the property tax study.

See James Morgan, Martin David, Wilbur Cohen, Harvey Brazer, *Income and Welfare in the United States* (New York: McGraw-Hill, 1962), chap. XIX.

8 Robert J. Lampman, "The American Tax System and Equalization of Income," *Proceedings of the National Tax Association* (1956), pp. 271–80.

9 We probably do not want to extend this equivalent-income approach to very high incomes. It is doubtful, for example, that we would want to contend that at high levels of income a family of five needs 120 per cent as much as a family of four while a family of two needs only two thirds as much as the family of four in order to attain the same level of welfare. This would be an extension of the view that taxable capacity or welfare should be related to "sacrifice" and that this should be regarded as a per capita matter. A more acceptable view today is that taxable capacity is a family matter and that there is a social interest—harking back to our concept of social utility (Chapter III)—in preserving from taxation basic private amenities of life; and that these amenities increase with family size. But after an allowance is made to safeguard the amenities, children may be regarded as a choice of consumption goods. That is, as we reach high-income levels, children should be regarded

as a choice of consumption, due no special state subsidy. At higher brackets, income is not so much an indicator of "consumption welfare" as it is an indicator of power—power to command all markets, shape the structure of society, etc.

10 This idea can be inferred from William Vickrey, "Resource Distribution Patterns and the Classification of Families," in *Studies in Income and Wealth* (New York: National Bureau of Economic Research, 1947), X, 276–77; perhaps from Friedman, *A Theory of the Consumption Function;* and perhaps from Modigliani and Brumberg, in *Post Keynesian Economics.*

11 See, for example, Joseph P. Driscoll, "Income Averaging for Individual Income Tax Purposes," *Federal Tax Policy for Economic Growth and Stability*, 84th Cong., 1st sess., November 9, 1955, pp. 176–77.

12 It should be kept in mind that our conclusion—that taxing current consumption provides greater neutrality (according to permanent income) than taxing current income—depends on the definition of consumption which we have stipulated. We assume that consumption includes only the use value of durables. It is this consumption which Friedman takes to be a constant percentage of permanent income. To levy taxes on such a base poses administrative problems even for the personalized expenditure tax, as, for example, that proposed by Nicholas Kaldor, *An Expenditure Tax,* especially pp. 195–201. A retail sales tax could not hope to tax consumption as Friedman defines it—as a flow of services in the year of enjoyment. Thus the Friedman hypothesis does not provide a firm foundation for the case for the sales tax on neutrality grounds. It is more convincing as a rationale for a progressive expenditure tax as opposed to a progressive income tax which lacks an averaging scheme. But because of the administrative difficulties of taxing the yearly flow of consumption services under a personal expenditure tax, it is not completely effective as a rationale here either.

13 I am not espousing these views but merely developing the conclusions that seem to follow from the reasoning which underlies the permanent-income hypothesis. My own view is that income averaging over a period of several years at the state level of government, compulsory for all taxpayers, is entirely unrealistic precisely because ability to pay taxes for most families is not a function of long-term (permanent) resource position. Rather, the timing of taxes, to strike when "ships are in rather than at sea," as Professor Harold M. Groves is fond of putting it, is of the essence. The experiments with moving average devices in Great Britain (3-year moving average period), Australia (5-year period), and Wisconsin (3-year period) foundered mainly because they allowed heavy tax liabilities, based on past good years, to fall in lean years. Popular reaction left many tax experts skeptical of the idea of taxpayer neutrality which encompasses a period of several years. My rejection of the idea that ability-to-pay is related to a permanent resource position is closely related to my reluctance to accept the Friedman proposition that consumption is so completely tied to a permanent resource position. If we are to put great emphasis on genuine long-term neutrality in taxation, the only way to do so fully is to encompass an entire lifetime. If we do this,

however, we need to do it at the end of life with a discount factor for the time pattern in which income is received, because leisure and light work loads must be given a value in equating people's relative capacities to pay taxes. Vickrey's lifetime averaging proposal (see note 10 above for Vickrey citation), for example, fails to do this. At the state level of government such an approach is unthinkable. In my opinion it is unfeasible and unnecessary even at the federal level.

14 Reed R. Hansen, "An Empirical Analysis of the Retail Sales Tax With Policy Recommendations," *National Tax Journal,* XV (March, 1962), 1–14.

15 *Ibid.,* 5–6.

16 Friedman, *A Theory of the Consumption Function,* chap. IV.

17 Daniel C. Morgan, Jr., "New Bases for Evaluating Retail Sales Taxation" (unpublished Ph.D. dissertation, Department of Economics, The University of Wisconsin), Appendix D.

18 For a balanced appraisal of the hypothesis, one which is more tentative in its conclusion than this one, see Robert Ferber, "Research on Household Behavior," *American Economic Review,* LII (March, 1962), especially 25–32.

19 L. R. Klein and N. Liviatan, "The Significance of Income Variability on Savings Behaviour," *Bulletin of Oxford University Institute of Statistics,* XIX (May, 1957), 151–60.

20 Ronald Bodkin, "Windfall Income and Consumption," *American Economic Review,* XLIX (September, 1959), 602–14; "Windfall Income and Consumption," in Irwin Friend and Robert Jones, eds., *Proceedings of the Conference on Consumption and Saving,* Philadelphia, 1960, II, 175–88.

21 Robert C. Jones, "Transitory Income and Expenditures on Consumption Categories," *Proceedings of the American Economic Association* (1959), *American Economic Review,* L (May, 1960), 565–73.

22 The difficulty with this interpretation is that if one third of windfall income is considered to be permanent income there is correlation between transitory income and permanent income. Thus Friedman's interpretation contradicts his own hypothesis. The Modigliani-Brumberg and the Modigliani-Ando versions of the permanent-income hypothesis are more flexible on this point. They allow for the possibility that transitory income and transitory consumption may be related to each other. For a simple presentation of this idea, see Robert Ferber, *op. cit.,* pp. 27–28.

23 Mordechai E. Kreinin, "Windfall Income and Consumption—Additional Evidence," *American Economic Review,* LI (June, 1961), 388–90.

24 Margaret G. Reid, "Consumption, Savings and Windfall Gains," *American Economic Review,* LII (September, 1962), 729–37.

25 The reader who wants a brief summary of the evidence favorable to Friedman on this tenet should read Robert Ferber, *op. cit.,* pp. 29–31. After a balanced and fair review, Ferber agrees with the position that the evidence is against the idea that the level of income has no influence on the consumption-income ratio.

26 Irwin Friend and Irving B. Kravis, "Consumption Patterns and Permanent Income," *Proceedings of the American Economic Association* (1956), *American Economic Review,* XLVII (May, 1957), 536–55.

27 *Ibid.,* pp. 544, 546.
28 Thomas Mayer, "The Permanent Income Theory and Occupation Groups," *The Review of Economics and Statistics,* XLV (February, 1963), 16–22.
29 Klein and Liviatan, *op. cit.*
30 *Ibid.,* p. 152.
31 *Ibid.,* p. 156.
32 Irwin Friend and Stanley Schor, "Who Saves?" *The Review of Economics and Statistics,* XLI (May, 1959) 213–48.

Chapter V

1 John Kenneth Galbraith, *The Affluent Society* (Boston: Houghton Mifflin, 1958).
2 Alvin Hansen has argued that children and adults devote more hours per year to radio, television, and movies than they do to school, church, and reading. The mechanical media are our most important educational institutions. And they are effectively under the control of advertisers whose mission is profit, not education. See Alvin H. Hansen, "Standards and Values in a Rich Society," in *The American Economy* (New York: McGraw-Hill, 1957).
3 Galbraith, *op. cit.,* p. 253.
4 *Ibid.,* p. 315.
5 Income elasticity as used here signifies: percentage change in a tax base ÷ percentage change in income—over a specified period of time. Whether tax rates have to rise over time depends in part on how "income elastic" the base of the tax structure is. If the value of the base increases faster than income—income elasticity greater than unity—there may be no necessity for rate increases when the governmental share of social product (income) is rising. On the other hand, if the tax base grows less rapidly than income, it will be necessary to raise rates periodically even if the governmental share is constant.
6 Galbraith, *op. cit.,* p. 316.
7 *Ibid.*
8 See Chapter III.
9 Surprisingly, Galbraith does not advocate a tax or a constraint on advertising despite the fact that he makes it appear to be the major cause of the social imbalance.
10 See, for example, Henry C. Wallich, "Public versus Private: Could Galbraith Be Wrong?" *Harper's Magazine,* October, 1961; Frederick A. Hayek, "The Non Sequitur of the 'Dependence Effect,'" *Southern Economic Journal,* XXVII (April, 1961), 346–48; Bertrand de Jouvenel, "On State Expenditures," in *The Ethics of Redistribution* (Cambridge, England: Cambridge University Press, 1951). All of these are reprinted in Norton (paperback) Series, Problems of the Modern Economy. See Edmund S. Phelps, ed., *Private Wants and Public Needs* (New York: Norton, 1962).
11 See Galbraith, *op. cit.,* chaps. XVIII, XIX, and XXII.
12 For actual projections see the following: Robert J. Lampman, "How Much Government Spending in the 1960's?" *The Quarterly Review of Economics*

and Business (February, 1961), pp. 7–17; Dick Netzer, "Financial Needs and Resources Over the Next Decade: State and Local Governments" in *Public Finances, Needs, Sources and Utilization* (Princeton: Princeton University Press, 1961), pp. 23–78; Gerhard Colm and Manuel Helzner (both of the National Planning Association), "Financial Needs and Resources Over the Next Decade: At All Levels of Government," *ibid.,* pp. 3–21; Otto Eckstein, *Trends in Public Expenditures in the Next Decade* (New York: The Committee for Economic Development, 1959); Rockefeller Brothers Fund Special Studies Project, Report IV, *The Challenge to America: Its Economic and Social Aspects* (New York, 1958).

13 Dick Netzer points out that this might not always be true. In a period in which defense, space, and foreign outlay cause the federal government to take the bulk of increases in GNP, federal personal and corporate income taxes can pre-empt the additional income before it affects the state and local bases. See Netzer, *op. cit.,* p. 33.

14 See Mabel Newcomer, "State and Local Financing in Relation to Economic Fluctuations," *National Tax Journal,* VII (June, 1954), 97–109.

15 See David M. Blank, "The Role of the Real Property Tax in Municipal Finance," *National Tax Journal,* VII (December, 1954), 319–26.

16 Netzer, *op. cit.,* p. 19.

17 For references, see Table 11.

18 Daniel Creamer, "Methods of Inquiry—an Income Approach," *Proceedings, Business and Economics Statistics Section, American Statistical Association* (1957), pp. 125–30.

19 John G. Myers, "Methods of Inquiry—The Consumption Approach," *Proceedings, Business and Economics Statistics Section, American Statistical Association* (1957), pp. 130–32.

20 Eleanor Snyder, "Measurement of the Size of the Urban Population with Chronic Low Income Status," *Proceedings, Business and Economics Statistics Section, American Statistical Association* (1957), pp. 132–35; Eleanor Snyder, "Families and Individuals at Permanently Depressed Income Levels: Summary of Findings, Franklin D. Roosevelt Foundation Study, 'Freedom from Want,' " in Sec. 5 of U.S. Congress, Subcommittee on Low-Income Families, Joint Committee on the Economic Report, *Characteristics of the Low-Income Population and Related Federal Programs,* 84th Cong., 1st sess., 1955, pp. 43–51; and Eleanor Snyder, "A Method of Identifying Chronic Low Income Groups from Cross-Section Survey Data," *Studies in Income and Wealth* (Princeton, New Jersey: Princeton University Press for the National Bureau of Economic Research, 1958), XXIII, 321–44.

21 Martin David, "Welfare, Income and Budget Needs," *Review of Economics and Statistics,* XLI (November, 1959), 393–99.

22 For a critique of the consumption-discriminant method of identifying permanent poverty, see Jenny Poduluk, Peter O. Steiner, Robert Summers, Irwin Wolkstein and Marie Delaney, and George Garvy, "Comment," following Eleanor Snyder, *Studies in Income and Wealth,* XXIII, 344–54.

23 Galbraith, *op. cit.,* p. 325.

24 A very readable review of the recent studies is: Dwight MacDonald, "Our Invisible Poor," *The New Yorker*, January 19, 1963.

25 Galbraith, *op. cit.*, p. 324.

26 Robert J. Lampman, "The Low Income Population and Economic Growth," *Study Paper No. 12*, Study of Employment, Growth, and Price Levels for Consideration by the Joint Economic Committee, 86th Cong., 1st sess., 1959.

27 *Ibid.*, p. 26–29.

28 *Ibid.*, p. 24.

29 James Morgan, Martin David, Wilbur Cohen, and Harvey Brazer, *Income and Welfare in the United States* (New York: McGraw-Hill, 1962).

30 *Ibid.*, p. 9.

31 *Ibid.*, p. 10.

32 John H. Adler, "The Fiscal System, the Distribution of Income, and Public Welfare," in Kenyon E. Poole, ed., *Fiscal Policies and the American Economy* (Englewood Cliffs, N.J.: Prentice-Hall, 1951), pp. 359–409; Allan M. Cartter, *The Redistribution of Income in Postwar Britain* (New Haven: Yale University Press, 1955); Tibor Barna, *The Redistribution of Incomes through Public Finance in 1937* (Oxford: The Clarendon Press, 1945); Alfred H. Conrad, "Redistribution through Government Budgets in the United States, 1950," in Alan T. Peacock, ed., *Income Redistribution and Social Policy* (London: Jonathan Cape, Ltd., 1954), pp. 178–267.

33 Many state income taxes are probably no more effectively progressive than typical retail sales taxes, even though they employ graduated rates and provide additional exemptions for extra family members. This can happen when the state allows the federal income tax liability to be deducted in computing the state tax. (Of course, the state tax is deductible in all states in computing the federal income tax for those persons who itemize deductions.) Effective regressivity can also arise from a failure to tax property income, fiduciary income, and capital gains adequately, and from poor administration and compliance. See Violet J. Sollie, "Are Personal Income Taxes Regressive?" *Taxes* (February, 1959), pp. 169–80.

Chapter VI

1 Harry Gunnison Brown, "The Incidence of a General Output or a General Sales Tax," *Journal of Political Economy*, XLVII (April, 1939), 254–62, reprinted in Richard A. Musgrave and Carl S. Shoup, eds., *American Economic Association Readings in the Economics of Taxation* (Homewood, Illinois: Richard D. Irwin, Inc., 1959), pp. 330–39.

2 Earl R. Rolph, "A Proposed Revision of Excise Tax Theory," *Journal of Political Economy*, LX (April, 1952), 102–17; see also *The Theory of Fiscal Economics* (Berkeley: The University of California Press, 1954), chaps. VI, VII; and see Earl Rolph and George Break, *Public Finance* (New York: The Ronald Press Co., 1961), pp. 287–309.

3 "Income effects" is Rolph's term and is not to be confused with J. R. Hicks' use of the same term. See text for Rolph's meaning.

4 *The Theory of Fiscal Economics*, p. 123.

5 Earl Rolph and George Break, "The Welfare Aspects of Excise Taxes," *Journal of Political Economy*, LVII (February, 1949), 46–54, reprinted in Richard Musgrave and Carl Shoup, eds., *American Economic Association Readings in the Economics of Taxation*, pp. 110–122.

6 *The Theory of Fiscal Economics*, pp. 124–25.

7 John Due notes Rolph's obscurity on this point. Due observes that both Brown and Rolph are fuzzy in their assumptions concerning the level and pattern of government expenditure accompanying the tax hike. In their initial presentations, Due notes, it seemed that they were assuming tax revenues to be sterilized. But this is an untenable assumption because it leads to a deflationary process. They do not intend this. Evidently they mean to assume that revenues are used so that aggregate money demand remains constant. We have followed Due in interpreting their position. In other words, we have presented the assumptions which Brown and Rolph must be operating under whether they so state it or not. See John F. Due, "Toward a General Theory of Sales Tax Incidence," *Quarterly Journal of Economics*, LXVII (May, 1953), 258.

James Buchanan stresses the same point. "Rolph commits a fundamental methodological error," says Buchanan, "when he attempts to analyze a new tax independently of change either in other taxes or in public expenditures and fails to follow through to the full consequences of the tax-induced monetary deflation." Rolph tries to impound under *ceteris paribus* both public expenditures and other taxes. Buchanan correctly points out that it is legitimate to take any of three approaches: (1) to assume that when the tax is raised another is lowered as an offset; (2) to assume that government expenditure and the tax are raised together; (3) to assume that the tax is raised, and then to trace the deflationary effects. (In Richard Musgrave's framework these approaches are, respectively, differential, balanced-budget, and absolute incidence.) See James M. Buchanan, *Fiscal Theory and Political Economy* (Chapel Hill: University of North Carolina Press, 1960), pp. 142–43.

8 Rolph and Break, *Public Finance*, pp. 306–307.

9 *The Theory of Fiscal Economics*, chap. VII.

10 Richard A. Musgrave, "On Incidence," *Journal of Political Economy*, LXI (August, 1953), 306–23; see also Musgrave, *The Theory of Public Finance* (New York: McGraw-Hill Book Company, 1959), chaps. X, XV, XVI. Most of the ideas of this section were suggested by Musgrave's penetrating work.

For a brilliant review and criticism of the major participants in this debate—Rolph, Brown, Musgrave, John Due, H. P. B. Jenkins, and Giannino Parravicini—see James Buchanan, *op. cit.*, chap. VI.

11 All of this assumes that there are no income or output effects from fiscal policy. Nowadays most of us believe that output effects are indeed likely. But many students of incidence assume them away. Earl Rolph does so explicitly. Output effects complicate things mightily.

12 However, the new tax does redistribute income because it alters relative prices and relative factor returns.

13 This is the nub of the criticism of Rolph's doctrine which Harold M. Groves advances in his oral tradition at The University of Wisconsin.

14 Richard Musgrave, *The Theory of Public Finance,* pp. 207–208 ff.

15 *Public Finance,* pp. 292–95.

16 Musgrave, "On Incidence," *loc. cit.;* and *The Theory of Public Finance,* pp. 380 ff.

17 Challis A. Hall, Jr., review of *Public Finance* by Earl R. Rolph and George F. Break, *The Amercian Economic Review,* LII (March, 1962), 267–69.

18 Differential incidence, Musgrave shows, is completely a matter of relative prices, not of absolute prices, under competitive assumptions. Under rigorous competition the distribution of real income and the distribution of output between public and private sectors is the same whether excises are shifted forward to consumers or backward to factors of production, and no matter what happens to an aggregate price index after an excise tax is imposed. See Musgrave, in *Journal of Political Economy,* LXI (August, 1953), and *The Theory of Public Finance,* chap. XV.

Chapter VII

1 Felix S. Wahraftig, "Meaning of Retail Sales and Storage, Use or Other Consumption Taxes," *Law and Contemporary Problems,* VIII, No. 3 (Duke University School of Law, 1941), 542–60.

2 John F. Due, "Retail Sales Taxation in Theory and Practice," *National Tax Journal,* III (December, 1950), 320.

3 This assumes absolute or specific incidence (see Chapter VI).

4 In a self-sufficient economy that is not accumulating capital, the two values are equal. But in an open and/or capital-accumulating economy they are not exactly the same.

5 See Federation of Tax Administrators, "Sales Tax Base—Services," RM366, December, 1960; James R. Stanford, "Broadening the Sales Tax Base: Recent Trends and Impending Developments," *Proceedings of the National Tax Association, 1960,* pp. 534–41; Denzel C. Cline, "Expanding Scope of Sales Taxes," *Proceedings of the National Tax Association, 1953,* pp. 296–99; *Michigan Tax Survey 1952,* A Report to the Legislative Interim Tax and Revenue Study Committee, submitted February 21, 1952, pp. 100-105; *Michigan Tax Study, 1958;* and State of Washington, *Report of the 1958 Tax Advisory Council.*

6 Reed R. Hansen, "An Empirical Analysis of the Retail Sales Tax with Policy Recommendations," *National Tax Journal,* XV (March, 1962), 1–14. Service inclusion is not as effective in alleviating regressivity as many people believe, however. The reason is that the expenditures on services that increase rapidly with rising incomes are not the services which are commonly sales taxed. We have in mind education, medical and hospital care, and foreign and distance travel.

7 Federation of Tax Administrators, "Sales Tax Base—Services," *op. cit.,* p. 6; research for Texas indicates that had the present sales tax been in operation since 1954, growth in its value base would have been only about 85 per

cent as rapid as the growth of personal income in the state, whereas the value base of a selection of services similar to the one suggested here would have grown about 1.4 per cent for each 1 per cent growth of personal income. Source: Lee Van Zant, forthcoming master's thesis, Department of Economics, The University of Texas, Austin.

8 From the 1958 *Michigan Tax Study* one infers that a limited range of proposed services would have added about 6 per cent to the sales-tax base of that state. A rough-and-ready estimate for Washington is that taxation of a broad range of services at regular sales-tax rates might add about 13 per cent in base value. In Texas a range of services similar to our proposals would have added between 15 per cent and 20 per cent to the base in 1961. Source: Lee Van Zant, *op. cit.* In making these estimates it must be remembered that if a state taxes services the entire value of the services is not gained because the state will probably sacrifice the revenue it now enjoys from the sale of tangibles to firms which perform services.

9 The state of Washington reports no particular administration or enforcement problems for its business and occupation tax and its administrators welcome the opportunity to add more services. Michigan expects no administrative disadvantages. It points out that it already deals with most of the firms which would be further taxed because they sell tangible property as part of the services they render. Auditing for most of these firms would actually be simplified.

10 Oster, *op. cit.*, chap. VII.

11 For a good, but dated, discussion of the problems and a review of decisions, see George T. Frampton and Numa L. Smith, "Commodities and Transactions Exempt from Consumption Taxes," *Law and Contemporary Problems,* VIII, No. 3 (Duke University School of Law, 1941), 580–82.

12 See, for example, Reed R. Hansen, "The Tax Treatment of Family Income" (unpublished Ph. D. dissertation, Department of Economics, The University of Wisconsin, Madison, 1960), p. 155.

13 Martin David, "Welfare, Income and Budget Needs," *Review of Economics and Statistics,* XLI (November, 1959), 395.

14 Some modification of the form proposed here would have to be made, depending on what items of family expenditure are excluded or exempted from tax. For example, if rent is exempted, as has been proposed here, the relative credit proposed would have to be altered. In other words, the relative credits now being proposed rest on the assumption that the sales-tax scheme levies on all consumption expenditure. If everything is not taxed, we must take account of exemptions in computing the relative credits for families of various compositions.

15 David, in *Review of Economics and Statistics,* p. 399.

16 All of the credits suggested in Table 16 do not correspond as closely with the actual welfare schedule of Table 14, however.

17 Reed R. Hansen, "The Tax Treatment of Family Income," documents this extensively.

18 This scale suggests that a variation of the French "quotient system" might

approximate the desired pattern for families. We could say that the spouses are together entitled to a certain credit (in our example, $20), and each additional child receives one fourth of this credit (in our example, $5). This does not quite fit the actual pattern of declining cost per marginal child, but it approximates it and provides a very simple conceptual scheme. The single person might receive a credit three fourths that of the married couple ($15 in our example).

19 It would not be hard to convince residents of Texas of the validity of this statement. Since the adoption of its food exemption sales tax in late 1961, Texas has had no end of administrative and compliance headaches arising from the exemption.

20 For the citations of these cases, see Frampton and Smith, *Law and Contemporary Problems,* VIII, No. 3, 583.

21 For citations of these additional examples of Ohio rulings, see Oster, *op. cit.,* p. 123.

22 The basic idea and merit of the sales-tax–income-tax integration, not connected with a stamp plan, was carefully explored by the Minnesota Tax Study Committee. The results are reported by Alek A. Rozental (see "Integration of Sales and Income Taxes at the State Level," *National Tax Journal,* IX [December, 1956], 370–77). There is one issue which deserves special emphasis here, beyond that given by Rozental and the Minnesota study. It is that the sales-tax credit refund should not be integrated with the income tax in the orthodox sense that refund may be avoided in cases where no income-tax liability accrues for the year. The sales-tax refund should be paid even if the individual or the spouses have no income-tax liability. The idea is that they have presumably already paid the sales tax, were unable to avoid doing so, and the refund is due them.

There are some administrative problems involved in integration since mandatory joint returns are not the prevailing practice. We are, remember, thinking of the sales tax as a tax on the family unit. These problems are not evaluated here. It should be noted that the same reasoning here applied to sales tax may also be applied for the personal income tax. This suggests mandatory joint returns for the entire family unit.

23 See Oster, *op. cit.,* pp. 166–80, for a discussion of Ohio's experience and its costs. Also see Appendix Table I.

24 A graduated sales tax may take several forms. See, for example, Walter A. Morton, "A Progressive Consumption Tax," *National Tax Journal,* IV (June, 1951), 160–66; United States Treasury, Division of Tax Research, "Considerations Respecting a Federal Retail Sales Tax" in U.S. Congress, Revenue Revision of 1943, *Hearings before the Committee on Ways and Means,* 78th Cong., 1st sess., pp. 1175–78; and Nevada, Legislative Counsel Bureau, *Survey of Sales Taxes Applicable to Nevada,* Bulletin No. 3, May, 1948.

BIBLIOGRAPHY

Books

Barna, Tibor. *The Redistribution of Income through Public Finance in 1937.* Oxford: The Clarendon Press, 1945.

Blum, Walter, and Harry Kalven. *The Uneasy Case for Progressive Taxation.* Chicago: University of Chicago Press, 1953.

Brownlee, O. H. *Estimated Distribution of Minnesota Taxes and Public Expenditure Benefits.* Minneapolis: The University of Minnesota Press, 1960.

Buchanan, James M. *Fiscal Theory and Political Economy.* Chapel Hill: University of North Carolina Press, 1960.

Cartter, Allan M. *The Redistribution of Income in Postwar Britain.* New Haven: Yale University Press, 1955.

Due, John F. *Sales Taxation.* Urbana: University of Illinois Press, 1957.

Duesenberry, James S. *Income, Saving and the Theory of Consumer Behavior.* Cambridge: Harvard University Press, 1952.

Eckstein, Otto. *Trends in Public Expenditures in the Next Decade.* New York: The Committee for Economic Development, 1959.

Fisher, Irving. *The Theory of Interest.* New York: The Macmillan Company, 1930.

Friedman, Milton. *A Theory of the Consumption Function.* Princeton, New Jersey: Princeton University Press, for the National Bureau of Economic Research, 1957.

Frisch, Ragnar. *New Methods of Measuring Marginal Utility.* Tubingen, Germany: J. C. B. Mohr, 1932.

Galbraith, John Kenneth. *The Affluent Society.* Boston: Houghton-Mifflin Company, 1958.

Groves, Harold M. *Financing Government.* 5th ed. New York: Henry Holt and Company, 1958.

Kaldor, Nicholas. *An Expenditure Tax.* London: George Allen & Unwin, Ltd., 1955.

Little, I. M. D. *A Critique of Welfare Economics.* London: Clarendon Press, 1950.

Morgan, James, Martin David, Wilbur Cohen, and Harvey Brazer. *Income and Welfare in the United States.* New York: McGraw-Hill Book Company, 1962.

Musgrave, Richard A. *The Theory of Public Finance.* New York: McGraw-Hill Book Company, 1959.

Oster, Clinton V. *State Retail Sales Taxation.* Columbus: Ohio State University Bureau of Business Research, 1957.

176

Pigou, A. C. *A Study in Public Finance*. 3rd ed. rev. New York: The Macmillan Company, 1960.

Rolph, Earl R. *The Theory of Fiscal Economics*. Berkeley: The University of California Press, 1954.

Rolph, Earl R., and George Break. *Public Finance*. New York: The Ronald Press Company, 1961.

Samuelson, Paul A. *Foundations of Economic Analysis*. Cambridge: Harvard University Press, 1958.

Simons, Henry C. *Personal Income Taxation*. Chicago: University of Chicago Press, 1938.

Zehor, Dean, and Edward Failor. *State Sales Taxes on Services*. Ames, Iowa: Institute of Public Affairs, State University of Iowa, December, 1954.

Articles and Periodicals

Adams, T. S. "Fundamental Problems of Federal Income Taxation," *Quarterly Journal of Economics*, XXXV (August, 1921), 551–52.

Adler, John H. "The Fiscal System, the Distribution of Income and Public Welfare," in Kenyon Poole, ed. *Fiscal Policies and the American Economy*. Englewood Cliffs, New Jersey: Prentice Hall, 1951, pp. 359–409.

Blank, David M. "The Role of the Real Property Tax in Municipal Finance," *National Tax Journal*, VII (December, 1954), 319–26.

Bodkin, Ronald. "Windfall Income and Consumption," *American Economic Review*, XLIX (September, 1959), 602–14.

Brabson, George D. "Analysis of Sales and Use Tax Exemptions with Comment as to More Uniform Applications," *Symposium on Sales Taxation, Vanderbilt Law Review*, IX (February, 1956), 294–315.

Brady, Dorothy S. "Family Saving, 1888–1950," in Raymond W. Goldsmith, Dorothy S. Brady, and Horst Mendershausen. *A Study of Saving in the United States*. Princeton: Princeton University Press, for the National Bureau of Economic Research, 1956, pp. 139–255.

Brady, Dorothy S., and Rose D. Friedman. "Savings and the Income Distribution," *Studies in Income and Wealth*. New York: National Bureau of Economic Research, 1947, X, 247–65.

Brand, H. "Poverty in the United States: How Affluent Is the Affluent Society?" *Dissent* (August, 1960), pp. 334–54.

Brown, Harry G. "The Incidence of a General Output or a General Sales Tax," *Journal of Political Economy*, XLVII (April, 1939), 254–62, reprinted in Richard A. Musgrave and Carl S. Shoup, eds. *American Economic Association Readings in the Economics of Taxation*. Homewood, Illinois: Richard D. Irwin, Inc., 1959, pp. 330–39.

Cline, Denzel C. "Expanding Scope of Sales Taxes," *Proceedings of the National Tax Association* (1953), pp. 296–99.

———. "Sales Tax Exemption of Producer Goods," *Proceedings of the National Tax Association* (1952), pp. 618–31.

Colm, Gerhard, and Manuel Helzner. "Financial Needs and Resources over the Next Decade: At All Levels of Government," in *Public Finances, Needs, Sources and Utilization*. A Conference of the Universities—National Bureau Committee for Economic Research. Princeton: Princeton University Press, for the National Bureau of Economic Research, 1961, pp. 3–21.

Conrad, Alred H. "Redistribution through Government Budgets in the United

States, 1950," in Alan T. Peacock, ed. *Income Redistribution and Social Policy.* London: Jonathan Cape, Ltd., 1954, pp. 178–267.

Creamer, Daniel. "Methods of Inquiry—An Income Approach," *Proceedings, Business and Economic Statistics Section, American Statistical Association* (1957), pp. 125–30.

David, Martin. "Welfare, Income and Budget Needs," *The Review of Economics and Statistics,* XLI (November, 1959), 393–99.

Davies, David G. "An Empirical Test of Sales Tax Regressivity," *Journal of Political Economy,* LXVII (February, 1959), 72–78.

———. "Progressiveness of Sales Taxes in Relation to Various Income Bases," *American Economic Review,* L (December, 1960), 987–95.

———. "The Sensitivity of Consumption Taxes to Fluctuations in Income," *National Tax Journal,* XV (September, 1962), 281–90.

de Jouvenel, Bertrand. "On State Expenditure," in *The Ethics of Redistribution.* Cambridge, England: Cambridge University Press, 1951, reprinted in paperback Norton Series, Problems of the Modern Economy. See Edmund S. Phelps, ed. *Private Wants and Public Needs.* New York: Norton, 1962.

Driscoll, Joseph P. "Income Averaging for Individual Income Tax Purposes," *Federal Tax Policy for Economic Growth and Stability,* 84th Cong., 1st sess., November 9, 1955, pp. 176–77.

Due, John F. "Retail Sales Taxation in Theory and Practice," *National Tax Journal,* III (December, 1950), 314–25.

———. "Toward a General Theory of Sales Tax Incidence," *Quarterly Journal of Economics,* LXVII (May, 1953), 253–67.

Eisner, Robert. "The Permanent Income Hypothesis, Comment," *American Economic Review,* XLVII (December, 1958), 972–90.

Fagan, Elmer D. "Recent and Contemporary Theories of Progressive Taxation," *Journal of Political Economy,* XLVI (August, 1938), 457–97, reprinted in Richard A. Musgrave and Carl S. Shoup, eds. *American Economic Association Readings in the Economics of Taxation.* Homewood, Illinois: Richard D. Irwin, Inc., 1959, pp. 19–53.

Fellner, William. "Relative Permanent Income: Elaboration and Synthesis," *Journal of Political Economy,* LXVII (October, 1959), 508–11.

Ferber, Robert. "Research on Household Behavior," *American Economic Review,* LII (March, 1962).

Fisher, Franklin, and Jerome Rothenberg. "How Income Ought to Be Distributed: Paradox Lost," *Journal of Political Economy,* LXIX (April, 1961), 162–80.

Fisher, Irving. "A Statistical Method for Measuring 'Marginal Utility' and Testing the Justice of a Progressive Income Tax," in Jacob H. Hallender, ed. *Economic Essays: Contributed in Honor of John Bates Clark.* New York: The Macmillan Company, 1927.

Fisher, Malcolm. "Explorations in Savings Behaviour," *Bulletin of Oxford University Institute of Statistics,* XVIII (August, 1956), 201–77.

Frampton, George T., and Numa L. Smith. "Commodities and Transactions Exempt from Consumption Taxes," *Law and Contemporary Problems,* VIII, No. 3 (Duke University School of Law, 1941), 579–93.

Friend, Irwin, and Irving B. Kravis. "Consumption Patterns and Permanent Income," *Proceedings of the American Economic Association* (1956), *American Economic Review,* XLVII (May, 1957), 536–55.

Friend, Irwin, and Stanley Schor. "Who Saves?" *The Review of Economics and Statistics,* XLI (May, 1959), 213–48.

Groves, Harold M. "Toward a Social Theory of Progressive Taxation," *National Tax Journal,* IX (March, 1956), 27–34.

Groves, Harold M., and C. Harry Kahn. "The Stability of State and Local Tax Yields," *American Economic Review,* XLII (March, 1952), 87–102.

Haig, Robert M. "The Concept of Income: Economic and Legal Aspects," *The Federal Income Tax.* New York: Columbia University Press, 1921, reprinted in Richard A. Musgrave and Carl S. Shoup, eds. *American Economic Association Readings in the Economics of Taxation.* Homewood, Illinois: Richard D. Irwin, Inc., 1959, pp. 54–76.

Hall, Challis A., Jr. Review of *Public Finance* by Earl R. Rolph and George F. Break, *American Economic Review,* LII (March, 1962), 267–69.

Hamburger, William. "The Relation of Consumption to Wealth and the Wage Rate," *Econometrica,* XXIII (January, 1955), 1–17.

Hansen, Alvin H. "Standards and Values in a Rich Society," in *The American Economy.* New York. McGraw-Hill Book Company, 1957.

Hansen, Reed R. "An Empirical Analysis of the Retail Sales Tax With Policy Recommendations," *National Tax Journal,* XV (March, 1962), 1–14.

Hayek, Frederick A. "The Non Sequitur of the 'Dependance Effect,'" *Southern Economic Journal,* XXVII (April, 1961), 346–48, reprinted in paperback Norton Series, Problems of the Modern Economy. See Edmund S. Phelps, ed. *Private Wants and Public Needs.* New York: Norton, 1962.

Houthakker, H. S. "The Permanent Income Hypothesis," *American Economic Review,* XLVII (June, 1958), 396–404.

Johnson, Harry G. "A Note on the Effect of Income Redistribution on Aggregate Consumption with Interdependent Consumer Preferences," *Econometrica,* XVIII (August, 1951), 295–97.

Jones, Robert C. "Transitory Income and Expenditures on Consumption Categories," *Proceedings of the American Economic Association* (1959), *American Economic Review,* L (May, 1960), 565–73.

Katona, George, Lawrence Klein, John Lansing, and James Morgan. "Statistical Elimination of Economic Relations from Survey Data," *Contributions of Survey Methods to Economics.* New York: Columbia University Press, 1954, pp. 189–240.

Klein, Lawrence R. "Estimating Patterns of Savings Behavior from Sample Survey Data," *Econometrica,* XIX (October, 1951), 438–54.

Klein, L. R., and N. Liviatan. "The Significance of Income Variability on Savings Behavior," *Bulletin of Oxford University Institute of Statistics,* XIX (May, 1957), 151–60.

Kreinin, Mordechaii E. "Windfall Income and Consumption—Additional Evidence," *American Economic Review,* LI (June, 1961), 388–90.

Lamale, Helen, and Margaret Stotz. "The Interim City Worker's Budget," *Monthly Labor Review,* LXXXIII (August, 1960), 785–808.

Lampman, Robert J. "The American Tax System and Equalization of Income," *Proceedings of the National Tax Association* (1956), pp. 271–80.

———. "How Much Government Spending in the 1960's?" *The Quarterly Review of Economics and Business,* I (February, 1961), 7–17.

———. "The Low-Income Population and Economic Growth," *Study Paper No. 12,* Study of Employment, Growth, and Price Levels for Consideration by the

Joint Economic Committee, 86th Cong., 1st sess., 1959.

———. "Making Utility Predictions Verifiable," *The Southern Economic Journal*, XXII (January, 1956), 360–66.

———. "Paying the Price for Higher Fertility," in *Problems of U.S. Economic Development*, Committee for Economic Development Essay Contest, Volume 2.

MacDonald, Dwight. "Our Invisible Poor." *The New Yorker*, January 19, 1963.

Mayer, Thomas. "The Permanent Income Theory and Occupation Groups," *The Review of Economics and Statistics*, XLV (February, 1963), 16–22.

Miller, Donald C. "Sales-Tax Progressivity Attributable to a Food Exemption," *National Tax Journal*, IV (June, 1951), 148–50.

Mincer, Jacob. "Income Distribution and Substandard Levels of Living," *Proceedings, Business and Economic Statistics Section, American Statistical Association* (August, 1957), pp. 138–39.

Modigliani, Franco, and Richard Brumberg. "Utility Analysis and the Consumption Function: An Interpretation of Cross Section Data," in Kenneth Kurihara, ed. *Post Keynesian Economics*. New Brunswick, New Jersey: Rutgers University Press, 1954, pp. 383–436.

Morgan, James N. "The Motivation of Savers," in Walter H. Heller, Francis M. Boddy, and Carl N. Nelson, eds. *Savings in the Modern Economy*. Minneapolis: Minnesota Press, 1953, pp. 213–17.

Morton, Walter A. "A Progressive Consumption Tax," *National Tax Journal*, IV (June, 1951), 160–66.

Musgrave, Richard A. "On Incidence," *Journal of Political Economy*, LXI (August, 1953), 306–23.

Musgrave, Richard A., and Darwin W. Daicoff, "Who Pays the Michigan Taxes?" Michigan Tax Study *Staff Papers*. Lansing: October, 1958.

Musgrave, Richard A., *et al.* "Distribution of Tax Payments by Income Groups: A Case Study for 1948," *National Tax Journal*, IV (March, 1951), 1–53.

Myers, John G. "Methods of Inquiry—The Consumption Approach," *Proceedings, Business and Economics Statistics Section, American Statistical Association* (1957), pp. 130–32.

Netzer, Dick. "Financial Needs and Resources Over the Next Decade: State and Local Governments," in *Public Finances, Needs, Sources and Utilization*. A Conference of the Universities–National Bureau Committee for Economic Research. Princeton: Princeton University Press, for the National Bureau of Economic Research, 1961, pp. 23–78.

Newcomer, Mabel. "State and Local Financing in Relation to Economic Fluctuations," *National Tax Journal*, VII (June, 1954), 97–109.

Northrup, Arthur S. "The Measure of Sales Taxes," *Symposium on Sales Taxation, Vanderbilt Law Review*, IX (February, 1956), 237–80.

Penniman, Clara. "The Role of the Property Tax in Wisconsin Since 1929, *National Tax Journal*, IX (December, 1956).

Poduluk, Jenny, Peter O. Steiner, Robert Summers, Irwin Wolkstein, Marie Delaney, and George Garvey. "Comment" following Eleanor Snyder in *Studies in Income and Wealth*. Princeton: Princeton University Press, for the National Bureau of Economic Research, 1958, XXIII, 344–54.

Reid, Margaret G. "Consumption, Savings and Windfall Gains," *American Economic Review*, LII (September, 1962), 729–37.

Rivoire, Charles. "The Retailer Looks at Sales Taxes," *Proceedings of the National Tax Association* (1948), pp. 318–24.

Rolph, Earl R. "A Proposed Revision of Excise Tax Theory," *Journal of Political Economy*, LX (April, 1952), 102–17.

Rolph, Earl R., and George F. Break. "The Welfare Aspects of Excise Taxes," *Journal of Political Economy*, LVII (February, 1949), 46–54, reprinted in Richard A. Musgrave and Carl S. Shoup, eds. *American Economic Association Readings in the Economics of Taxation.* Homewood, Illinois: Richard D. Irwin, Inc., 1959, pp. 110–22.

Rozental, Alek A. "Integration of Sales and Income Taxes at the State Level," *National Tax Journal*, IX (December, 1956), 370–77.

Shoup, Carl S. "Theory and Background of the Value-added Tax," *Proceedings of the National Tax Association* (1955), pp. 6–19.

Smithies, Arthur, and J. Mosak. "Forecasting Postwar Demand," *Econometrica*, XIII (January, 1945), 1–14 and 25–53.

Snyder, Eleanor. "Families and Individuals at Permanently Depressed Income Levels: Summary of Findings, Franklin D. Roosevelt Foundation Study, 'Freedom from Want,'" in Sec. 5 of U.S. Congress, Subcommittee on Low-Income Families, Joint Committee on the Economic Report, *Characteristics of the Low-Income Population and Related Federal Programs*, 84th Cong., 1st sess., 1955, pp. 43–51.

———. "Measurement of the Size of the Urban Population with Chronic Low Income Status," *Proceedings, Business and Economics Statistics Section, American Statistical Association* (1957), pp. 132–35.

———. "A Method of Identifying Chronic Low Income Groups from Cross-Section Survey Data," in *Studies in Income and Wealth.* Princeton: Princeton University Press, for the National Bureau of Economic Research, 1958, XXIII, 321–44.

Sollie, Violet J. "Are Personal Income Taxes Regressive?" *Taxes* (February, 1959), pp. 169–80.

Soltow, Lee "The Historic Rise in the Number of Taxpayers in a State with Constant Tax Law," *National Tax Journal*, VIII (December, 1955), 371–81.

Stanford, James R. "Broadening the Sales Tax Base: Recent Trends and Impending Developments," *Proceedings of the National Tax Association* (1960), pp. 534–41.

Studenski, Paul. "Toward a Theory of Business Taxation," *Journal of Political Economy*, XLVIII (October, 1940), 621–54.

Taylor, Milton C. "Toward Rationality in a Retail Sales Tax," *National Tax Journal*, III (March, 1952), 79–85.

Texas Research League, "The Sales Tax and Business," *Analyzes*, June, 1961, p. 8.

Tobin, James. "Relative Income, Absolute Income and Savings," in *Money, Trade and Economic Growth: In Honor of John Henry Williams.* New York: The Macmillan Company, 1951, pp. 135–56.

Vickrey, William. "Resource Distribution Patterns and the Classification of Families," in *Studies in Income and Wealth.* New York: National Bureau of Economic Research, 1947, X, 276–77.

———. "Some Limits to the Income Elasticity of Income Tax Yields," *Review of Economics and Statistics*, XXXI (May, 1949), 140–44.

Wahraftig, Felix S. "Meaning of Retail Sales and Storage, Use or Other Consumption Taxes," *Law and Contemporary Problems*, VIII, No. 3 (Duke University School of Law, 1941), 542–60.

Wallich, Henry C. "Public versus Private: Could Galbraith Be Wrong?" *Harper's Magazine,* October, 1961, reprinted in paperback Norton Series, Problems of the Modern Economy. See Edmund S. Phelps, ed. *Private Wants and Public Needs.* New York: Norton, 1962.

Zellner, Arnold. "Tests of Some Basic Propositions in the Theory of Consumption," *Proceedings of the American Economic Association* (1959), *American Economic Review,* L (May, 1960), 565–73.

Reports and Public Documents

Bureau of Labor Statistics–Wharton. *1950 Study of Consumer Expenditure.*

Commerce Clearing House. *All-State Tax Reporter.*

Commerce Clearing House. *Sales and Use Tax Statutes,* Rules and Regulations of the Various States.

Committee for Economic Development. *Trends in Public Expenditures in the Next Decade,* 1959.

Community Council of Greater New York. *Annual Price Survey and Family Budget Costs,* October, 1959. New York: December, 1959.

Conference on Economic Progress. *Poverty and Deprivation in the United States: The Plight of Two-fifths of the Nation.* Washington, D.C., 1962.

Federation of Tax Administrators, *Administrators News.*

———. "Sales Tax Base—Services," RM366, December, 1960.

Michigan Tax Study 1958.

Michigan Tax Survey 1952. A Report to the Legislative Interim Tax and Revenue Study Committee, submitted February 21, 1952.

National Planning Association. *Long-range Projections for Economic Growth: The American Economy in 1970.* Planning Pamphlet No. 107, 1959.

Nevada Legislative Counsel Bureau. *Survey of Sales Taxes Applicable to Nevada,* Bulletin No. 3, May, 1948.

Nevada Legislative Tax Study Group. *Financing State and Local Government in Nevada,* January, 1960.

Rockefeller Brothers Fund Special Studies Project, Report IV, *The Challenge to America: Its Economic and Social Aspects.* New York, 1958.

State of Washington. *Report of the 1958 Tax Advisory Council.*

Tax Foundation, Inc. *Retail Sales and Individual Income Taxes in State Tax Structures.* Project Note No. 48, January, 1962,

United States Bureau of the Census. *Current Population Reports,* series P-25, No. 187.

United States Bureau of Labor Statistics. *Monthly Labor Review,* LXVII (February, 1948), 179.

———. *Monthly Labor Review,* LXXXIII (August, 1960), 785–808.

———. *Monthly Labor Review,* LXXXIII (November, 1960), 1197–1200.

———. *Workers' Budget in the United States: City Families and Single Persons, 1946 and 1947,* BLS Bulletin No. 927 (1948), pp. 6–9.

United States Congress, Subcommittee on Low-Income Families, Joint Committee on the Economic Report. *Characteristics of the Low-Income Population and Related Federal Programs.* 84th Cong., 1st sess., 1955.

United States Treasury, Division of Tax Research. "Considerations Respecting a Federal Retail Sales Tax," in United States Congress, Revenue Revision of 1943. *Hearings Before the Committee on Ways and Means,* 78th Cong., 1st sess., pp. 1175–178.

University of Wisconsin Tax Study Committee. *Wisconsin's State and Local Tax Burden: Impact, Incidence and Tax Revision Alternatives.* Madison: September, 1959.

Unpublished Material

Hansen, Reed R. "The Tax Treatment of Family Income." Unpublished Ph.D. dissertation, Department of Economics, The University of Wisconsin, Madison, 1960.

Houthakker, H. S. "An International Comparison of Personal Savings," *Stanford Project for Quantitative Research in Economic Development.* Unpublished memorandum, Department of Economics, Stanford University, January, 1960.

Lewis, David P. "The Permanent Income Hypothesis: Its Assumptions and Theoretical Basis—A Critical Inquiry." Unpublished Master's thesis, Department of Economics, University of Tennessee, Knoxville, 1959.

Morgan, Daniel C., Jr. "New Bases for Evaluating Retail Sales Taxation." Unpublished Ph.D. dissertation, Department of Economics, The University of Wisconsin, Madison, 1961.

———. "Toward Rationality in Retail Sales Taxation." Unpublished seminar paper, Department of Economics, The University of Wisconsin, Madison.

INDEX

DATE DUE